COUNTY STREET ATLAS

TOWN CENTRE STREET MAPS

C000259397

CONTENTS

Index to Street Maps 3

Administrative District Map 4-5

Gazetteer Index to Road Map 6-7

County Road Map 8-11

Town Centre Street Maps 12-60
4 Inches to 1 Mile

Index to Streets 61

www.philips-maps.co.uk

This edition published by Philip's,
a division of Octopus Publishing Group Ltd
www.octopusbooks.co.uk
2–4 Heron Quays, London E14 4JP
An Hachette Livre UK Company
www.hachettelivre.co.uk

First published in 1975 by Estate Publications
First Philip's edition 2008
First impression 2008
15/10-05

ISBN 978-0-540-09470-7

© Philip's 2008

Ordnance Survey®

This product includes mapping data licensed
from Ordnance Survey®, with the permission
of the Controller of Her Majesty's Stationery
Office.© Crown copyright 2005. All rights
reserved. Licence number 100011710

	Symbol	Description
		Pedestrianized / Restricted Access
		Track
		Built Up Area
		Footpath
		Stream
		River
	Lock	Canal
		Railway / Station
	●	Post Office
	P P+	Car Park / Park & Ride
	C	Public Convenience
	+	Place of Worship
	→	One-way Street
	i	Tourist Information Centre
	8 8	Adjoining Pages
		Area Depicting Enlarged Centre
		Emergency Services
		Industrial Buildings
		Leisure Buildings
		Education Buildings
		Hotels etc.
		Retail Buildings
		General Buildings
		Woodland
		Orchard
		Recreational / Parkland
		Cemetery

Scale of street plans: 4 Inches to 1 Mile (unless otherwise stated)

TOWN	Page	TOWN	Page
Ashford	12	Marden	34
Biddenden	13	Margate	36
Birchington	14	Minster	37
Borough Green	13	New Romney	38
Broadstairs	15	Northfleet	39
Canterbury (8 Inches to 1 Mile)	16	Paddock Wood	40
Charing	17	Queenborough	41
Chatham	18	Rainham	42
Cliftonville	19	Ramsgate	43
Cranbrook	20	Rochester	44
Dartford	21	Royal Tunbridge Wells (8 Inches to 1 Mile)	56
Deal	22	Saint Margarets at Cliffe	41
Dover (5 Inches to 1 Mile)	23	Sandwich	45
Edenbridge	24	Sevenoaks	46
Faversham	25	Sheerness	47
Folkestone (6 Inches to 1 Mile)	26	Sittingbourne	48
Gillingham	27	Snodland	49
Gravesend	28	Southborough	50
Greenhithe	29	Staplehurst	51
Hadlow	17	Strood	52
Hamstreet	30	Swanley	53
Harrietsham	30	Swanscombe	29
Hawkhurst	31	Tenterden	54
Headcorn	31	Tonbridge	55
Herne Bay	32	Westerham	57
Hythe	33	Westgate on Sea	58
Lenham	32	Whitstable	59
Lydd	34	Woodchurch	60
Maidstone	35	Wye	60

COUNTY STREET ATLASES

This atlas is intended for those requiring street maps of the historical and commercial centres of towns within the county. Each locality is normally presented on one or two pages and although, with many small towns, this space is sufficient to portray the whole urban area, the maps of large towns and cities are for centres only and are not intended to be comprehensive. Such coverage is offered in the Local Street Atlases

Shoeburyness

Minster
Warden
Eastchurch
Leysdown-on-Sea

Birchington
Margate
Cliftonville
Kingsgate

Reculver
Westgate-on-Sea
St. Peter's

Herne Bay
Broadstairs

Whitstable
Tankerton
Beltinge
Hillborough
St. Nicholas at Wade
Acol
Manston
Ramsgate

Chestfield
Swalecliffe
Broomfield
Herne
Marshside
Sarre
Monkton
Minster
Cliffs End
Dumpton

THANET

Seasalter
Clapham Hill
Maypole
Chislet
West Stourmouth

Conyer

Teynham
Yorkletts
Honey Hill
Hoath
Upstreet
East Stourmouth
Westmarsh

Oare
Graveney
Dargate
Hersden
Grove
Preston
Ware
Great Stonar

Goodnestone
Tyler Hill
Westbere
Stodmarsh
Elmstone

Faversham
Lynsted
Osprenge
Hernhill
Blean
Sturry
Fordwich
Wickhambreaux
Hoaden
Ash
Sandwich

SWALE
Painter's Forstal
Boughton Street
Dunkirk
Rough Common
CANTERBURY
Littlebourne
Marshborough
Stone Cross

Newnham
Sheldwich
Harbledown
Canterbury
Ickham
Wingham
Woodnesborough
Worth

Eastling
Throwley
Chartham Hatch
Thanington
Patrixbourne
Staple
Eastry
Ham

Badlesmere
Old Wives Lees
Chartham
Nackington
Bekesbourne
Chillenden
DOVER
Finglesham

Selling
Shalmsford Street
Lower Hardres
Adisham
Goodnestone
Knowlton
Betteshanger
Sholden

Leaveland
Shottenden
Chilham
Bishopsbourne
Aylesham
Northbourne

Stalisfield Green
Molash
Petham
Upper Hardres Court
Kingston
Nonington
Tilmanstone
Great Mongeham
Deal

Challock
Godmersham
Sole Street
Barham
Womenswold
Elvington
East Studdal
Walmer

Charing
Boughton Aluph
Bilting
Cruddale
Bossingham
Derringstone
Woolage Green
Barfreston
Eythorne
Sutton
Ripple
Ringwould

Westwell
Boughton Lees
Wye
Hassell Street
Waltham
Stelling Minnis
Denton
Shepherdswell or Sibertswold
West Langdon
Martin
Kingsdown

Little Chart
Kennington
Bodsham
Elmsted
Wootton
Coldred
Lydden
Whitfield
East Langdon
Martin Mill

Hothfield
Brook
Hastingleigh
Lymbridge Green
Elham
Swingfield Minnis
Ewell Minnis
Temple Ewell
Guston
West Cliffe
St. Margaret's at Cliffe

Ashford
Hinxhill
Brabourne
Rhodes Minnis
Alkham
Buckland

Great Chart
Willesborough
Stowting
Lyminge
Densole
West Hougham

ASHFORD
Sevington
Brabourne Lees
Paddlesworth
Hawkinge
Dover

Kingsnorth
Mersham
Cheeseman's Green
Smeeth
Postling
Etchinghill
Capel-le-Ferne

Shadoxhurst
Sellindge
Channel Tunnel Terminal

Aldington Frith
Aldington
Stanford
Newington
Cheriton

Bromley Green
Bonnington
SHEPWAY
Saltwood
Sandgate
Folkestone

Hamstreet
Bilsington
Lympne
Hythe

Warehorne
Ruckinge
Newchurch
Burmarsh

Snave
St. Mary in the Marsh
Dymchurch

Snargate
Ivychurch
St Marys Bay

Brenzett
Littlestone-on-Sea

Brookland
New Romney
Old Romney
Greatstone-on-Sea

East Guldeford
Lydd
Lydd-on-Sea

Camber

	County Boundary
	District Boundary

County of Kent, estimated population 1,329,718
Medway Unitary Authority, estimated population 249,488

Districts: Boundaries of the districts are shown on pages 4-5.

Ashford	**102,661**	Gravesham	**95,717**	Swale	**122,80**
Canterbury	**135,278**	Maidstone	**138,948**	Thanet	**126,70**
Dartford	**85,911**	Sevenoaks	**109,305**	Tonbridge & Malling	**107,56**
Dover	**104,566**	Shepway	**96,238**	Tunbridge Wells	**104,03**

Acol 10 E3
Addington 8 D4
Adisham 10 D4
Aldington 11 C6
Aldington Frith 11 B6
Alkham 11 D5
Allhallows 8 E2
Allhallows-on-Sea 8 E2
Appledore 11 A7
Ash 8 C3
Ash 10 E4
Ashford 11 B5
Ashurst 9 B6
Aylesford 8 D4
Aylesham 10 D4

Badgers Mount 8 B3
Badlesmere 10 B4
Bapchild 10 A3
Barfreston 11 E5
Barham 11 D5
Bean 8 C3
Bearsted 8 E4
Bekesbourne 10 D4
Beltinge 10 D3
Benenden 9 E6
Benover 9 D5
Bethersden 11 A6
Betsham 8 C3
Betteshanger 10 E4
Bicknor 8 F4
Bidborough 9 C5
Biddenden 9 E6
Bilsington 11 B6
Bilting 11 B5
Birchington 10 E3
Birling 8 D4
Bishopsbourne 10 D4
Blean 10 C4
Blue Bell Hill 8 D3
Bobbing 8 F3
Bodsham 11 C5
Bonnington 11 B6
Borden 8 F3
Borough Green 8 C4
Borstal 8 D3
Bossingham 11 C5
Bough Beech 9 B5
Boughton Aluph 11 B5
Boughton Lees 11 B5
Boughton Monchelsea 8 E4
Boughton Street 10 C4
Boxley 8 E4
Brabourne 11 C5
Brabourne Lees 11 C5
Brasted 8 B4
Brasted Chart 8 B4
Bredgar 8 F4
Bredhurst 8 E4
Brenchley 9 D5
Brenzett 11 B7
Bridge 10 D4
Broad Oak 10 D4
Broad Street 8 E4
Broadstairs 10 F3

Bromley Green 11 B6
Brompton 8 E3
Brook 11 C5
Brookland 11 B7
Broomfield 8 E4
Broomfield 10 D3
Buckland 11 E5
Burham 8 D4
Burmarsh 11 C6

Canterbury 10 D4
Capel-le-Ferne 11 D6
Chainhurst 9 D5
Chalk 8 D3
Challock 11 B5
Channel Tunnel Terminal 11 D6
Charing 11 B5
Charing Heath 11 A5
Chart Sutton 9 E5
Chartham 10 C4
Chartham Hatch 10 C4
Chatham 8 E3
Chattenden 8 E3
Cheeseman's Green 11 B6
Cheriton 11 D6
Chestfield 10 C3
Chevening 8 B4
Chiddingstone 9 B5
Chiddingstone Causeway 9 B5
Chilham 10 C4
Chillenden 10 E4
Chislet 10 D3
Church Street 8 D2
Clapham Hill 10 C3
Claygate 9 D5
Claygate Cross 8 C4
Cliffe 8 D2
Cliffe Woods 8 D2
Cliffs End 10 E3
Cliftonville 10 F3
Cobham 8 D3
Coldred 11 E5
Collier Street 9 D5
Conyer 10 B3
Cooling 8 E2
Cowden 9 A6
Coxheath 9 D5
Cranbrook 9 E6
Cranbrook Common 9 E6
Crockenhill 8 B3
Crockham Hill 9 A5
Cross-at-Hand 9 E5
Crundale 11 C5
Culverstone Green 8 C3
Curtisden Green 9 D5
Cuxton 8 D3

Darenth 8 C3
Dargate 10 C4
Dartford 8 B2
Deal 10 F4
Densole 11 D5
Denton 11 D5
Derringstone 11 D5
Detling 8 E4

Ditton 8 D4
Doddington 10 A4
Dover 11 E6
Dumpton 10 F3
Dungeness 11 C8
Dunk's Green 8 C4
Dunkirk 10 C4
Dunton Green 8 B4
Dymchurch 11 C7

East Barming 8 D4
East End 9 E6
East Farleigh 8 D4
East Langdon 11 E5
East Malling 8 D4
East Peckham 9 D5
East Stourmouth 10 E3
East Studdal 11 E5
Eastchurch 10 B3
Eastling 10 B4
Eastry 10 E4
Eccles 8 D4
Edenbridge 9 A5
Egerton 11 A5
Egerton Forstal 11 A5
Elham 11 D5
Elmsted 11 C5
Elmstone 10 D4
Elvington 11 E5
Etchinghill 11 D6
Ewell Minnis 11 E5
Eynsford 8 B3
Eythorne 11 E5

Fairseat 8 C4
Farningham 8 B3
Faversham 10 B3
Fawkham Green 8 C3
Finglesham 10 E4
Five Oak Green 9 C5
Fleet Downs 8 C2
Folkestone 11 D6
Fordcombe 9 B6
Fordwich 10 D4
Four Elms 9 B5
Four Throws 9 E6
Frindsbury 8 D3
Frinsted 8 F4
Frittenden 9 E5

Gillingham 8 E3
Godmersham 11 B5
Golden Green 9 C5
Goodnestone 10 B4
Goodnestone 10 D4
Goudhurst 9 D6
Grafty Green 9 F5
Grain 8 F2
Graveney 10 C3
Gravesend 8 D2
Great Chart 11 B5
Great Mongeham 11 E5
Great Stonar 10 E4
Greatstone-on-Sea 11 C7
Greenhithe 8 C2

Grove 10 D
Guston 11 E

Hadlow 9 C
Haffenden Quarter 9 F
Hale Street 9 D
Halfway Houses 10 A
Halling 8 D
Halstead 8 B
Ham 10 E
Hamstreet 11 B
Harbledown 10 C
Harrietsham 8 F
Hartley 8 C
Hartley 9 D
Hartlip 8 E
Hassell Street 11 C
Hastingleigh 11 C
Hawkenbury 9 E
Hawkhurst 9 D
Hawkinge 11 D
Hawley 8 B
Headcorn 9 E
Heaverham 8 C
Hempstead 8 E
Herne 10 D
Herne Bay 10 C
Hernhill 10 C
Hersden 10 D
Hever 9 B
Hextable 8 B
High Halden 9 F
High Halstow 8 E
Higham 8 D
Higham Wood 9 C
Highsted 8 F
Hildenborough 9 C
Hillborough 10 D
Hinxhill 11 B
Hoaden 10 E
Hoath 10 D
Hollingbourne 8 F
Honey Hill 10 C
Hoo Saint Werburgh 8 E
Horsmonden 9 D
Horton Kirby 8 C
Hothfield 11 A
Hucking 8 E
Hunton 9 D
Hythe 11 D

Ickham 10 D
Ide Hill 8 B
Iden Green 9 E
Ightham 8 C
Istead Rise 8 C
Ivy Hatch 8 C
Ivychurch 11 B
Iwade 10 A

Kemsing 8 B
Kemsley 8 F
Kenardington 11 A
Kennington 11 B
Kilndown 9 D

ing's Hill	8 D4	**N**ackington	10 C4	Sandhurst	9 E7	Thurnham	8 E4
ingsdown	11 F5	Nettlestead	8 D4	Sandwich	10 E4	Tilmanstone	10 E4
ingsgate	10 F3	Nettlestead Green	8 D4	Sarre	10 E3	Tonbridge	9 C5
ingsnorth	8 E3	New Ash Green	8 C3	Seal	8 C4	Tovil	8 E4
ingsnorth	11 B6	New Barn	8 C3	Seasalter	10 C3	Toy's Hill	9 B5
ingston	11 D5	New Hythe	8 D4	Sellindge	11 C6	Trottiscliffe	8 C4
ingswood	9 F5	New Romney	11 B7	Selling	10 B4	Tudeley	9 C5
nockholt	8 B4	Newchurch	11 B6	Sevenoaks	8 B4	Tunstall	8 F4
nowlton	10 E4	Newenden	9 E7	Sevenoaks Weald	9 B5	Tyler Hill	10 C4
		Newington	8 F3	Sevington	11 B6		
addingford	9 D5	Newington	11 D6	Shadoxhurst	11 B6	**U**lcombe	9 F5
amberhurst	9 D6	Newnham	10 A4	Shalmsford Street	10 C4	Underriver	8 B4
angley Heath	9 E5	Nonington	10 E4	Sheerness	10 A2	Upchurch	8 E3
angton Green	9 B6	Northbourne	10 E4	Sheldwich	10 B4	Upnor	8 E3
arkfield	8 D4	Northfleet	8 C2	Shepherdswell	11 D5	Upper Hardres Court	11 C5
aveland	10 B4			Shepway	8 E4	Upstreet	10 D3
eeds	8 E4	**O**ad Street	8 F3	Shipbourne	8 C4		
eigh	9 B5	Oare	10 B3	Sholden	10 F4	**V**igo Village	8 D3
eigh Green	9 F6	Offham	8 D4	Shoreham	8 B4		
enham	8 F4	Old Romney	11 B7	Shorne	8 D3	**W**ainscott	8 D3
enham Heath	9 F5	Old Wives Lees	10 C4	Shottenden	10 B4	Walderslade	8 E3
eybourne	8 D4	Ospringe	10 B4	Sibertswold	11 D5	Walmer	11 F5
eysdown-on-Sea	10 B3	Otford	8 B4	Singlewell	8 D3	Waltham	11 C5
inton	9 E5	Otham	8 E4	Sissinghurst	9 E6	Warden	10 B3
ttle Chart	11 A5			Sittingbourne	10 A3	Ware	10 E4
ttlebourne	10 D4	**P**addlesworth	11 D6	Small Hythe	9 F6	Warehorne	11 B6
ttlestone-on-Sea	11 C7	Paddock Wood	9 D5	Smarden	9 F5	Warren Street	10 A4
ongfield	8 C3	Painter's Forstal	10 B4	Smeeth	11 C6	Wateringbury	8 D4
oose	8 D4	Park Wood	8 E3	Snargate	11 B7	Wayfield	8 E3
ords Wood	8 E3	Patrixbourne	10 D4	Snave	11 B7	Well Hill	8 B3
ower Halstow	8 F3	Pembury	9 C5	Snodland	8 D4	West Cliffe	11 E5
ower Hardres	10 C4	Penshurst	9 B5	Sole Street	8 D3	West Farleigh	8 D4
ower Higham	8 D2	Petham	11 C5	Sole Street	11 C5	West Hougham	11 E5
ower Rainham	8 E3	Platt	8 C4	South Darenth	8 C3	West Kingsdown	8 C3
ower Stoke	8 E2	Platt's Heath	9 F5	Southborough	9 C5	West Langdon	11 E5
uddesdown	8 D3	Plaxtol	8 C4	Southfleet	8 C3	West Malling	8 D4
uton	8 E3	Pluckley	9 F5	Speldhurst	9 B5	West Peckham	8 C4
ydd	11 B7	Postling	11 C6	Stalisfield Green	10 B4	West Stourmouth	10 E3
ydden	11 D5	Preston	10 D4	Standen	9 F6	West Street	10 A4
ydd-on-Sea	11 C7			Stanford	11 C6	Westbere	10 D4
ymbridge Green	11 C5	**Q**ueenborough	10 A3	Stansted	8 C3	Westerham	8 B4
yminge	11 D5			Staple	10 E4	Westgate-on-Sea	10 E3
ympne	11 C6	**R**ainham	8 E3	Staplehurst	9 E5	Westmarsh	10 E4
ynsted	10 A4	Ramsgate	10 F3	Stelling Minnis	11 C5	Westwell	11 B5
		Reading Street	11 A6	Stockbury	8 E4	Whetsted	9 C5
Maidstone	8 D4	Reculver	10 D3	Stodmarsh	10 D4	Whitfield	11 E5
Maltmans Hill	9 F5	Redbrook Street	11 A6	Stoke	8 E2	Whitley Row	8 B4
Manston	10 E3	Rhodes Minnis	11 C5	Stone	8 C2	Whitstable	10 C3
Marden	9 E5	Ringwould	11 E5	Stone	11 A7	Wichling	10 A4
Margate	10 E3	Ripple	11 E5	Stowting	11 C5	Wickhambreaux	10 D4
Markbeech	9 B5	Riverhead	8 B4	Strood	8 D3	Wigmore	8 E3
Marlpit Hill	9 A5	Rochester	8 D3	Sturry	10 D4	Willesborough	11 B5
Marsh Green	9 A5	Rodmersham	10 A4	Sundridge	8 B4	Wilmington	8 B3
Marshborough	10 E4	Rolvenden	9 F6	Sutton	11 E5	Wingham	10 D4
Marshside	10 D3	Rolvenden Layne	9 F6	Sutton at Hone	8 B3	Wittersham	11 A7
Martin	11 E5	Rough Common	10 C4	Sutton Valence	9 E5	Womenswold	11 D5
Martin Mill	11 E5	Royal British Legion Village		Swalecliffe	10 C3	Woodchurch	11 A6
Matfield	9 C5		8 D4	Swanley	8 B3	Woodnesborough	10 E4
Maypole	10 D3	Royal Tunbridge Wells	9 C6	Swanscombe	8 C2	Woolage Green	11 D5
Meopham	8 D3	Ruckinge	11 B6	Swingfield Minnis	11 D5	Wootton	11 D5
Meopham Station	8 C3	Ryarsh	8 D4			Wormshill	8 F4
Mereworth	8 C4			**T**ankerton	10 C3	Worth	10 E4
Mersham	11 B6	**S**t Margaret's at Cliffe	11 F5	Temple Ewell	11 E5	Wouldham	8 D3
Milebush	9 E5	St Mary Hoo	8 E2	Tenterden	9 F6	Wrotham	8 C4
Milstead	8 F4	St Mary in the Marsh	11 C7	Teston	8 D4	Wrotham Heath	8 C4
Milton Regis	8 F3	St Marys Bay	11 C7	Teynham	10 A3	Wye	11 C5
Minster	10 B2	St Michaels	9 F6	Thamesport	8 F2		
Minster	10 E3	St Nicholas at Wade	10 D3	Thanington	10 C4	**Y**alding	9 D5
Molash	10 B4	St Peter's	10 F3	The Moor	9 E7	Yorkletts	10 C3
Monkton	10 E3	Saltwood	11 D6	Thong	8 D3		
		Sandgate	11 D6	Throwley	10 B4		

Population figures are based upon 2001 Census.

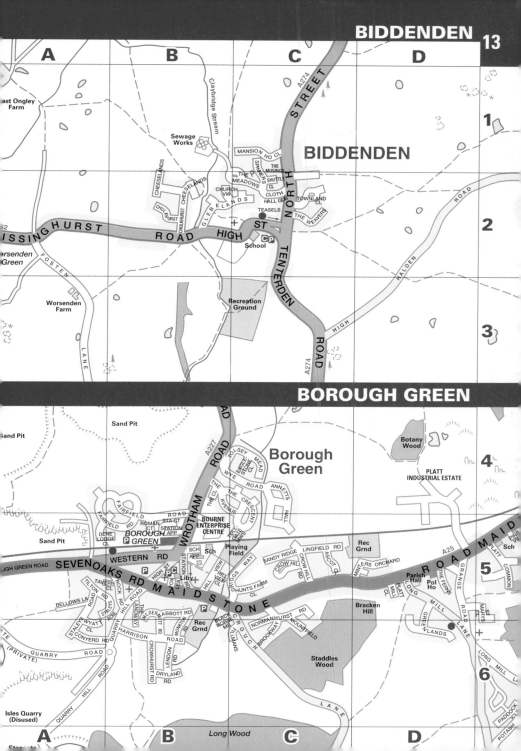

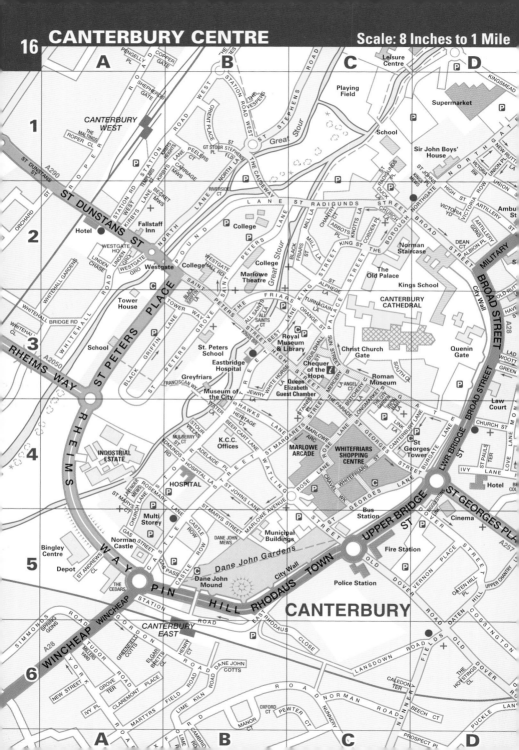

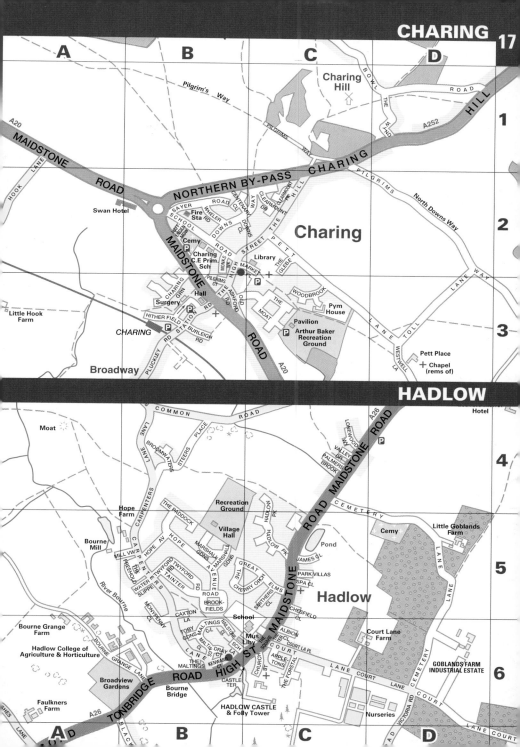

A   B   C   D

Walpole Bay

Walpole Rocks

Palm Bay

Bathing Pool

Newgate Gap Bridge

Hodges Bridge

PROMENADE

Miniature Golf Course

QUEENS

The Oval

EASTERN

LEWIS CRES

Bowling Green

Hodges Gap

Sacketts Gap

PRINCES

PALM

BAY

AVENUE

WALK GAP

FRIENDLY GAP

PRINCES

THE RIDINGS

School

ESPLANADE

BERESFORD

Grand Hotel

Hotel

Cliftonville

RUTLAND

Recreation Ground

MARGARET AV

SPRINGFIELD

Sch

Hall

DEVONSHIRE

NORTHUMBERLAND

LEICESTER

GLOUCESTER

CLARENCE

MAGNOLIA

PRINCESS

EASTCHURCH

SALTWOOD GDNS

Sch

Playing Field

Laleham School

Sch

OLD GREEN RD

WILLOW

FORELAND

DALMENY

Northdown

Liby

Northdown Park

THE PADDOCKS

WEST PARK

QUEEN ELIZABETH AV

East Northdown Farm

Victoria

Sch

ANTHONYS WAY

ADISHAM WAY

DENTON WY

St Anthonys School

AMHERST CL

Northdown House

B2052

MILLMEAD

Northdown C.P. Sch

NORTHDOWN PK RD

GEORGE HILL RD

Playground

Northdown C.P. Sch

HINCHLIFFE

ST MICHAELS AV

READING STREET ROAD

NORTHDOWN

GREEN LANE

ST MARYS AVENUE

Victoria AV

WHITFIELD

CAMDEN

FOSTERS

PEARSONS

B2053

ST PETERS RD

A255

Updown Farm

A   B   C   D

1 2 3 4 5 6

A B C D

1

2

3

4

5

6

Scamperdale

Gaywood Farm

ROAD MAIN
B2026

HOMESTEAD RD

FAIRMEAD RD

HIGHFIELDS

OAKFIELD RD

HILDERS CL

HILL-CREST RD

ELM COTTS

ASHCOMBE DR

YMEAD

BROWN INGS

ROAD

Swan Lane Farm

Marlpit Hill

MARLHURST

MEADOW LANE

HILDERS LANE

HILDERS

LANE

PIT

ROAD

SWAN

LANE

SWAN

LANE

RIDGE WY

RIDGE

SWAN RIDGE

CROWN ROAD

LANE

WAY

Mowshurst B2027

FOUR ELMS RD

Football Ground

Breezehurst Farm

Hamsell Mead Farm

ALBION

SUNNYSIDE

EDENBRIDGE

CROUCH HOUSE

St BRELADES CT
Caravan Park

ENTERPRISE WY

STATION

FIRCROFT

GREAT MEAD

COMMERCE

INDUSTRIAL ESTATE

INDUSTRIAL ESTATE

St JOHNS WY

NEWHOUSE TER

WAY

HERON

MALLARD WY

WOODLAND

MARLPIT

PLOVER CL

FIRCROFT

FARMSTEAD

PLOUGH WALK

HARROW

KESTREL

OXFIELD STACKFIELD

ROWFIELD

SPEEDWELL

BRIAR CT

FOXGLOVE CLOVER WAY

WAYSIDE DR

WAINHOUSE

GREENFIELD

HOPGARDEN CL

SKINNERS

SMITHYFIELD

1 WOODPECKER CL
2 SORRELL CL
3 BROOK CT
4 TEMPLARS CT

Sewage Works

Driving Range

Edenbridge Golf & Country Club

DALESHURST RD

GRESHAMS WY

GOODWYN CL

Crouch House Farm

Spitals Cross

WESTWAYS

FOUR

ELMS

Eden Valley School

Skinners Farm

Crouch House Green

CEDAR

HAW THORN

PARK AV

PARK

MOLES MEAD

ORCHARD

CROUCH HO COTTS

HOLLY COTTS

OAKS RD

STANBRIDGE RD

PINE GROVE

CHESTNUT

PINE

CROUCH

PARK VIEW CL

WELLINGTONIA WY

SCHOOL FIELD

Edenbridge Leisure Centre & Swimming Pool

PENLEE CL

STATION APPROACH

EDENBRIDGE TOWN

Edenbridge

Hall

Clinic

STANGROVE

GORDON

HENRY HO

GRANGE

HEADLEY CT

CLOSE

GREENFIELD

Sch

ROAD

HALLAND

St BARN HAWE

FALCONERS

CROFT LA

FORGE

CROFT

FRANT FLD

CHURCH FIELD

STREATFEILD

CROFT

Cemy

THE PLAT

Springfield

MANOR

MANOR HO GDNS

MANOR RD GDNS

LINGFIELD

THE LIMES

LIby

CP

P

SCHURCH

Cemy

STREET

SPRING

MANOR

ROAD

ROAD

SKEYNES

ASH CL

TANNERS

TAXED

Council Offices

Mus

Mkt

S/store

THE SQ

LEATHER

RIVERSIDE

CHURCH ST

RIVERSIDE CT

River Eden

Skeynes Park

LINGFIELD

Kent Brook

COOMB

LUCILINA DR

DOGGETTS CL

PENN

COBBETTS

LEATHER

CROFT

AUFAN WY

MONT

HIGH STREET

MILL STREET

Fire Sta

KATHERINE RD

VICTORIA RD

VICTORIA CL

MILL HILL COTTS

ASHBYS

ROBINS

HEVER

WATER MEADOWS

Recreation Ground

Mill Race

EDENBRIDGE TRADING CENTRE

WARSOP IND EST

ROAD

HOSPITAL

B2026

MEAD RD

A B C D

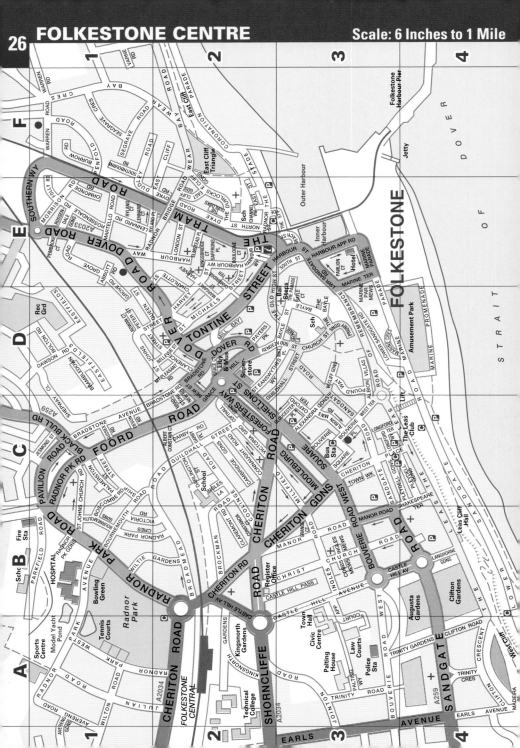

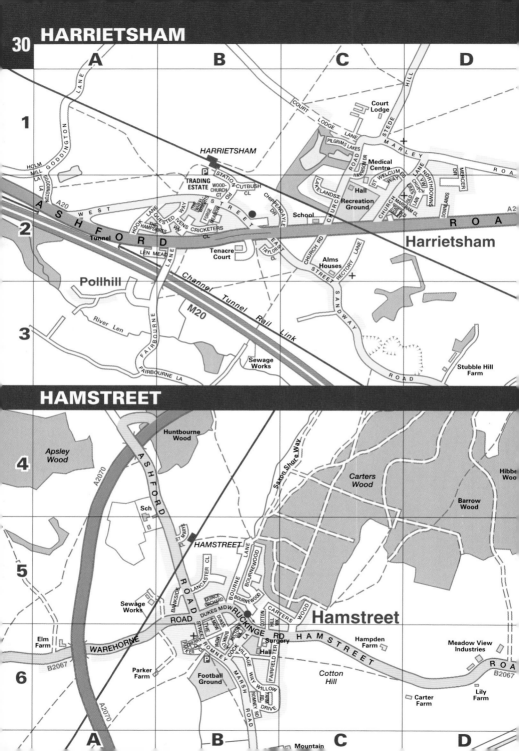

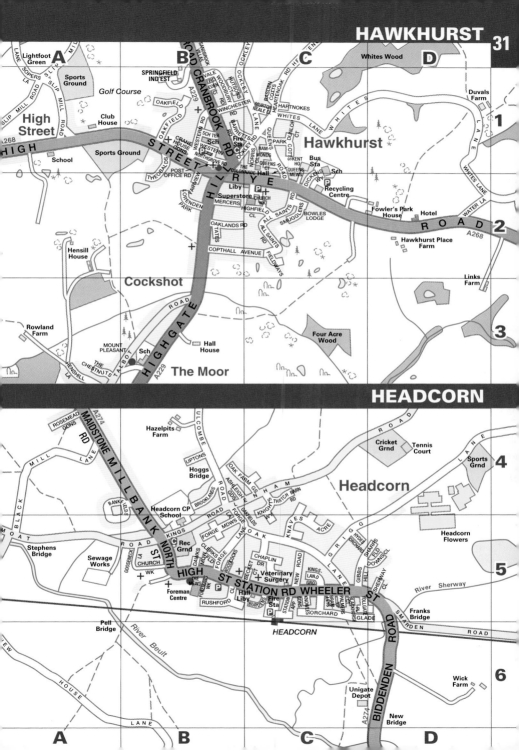

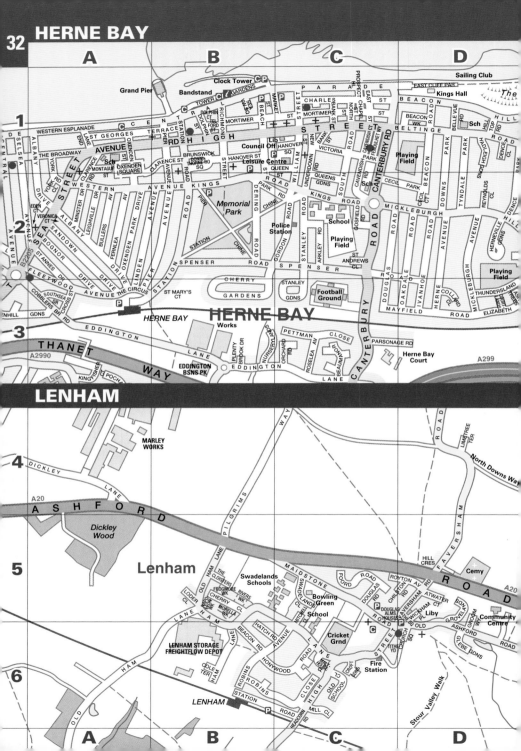

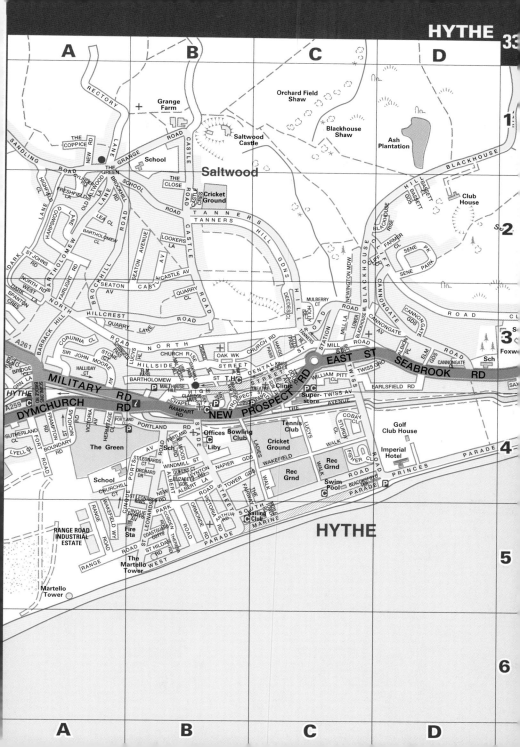

Saltwood

HYTHE

A B C D

Rectory Lane

Grange Farm

Orchard Field Shaw

Blackhouse Shaw

Ash Plantation

THE COPPICE

School

Saltwood Castle

BLACKHOUSE

Club House

HILL BASSETT GDS

BASSETT GDS

THE GREEN

NEW RD

GYLINGE ROAD

OLD SALTWOOD LANE

THE CLOSE

CASTLE ROAD

PLASTUS CRES

Cricket Ground

TANNERS HILL GDNS

BLACKHOUSE RISE

FARMER CL

SENE PK

SENE PARK

HIGHFIELD CL

FRESHFIELD LA

GRANGE ROAD

SCHOOL ROAD

TANNERS

CASTLE ROAD

DEDDES CL

HILL

CLIFF

CANNONGATE AV

CANNONGATE GDS

ROAD

DARK LA

ST JOHNS RD

HARPSWOOD LA

BARTHOLOMEW

BROCKHILL ROAD

LEA CL

LOOKERS LA

SEATON AVENUE

QUARRY CL

Mulberry CT

HOLLY

TANNERS

ROAD

CANNON GATE

ALBICH PL

ELM GDS

CANNONGATE

ROAD

Sch

Foxw

NORTH RD

DARK WEST

SPANTON CRES

BARTHOLOMEW CL

CASTLE AV

SEATON AV

CASTLE AV

QUARRY ROAD

NORTH

CHURCH RD

STATION ROAD

MILL LA

LOWER BLACKHOUSE HL

MILL RD

ELM GDS

SAXO

A261

BARRACK HILL

HILLCREST

QUARRY LANE

CORUNNA CL

SIR JOHN MOORE AV

CHURCH RISE

CHURCH HL

OAK WK

STREET

KINGS RIDE R

DENTAL STREET

THE STREET

EAST ST

SEABROOK RD

S

BRIDGE

A259

GRN LA

MILITARY RD

DYMCHURCH RD

HALLIDAY CT

STONE

LUCYS HILL

HILLSIDE

BARTHOLOMEW

MALTHOUSE

HIGH ST

CHAPEL ST

RAMPART

CLARIDGE RD

PROSPECT RD

NEW PROSPECT RD

THEATRE

Clinic

WILLIAM PITT AV

TWISS RD

WILLIAM PITT

TWISS AV

EARLSFIELD RD

T.H.C

P C

Super-store

SUTHERLAND CL

FRAMPTON RD

FORT RD

LYELL RD

BOUNDARY RD

ST NICHOLAS

VICTORIA AV

HERMITAGE

PORTLAND

PORTLAND RD

Offices

Bowling Club

Liby

Tennis Club

Cricket Ground

LUCYS WALK

STURDY CL

COBAY CL

WALK

Golf Club House

Imperial Hotel

PARADE

The Green

School

CHURCHILL CT

PORTS HILL

ORCHARD DR

LEONARDS CT

ST LEONARDS RD

Sch

WINDMILL ST

WOOD ST

QUEENS CT

ELIZABETH RD

LYNTON RD

ALBERT RD

ALBERT LA

NAPIER GDS

SLADE

LADIES WALK

WAKEFIELD

Rec Grnd

Rec Grnd

Swim Pool

FISHER ROAD

PRINCES PARADE

BEACONSFIELD RD

P

RANGE ROAD INDUSTRIAL ESTATE

WAKEFIELD RD

CINQUE PORTS

Fire Sta

ST LEONARDS ROAD

ST HILDAS RD

NEW RD

PARK

ORMONDE RD

COOPER THERESA

COASTGUARD COTTS

ARTHUR RD

SOUTH PARADE

TOWER GDS

THE FAIRWAY

ST FARMY

Sailing Club

MARINE

HYTHE

RANGE ROAD

The Martello Tower

WEST

Martello Tower

1

2

3

4

5

6

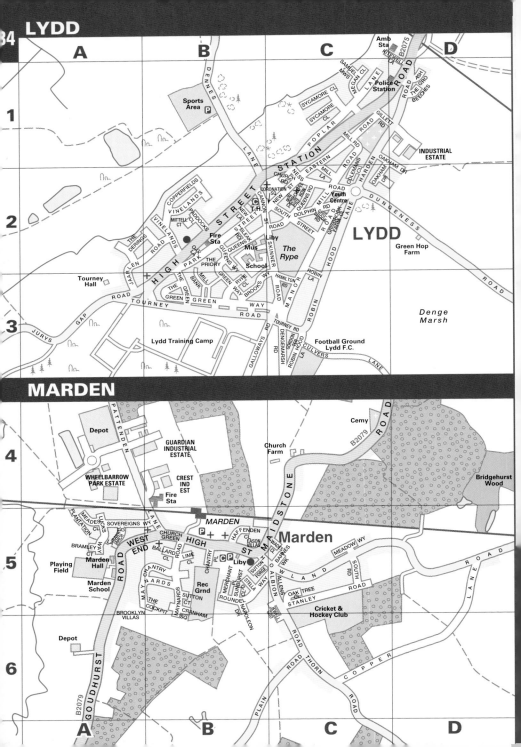

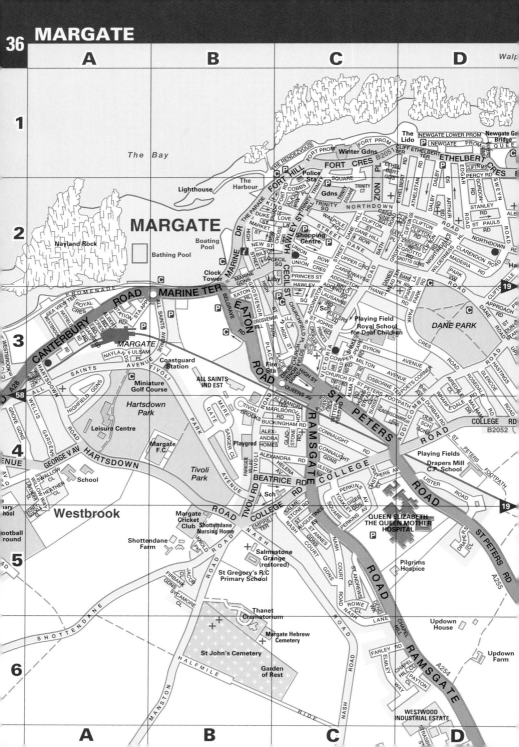

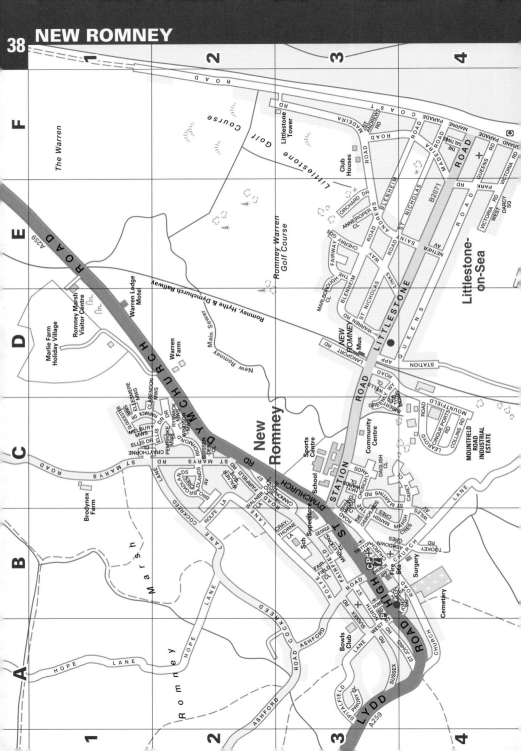

The Warren

Golf Course

Littlestone Tower

Littlestone Golf Course

Club Houses

ROAD

MADEIRA ST

ST ANDREWS RD

THE SALTINGS

GRAND PARADE

MARINE PARADE

MADEIRA ROAD

ORCHARD DR

ANNE ROPER CL

CHERRY GDS

FAIRWAY

THE FAIRWAY

BLENHEIM WAY

ST ANDREWS ROAD

ST NICHOLAS ST

MARLBOROUGH CL

BLENHEIM RD

WARREN RD

ST NICHOLAS RD

SAINT ANDREWS AV

PARK ROAD

B2071

QUEENS RD

VICTORIA ROAD

VICTORIA RD

WEST RD

D'ARCY SQ

NETHER ROAD

Littlestone-on-Sea

Romney Warren Golf Course

Romney, Hythe & Dymchurch Railway

New Romney Main Sewer

Warren Lodge Motel

Warren Farm

A259

ROAD

DYMCHURCH ROAD

Marlie Farm Holiday Village

Romney Marsh Visitor Centre

LITTLESTONE

QUEENS ROAD

NEW ROMNEY Mus

LANGPORT RD

APP ROAD

STATION

WELLS AM RD

GREAT HALL

MADEIRA RD

THE GRN

MOUNTFIELD ROAD

LEAFORD

CINQUE PORTS RD

COLLINS RD

MOUNTFIELD ROAD INDUSTRIAL ESTATE

New Romney

Brodynex Farm

ST MARYS ROAD

ROAD

GLOUCESTER MWS

ELLESMERE MWS

MELBURY MWS

HARROW DR

CLARENDON MWS

ELLIS DR

PEMBROKE DR

WINDSOR MWS

RICHMOND DR

RYSWICK MWS

ST MARYS AV

CANNON ST

FAIRFIELD ST

WALNER LANE

CRAY HOUSE

GRAYTHORNE

LANE

ROLFE LA

COCKEREED LANE

Romney Marsh

HOPE LANE

COCKEREED LANE

ASHFORD ROAD

SPITALFIELD LA

PRIORY RD

A259

LYDD ROAD

Sports Centre

Community Centre

DYMCHURCH RD

HIGH ST

STATION ROAD

School

Superstore

Sch

THORNE LA

GEORGE LA

MAGDALEN RD

ROLFE RD

FAIRFIELD RD

CHURCH RD

CP

Fire Sta

Surgery

TOOKEY RD

CHURCH RD

Cemetery

Bowls Club

SUSSEX LANE

WEST RD

NORTH RD

SUSSEX RD

ST JOHNS RD

TRITON RD

ASHDOWN CL

MARSH CRES

WILES AV

CAREY RD

DAGLISH CL

SOKARI DR

ST MARTINS RD

THE CHURCH ROAD

SANDS

MARSH CRES

WARREN RD

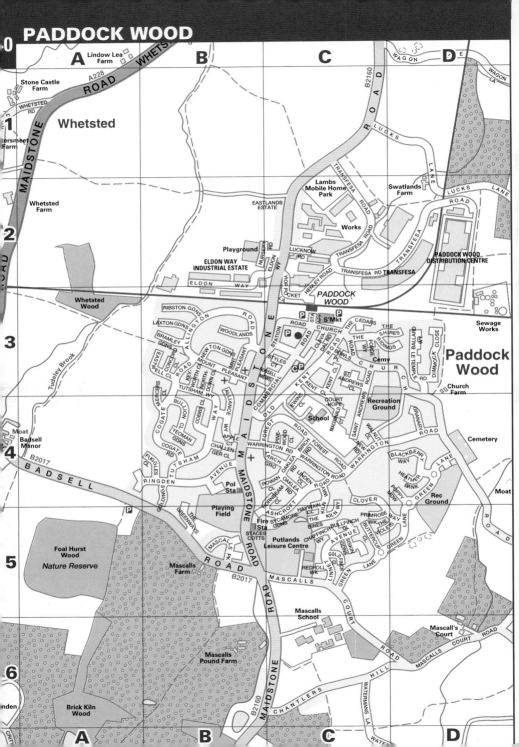

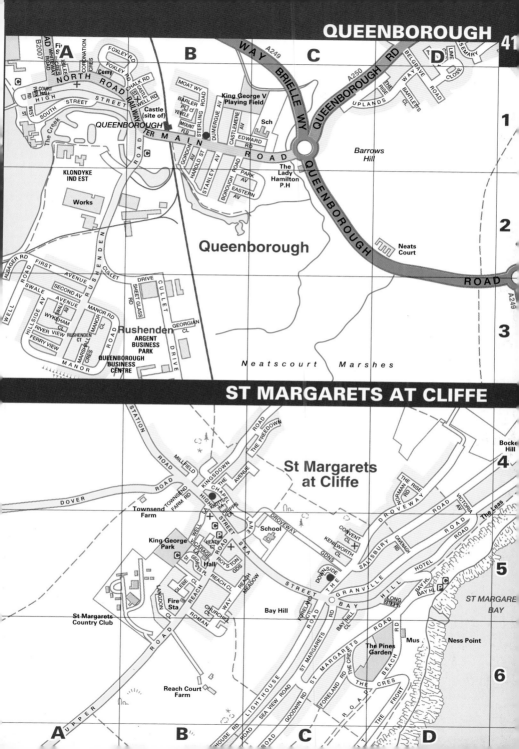

Queenborough

KLONDYKE IND EST

Works

Rushenden

ARGENT BUSINESS PARK

QUEENBOROUGH BUSINESS CENTRE

King George V Playing Field

Barrows Hill

Neats Court

The Lady Hamilton P.H

Neatscourt Marshes

ST MARGARETS AT CLIFFE

St Margarets at Cliffe

Townsend Farm

King George Park

St Margarets Country Club

Reach Court Farm

Bay Hill

The Pines Garden

St Margarets Country Club

Bocke Hill

ST MARGARE BAY

Ness Point

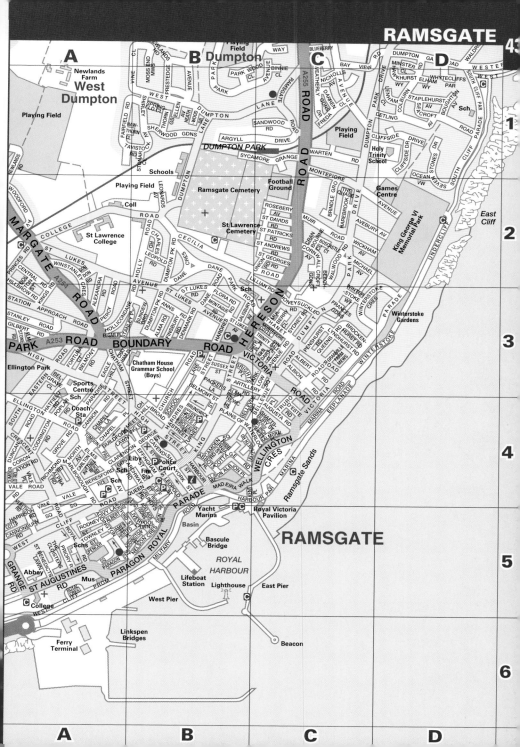

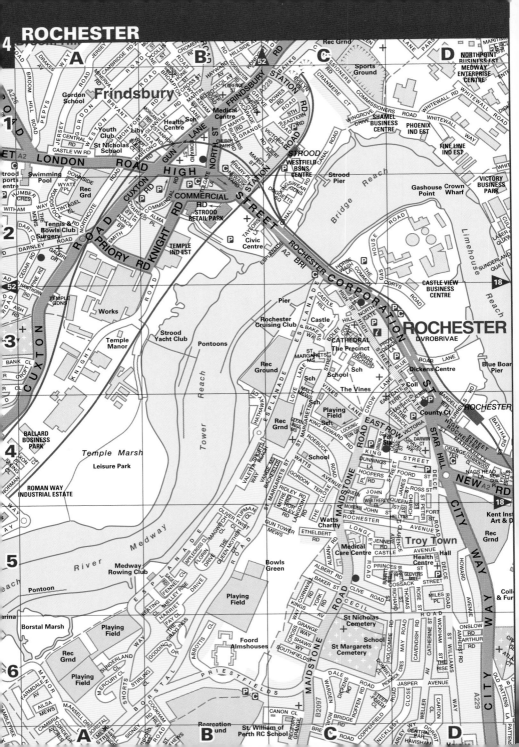

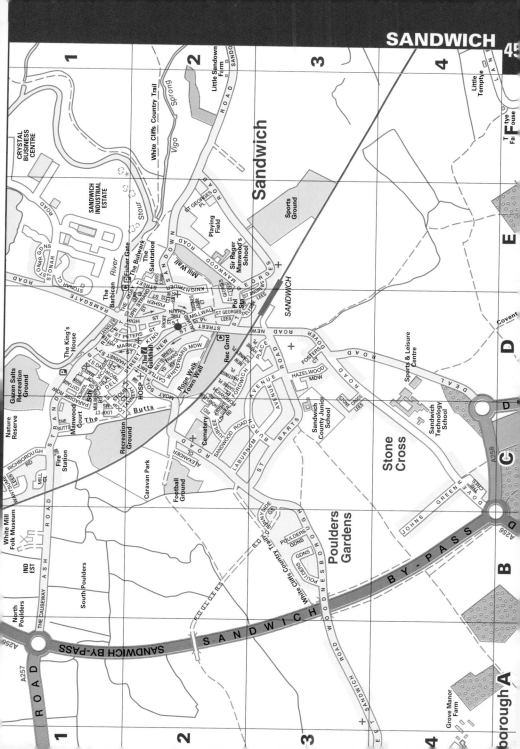

Sandwich

1
CRYSTAL BUSINESS CENTRE

White Cliffs Country Trail

Vigo Sprong

Little Sandown Farm

Little Temple

Tye Farm House

SANDWICH INDUSTRIAL ESTATE

STONAR CL
OMAR GDNS

River Stour

The Barbican
RAMSGATE ROAD

Fisher Gate
The Bulwark
The Salutation

St Georges PL

Playing Field

Sir Roger Manwood's School

Sports Ground

SANDWICH

Mill Wall
KNIGHTRIDER

MANWOOD ROAD

ST GEORGES

ST ANDREWS LEES

The King's House

Gazen Salts Recreation Ground

Nature Reserve

FISHER ST
SHORT

HIGH STREET

MARKET ST
KING ST

NEW ST

The Guildhall

Rec Grnd

Pol Sta
MILLWALL

ST GEORGES LEES

DELFSIDE

New ROAD

FOSTERS ROAD

DEAL ROAD

Sports & Leisure Centre

Covent

Town Wall
Rope Walk

HASTINGS PLACE
HAZELWOOD MDW

STONE CROSS LEES

Sandwich Technology School

White Mill Folk Museum

IND EST

MANTSURE LEES
RICHBOROUGH RD

MILL CL

Fire Station

Manwood Court

The Butts

Recreation Ground

Cemetery

Caravan Park

Football Ground

SANDWOOD ROAD

JUBILEE ROAD

ALEXANDER ROAD

LABURNUM RD

AVENUE ROAD

ST BARTS

Sandwich County Junior School

Stone Cross

JOHNS GREEN

DOVE CORNER

A258

North Poulders

THE CAUSEWAY
ASH ROAD

South Poulders

White Cliffs Country Trail

POULDERS ROAD
WOODNESBOROUGH ROAD

POULDERS GDNS

Poulders Gardens

SANDWICH BY-PASS

SANDWICH BY-PASS

Grove Manor Farm

borough A

1   **2**   **3**   **4**

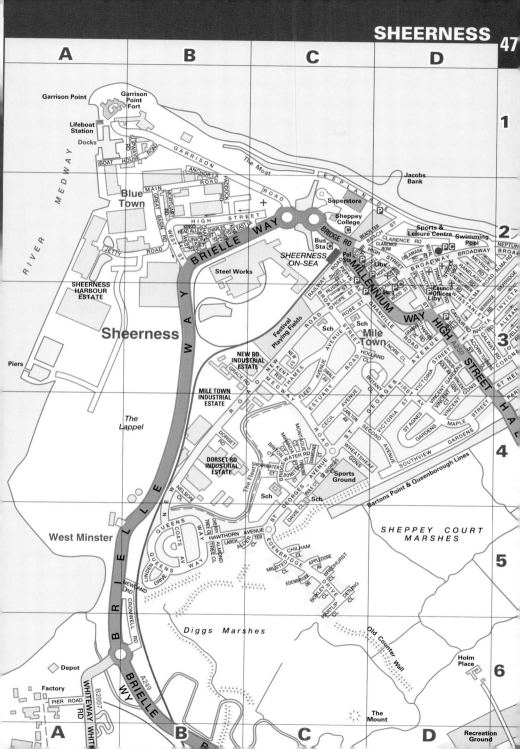

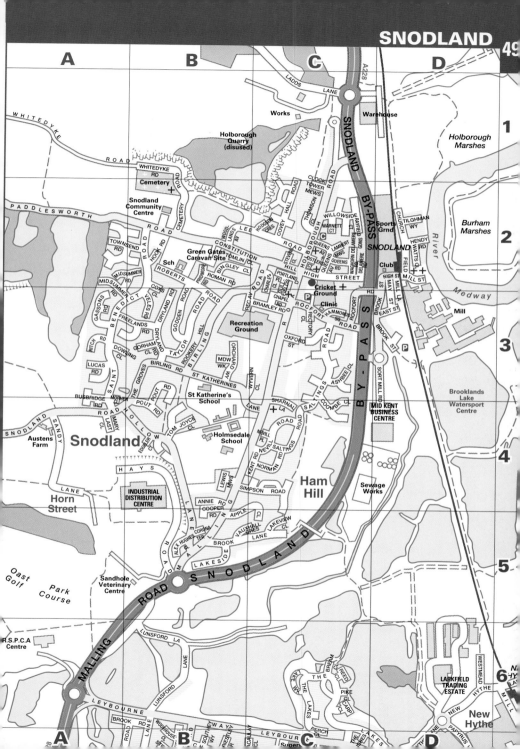

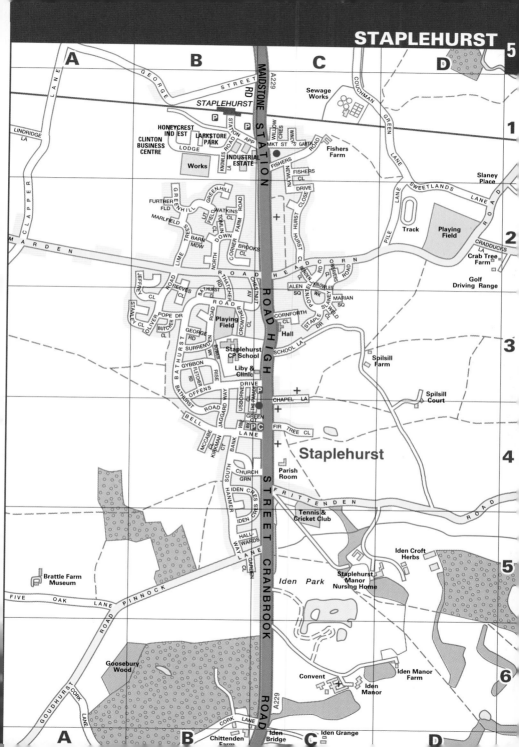

STAPLEHURST

A   **B**   **C**   **D**   5

GEORGE STREET

MAIDSTONE RD   A229

STAPLEHURST

LINDRIDGE LA

Sewage Works

COUGHMAN GREEN LANE

HONEYCREST IND EST

LARKSTORE PARK

CLINTON BUSINESS CENTRE

STATION APP

LODGE

KNOWLES LA

Works

INDUSTRIAL ESTATE

MKT ST

FISHERS

NEWLYN

FISHERS CL

DRIVE

Fishers Farm

Slaney Place

SWEETLANDS LANE

CLAPPER

MARDEN

FURTHER FLD

GREENHILL

MARLFIELD

GREENHILL

WATKINS CL

FARM ROAD

TOMLIN CL

LIME TREES

LITT

BARN MDW

DOWN

CORNER

BROOKS CL

NORTH

CHESTNUT AV

HURST CL

HEATH ROAD

CORN

Track

Playing Field

PILE LANE

CRADDUCKS LA

Crab Tree Farm

Golf Driving Range

JEFFREY CL

STANLEY CL

OLIVER CL

POPE DR

BUTCHER CL

REEVES CL

BATHURST ROAD

THATCHER

ROAD

Playing Field

CROWTHER

GEORGE RD

SURRENDEN WK

CORNFORTH CL

ALEN SQ

POYNTER

KNOWLES WK

SLANEY FIELD

STAPLE DR

MARIAN SQ

Hall

BATHURST ROAD

GYBBON RD

FLETCHER RD

RISE

OFFENS

USBORNE DRIVE

Staplehurst CP School

Liby & Clinic

SCHOOL LA

Spilsill Farm

Spilsill Court

BATHURST ROAD

BELL

JAGGARD WAY

VINE WK

THE HIGH

GREEN

PC

CHAPEL LA

FIR TREE CL

Staplehurst

MCCABE

KIRKMAN CT

BANK

SOUTH

CHURCH GRN

IDEN

HANNAM

Parish Room

FRITTENDEN

CRES

Tennis & Cricket Club

Brattle Farm Museum

FIVE OAK LANE

PINNOCK

Iden Park

Iden Croft Herbs

Staplehurst Manor Nursing Home

ROAD

GOUDHURST

CORK LANE

Goosebury Wood

Convent

Iden Manor

Iden Manor Farm

CORK LANE

Chittenden Farm

Iden Bridge

Iden Grange

CRANBROOK ROAD   A229

A   **B**   **C**   **D**

1

2

3

4

5

6

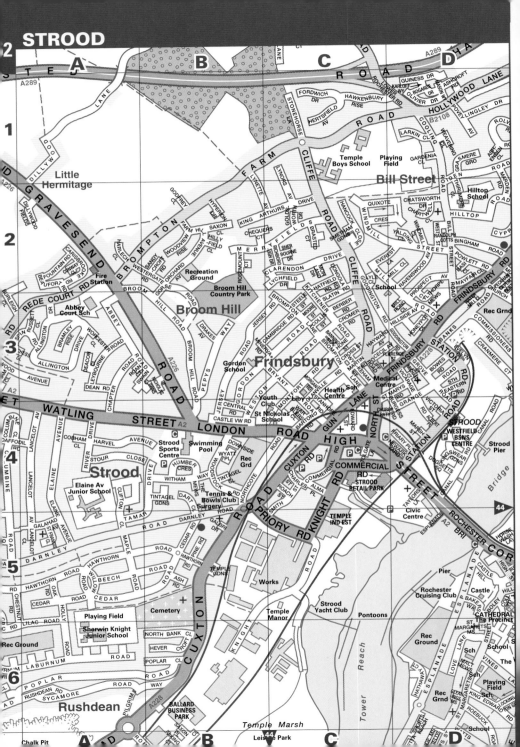

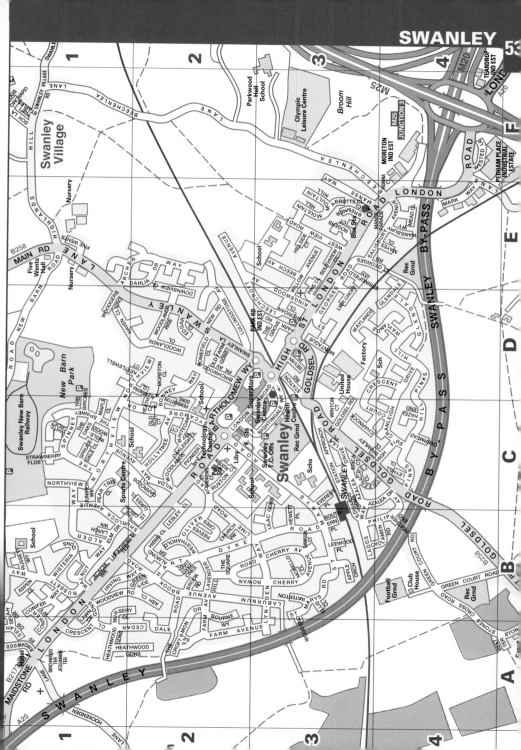

Swanley Village

TEARDROP IND EST

M20

M25

Parkwood Hall School

Olympic Leisure Centre

Broom Hill

M25 JUNCTION 3

MORETON IND EST

PEDHAM PLACE INDUSTRIAL ESTATE

LONDON ROAD

SWANLEY BY-PASS

Nursery

Five Wents Hall

MAIN RD

B258

School

New Barn Park

Swanley New Barn Railway

STRAWBERRY FLDS

NORTHVIEW

Sports Centre

School

Swanley Superstore

Swanley Health Centre

Swanley T.C. Offs

United House

Factory

GOLDSEL ROAD

SWANLEY BY-PASS ROAD

GOLDSEL ROAD B258

School

Football Grnd

Club House

GREEN COURT ROAD

Rec Grnd

STONES CROSS ROAD

School

B2173

MAIDSTONE RD

A20

SWANLEY LANE

HOCKENDEN LANE

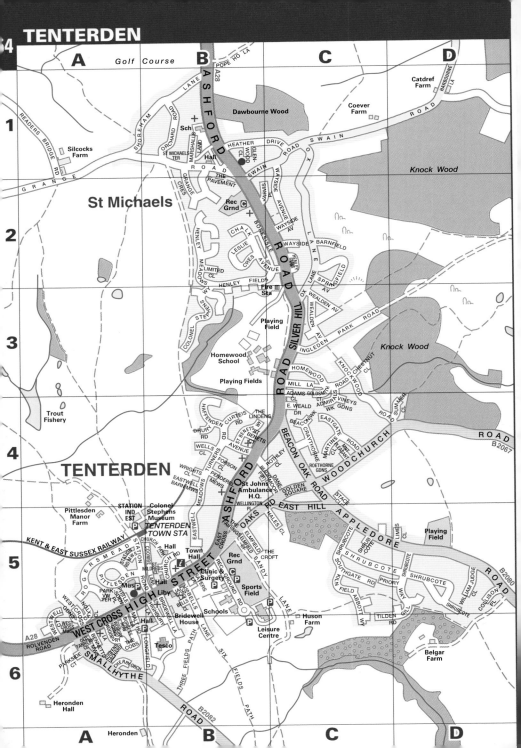

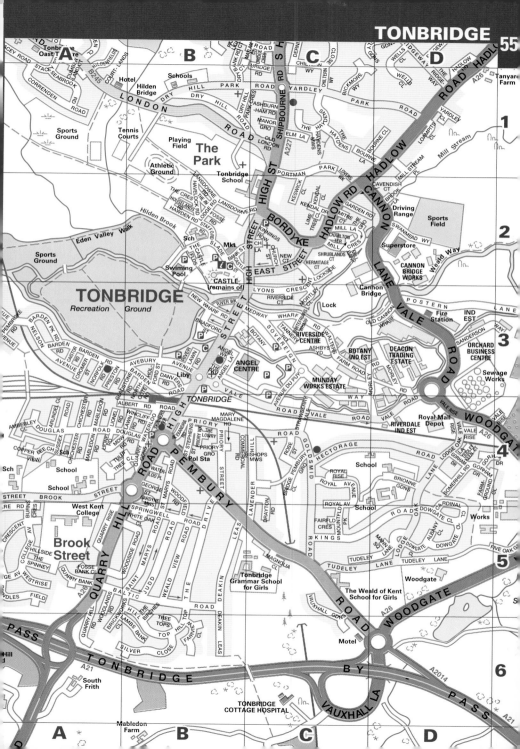

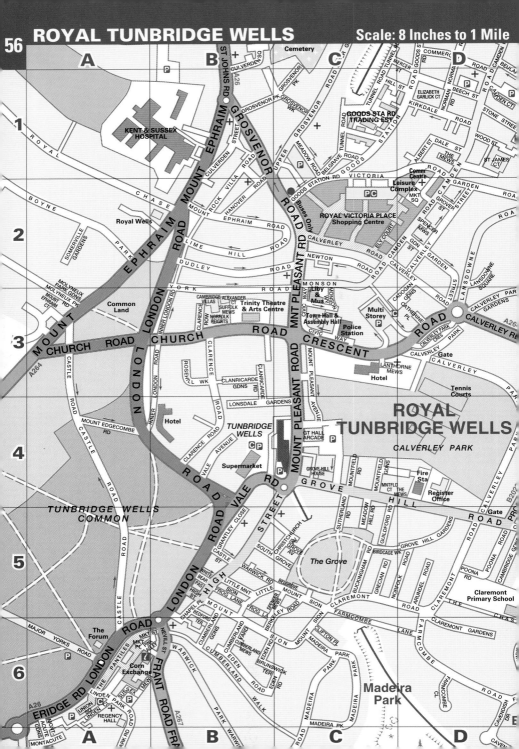

Westgate on Sea

Garlinge

Westbrook Bay

St Mildreds Bay

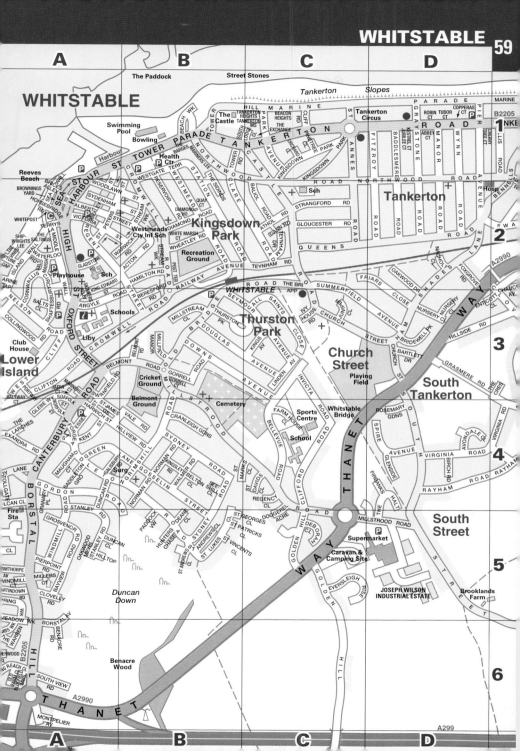

A   B   C   D

The Paddock   Street Stones

WHITSTABLE

Tankerton Slopes

MARINE

PARADE

Swimming Pool

Bowling

Harbour

Reeves Beach

Brownings Yard

Horsebridge

Whitepost

Ship-Wrights Saltings

The Castle
Tankerton Heights
Tankerton Mans
The Exchange
Beacon Heights

Tankerton Circus

Robin Tudor
COPPERAS

CHERRY TREE

Kestrel CT
Jubilee CT

ABBEY CT

Tankerton

Health Ctr

Westgate

Reservoir

Sydenham

Diamond Ho

Woodlawn

Westmeads
City Inf Sch

Kingsdown Park

White Marsh

Sch

Strangford RD

Gloucester RD

Queens

Northwood

Recreation Ground

Railway Avenue

Teynham RD

WHITSTABLE

THE BRI
APP

Summerfield

Friars
Oakwood Dr
Nursery

Hosp

Playhouse

Sch

Lower Island

Club House

Liby

Cromwell

Thurston Park

Church Street

Church Street

Playing Field

Whitstable

South Tankerton

Cricket Ground

Belmont Ground

Cemetery

Farm House

Sports Centre

School

Whitstable Bridge

Rosemary Gdns

Grasmere RD

South Tankerton

Sydney

Surg

Virginia RD

Virginia Road

Rayham Road

Fire Sta

Grosvenor

South Street

Windmill

Pierpoint

Millstrood Road

Supermarket

South Street

Duncan Down

Caravan & Camping Site

Eversleigh

JOSEPH WILSON INDUSTRIAL ESTATE

Brooklands Farm

Benacre Wood

Montpelier Av

A2990

THANET

A299

A   B   C   D

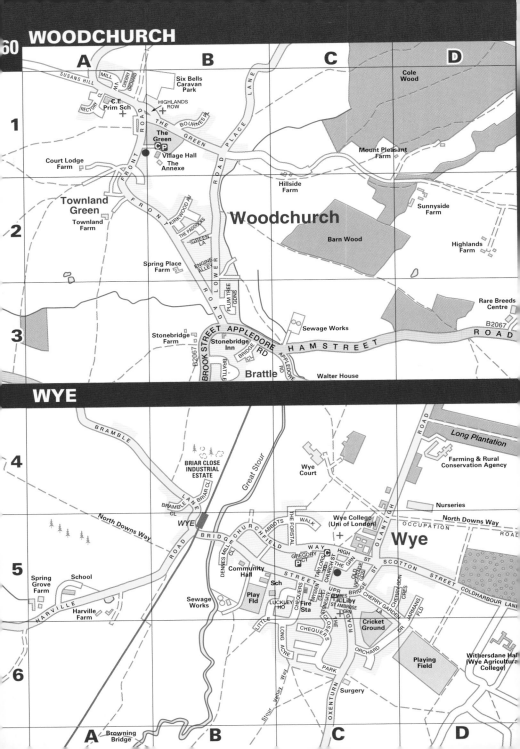

A   B   C   D

SUSANS HILL
MILL
CHERRY ORCHARD
Six Bells Caravan Park
Cole Wood
RECTORY CL
C.E. Prim Sch
HIGHLANDS ROW
LANE
1
THE GREEN
BOURNES PL
The Green
CP
Village Hall
Mount Pleasant Farm
Court Lodge Farm
The Annexe
FRONT ROAD
Hillside Farm

PLACE
Townland Green
KIRKWOOD AV
Woodchurch
Sunnyside Farm
2
Townland Farm
THE PADDOCKS
GREEN LA
Barn Wood
Highlands Farm
Spring Place Farm
ENGINE ALLEY
LOWER ROAD
PLUM TREE GDNS

Stonebridge Farm
APPLEDORE RD
Sewage Works
Rare Breeds Centre
B2067
3
BROOK STREET
Stonebridge Inn
BRIDGE
BRATTLE
APPLEDORE RD
H A M S T R E E T
R O A D
B2067
Brattle
Walter House

BRAMBLE
Long Plantation
4
BRIAR CLOSE INDUSTRIAL ESTATE
Great Stour
Wye Court
Farming & Rural Conservation Agency
BRAMBLE CL
BRIAR CL
ROAD
WYE
North Downs Way
Wye College (Uni of London)
Nurseries
North Downs Way
OCCUPATION ROAD
THE FORSTAL
WALK
CHURCHFIELD
ABBOTS
Wye
Spring Grove Farm
School
North Downs Way
BRIDGE
DENNES MILL CL
GREGORY PCT
WAY
TAYLORS
HIGH ST
THE GRN
OLD VICARAGE GDNS
SCOTTON STREET
5
Community Hall
Sch
CHURCH ST
KEMPES CL
CHERRY GARDEN LA
JARMANS FIELD
HARVILLE
Harville Farm
Play Fld
LUCKLEY HO
Fire Sta
STRACKS CLOSERS
ST AMBROSE
UPR BRIDGE ST
COLDHARBOUR LANE
Sewage Works
CHEQUERS
Liby
Cricket Ground
LONG ACRE
LITTLE
CHEQUERS
THE
6
PARK
ORCHARD
Surgery
Playing Field
Withersdane Hall (Wye Agricultural College)
Stour Valley Way
OXENTURN
Browning Bridge

A   B   C   D

The Index includes some names for which there is insufficient space on the maps. These names are indicated by an * and are followed by the nearest adjoining thoroughfare.

Abbey Cl, Deal CT14	22 A3
Abbey Ct, Sheerness ME12	37 D3
Abbey Ct, Birchington CT7	58 A4
Abbey Ct, Whitstable CT5	59 D1
Abbey Pl, Dartford DA1	21 B1
Abbey Pl, Faversham ME13	25 D2
Abbey Rd, Faversham ME13	25 D1
Abbey Rd, Gillingham ME8	27 D6
Abbey Rd, Greenhithe DA9	29 C2
Abbey Rd, Rochester ME2	52 A3
Abbey St ME13	25 D2
Abbeyview Dr ME12	37 B3
Abbots Hill CT11	43 B4
Abbots Pl CT1	16 C2
Abbots Walk TN25	60 B5
Abbott Rd, Folkestone CT20	26 E1
Abbott Rd, Sevenoaks TN15	13 B5
Abbott Way TN30	54 C5
Abbotts Cl, Rochester ME1	44 B6
Abbotts Cl, Swanley BR8	53 E3
Acacia Rd DA1	21 A5
Acacia Walk BR8	53 B1
Acorn Rd ME7	27 C4
Acorn St ME12	47 D3
Acre Ct CT17	23 A1
Acton Rd CT5	59 B2
Adams Cl TN30	54 C4
Addelam Cl CT14	22 A4
Addelam Rd CT14	22 A4
Addington Pl CT11	43 B5
Addington Rd, Margate CT9	36 C2
Addington Rd, Sittingbourne ME10	48 A3
Addington Sq CT9	36 C2
Addington St, Margate CT9	36 C3
Addington St, Ramsgate CT11	43 A5
Addiscombe Gdns CT9	36 C4
Addiscombe Rd CT9	36 D4
Adelaide Gdns CT11	43 B4
Adelaide Pl CT1	16 B4
Adelaide Rd ME7	27 A4
Adisham Way CT9	19 B4
Admirals Mews CT14	22 C4
Admirals Walk, Chatham ME4	18 B1
Admirals Walk, Greenhithe DA9	29 B1
Admirals Walk, Tenterden TN30	54 C4
Admirals Way DA12	28 D2
Admiralty Cl ME13	25 B2
Admiralty Ter ME7	18 C1
Adrian Mews CT8	58 C2
Adrian St CT8	58 C2
Adrian St CT17	23 C2
Afghan Rd ME4	18 A4
Ailsa Mews ME1	44 A6
Aintree Cl DA12	28 B6
Airedale Cl CT9	36 D3
Akehurst La TN13	46 C6
Alamein Rd DA10	29 D3
Alan Cl DA1	21 A1
Alaseun Ter ME12	37 A4
Albany Cl TN9	55 D5
Albany Dr CT6	32 A1
Albany Pl CT17	23 C2
Albany Rd, Gillingham ME7	27 B4
Albany Rd, Rochester ME1	44 C5
Albany Rd, Sittingbourne ME10	48 B4
Albany St ME14	35 C2
Albany Ter, Chatham ME4	18 A4
Albany Ter, Gillingham ME7	27 B4
Albert Constain Ct CT20	26 C2
Albert La CT21	33 B4
Albert Murray Cl DA12	28 C3
Albert Pl ME2	52 D4
Albert Rd, Ashford TN24	12 C3
Albert Rd, Broadstairs CT10	19 D6
Albert Rd, Chatham ME4	18 C5
Albert Rd, Deal CT14	22 C2
Albert Rd, Gillingham ME7	27 A4
Albert Rd, Hythe CT21	33 A3
Albert Rd, Margate CT9	36 A3
Albert Rd, Ramsgate CT11	43 C3
Albert Rd, Rochester ME1	44 C5
Albert Rd, Swanscombe DA10	29 F3
Albert Rd, Tonbridge TN9	55 A4
Albert Reed Gdns ME15	35 A6
Albert St, Maidstone ME14	35 B1
Albert St, Ramsgate CT11	43 A5
Albert St, Tunbridge Wells TN1	56 D1
Albert St, Whitstable CT5	59 A2
Albion Cl TN11	17 C6
Albion Hill CT11	43 B4
Albion Mews Rd CT20	26 D2
Albion Par DA12	28 D2
Albion Pl, Canterbury CT1	16 D2
Albion Pl, Faversham ME13	25 C2
Albion Pl, Hythe CT21	33 D3
Albion Pl, Maidstone ME15	35 C4
Albion Pl, Ramsgate CT11	43 B4
Albion Rd, Birchington CT7	14 D3
Albion Rd, Broadstairs CT10	15 A2
Albion Rd, Gravesend DA12	28 C3
Albion Rd, Margate CT9	19 A3
Albion Rd, Ramsgate CT11	43 C3
Albion Rd, Tonbridge TN12	34 C5
Albion St CT10	15 D4
Albion Ter DA12	28 C2
Albion Villas CT20	26 C3
Albion Way TN8	24 B2
Alder Cl ME12	47 B5
Alder Way BR8	53 B1
Alderney Gdns CT9	15 A3
Aldred Rd ME13	25 C3
Alen Sq TN12	51 C2
Alexander Cl, Faversham ME13	25 C2
Alexander Cl, Sandwich CT13	45 C2
Alexander Ct TN1	56 B3
Alexander Dr ME13	25 B2
Alexander Rd DA9	29 C2
Alexandra Av ME7	27 B4
Alexandra Cl BR8	53 D2
Alexandra Gdns CT20	26 C3
Alexandra Homes CT9	36 B4
Alexandra Rd, Birchington CT7	14 D4
Alexandra Rd, Broadstairs CT10	15 C4
Alexandra Rd, Chatham ME4	18 D6
Alexandra Rd, Deal CT14	22 D6
Alexandra Rd, Margate CT9	36 B4
Alexandra Rd, Ramsgate CT11	43 A3
Alexandra Rd, Tonbridge TN9	55 B4
Alexandra Rd, Whitstable CT5	59 A4
Alexandra St ME14	35 B2
Alexandra Ter CT9	36 C4
Alfred Cl ME4	18 C5
Alfred Rd, Ashford TN24	12 D6
Alfred Rd, Birchington CT7	14 B1
Alfred Rd, Gravesend DA11	28 B5
Alfred Rd, Margate CT9	19 A4
Alfred Row CT14	22 C1
Alfred Sq CT14	22 C1
Alicia Av CT9	58 D3
Alison Cl CT7	14 E2
Alkali Row CT9	36 C2
Alkerden La, Greenhithe DA9	29 C3
Alkerden La, Swanscombe DA10	29 D3
Alkham Rd ME14	35 D3
All Saints Av CT9	36 A3
All Saints Cl, Swanscombe DA10	29 F2
All Saints Cl, Whitstable CT5	59 C3
All Saints Ct CT1	16 B3
All Saints Ind Est CT9	36 B3
All Saints La CT1	16 B3
All Saints Rd, Cranbrook TN18	31 C2
All Saints Rd, Tunbridge Wells TN4	50 D5
All Saints Rise TN4	50 D5
Allanbrooke DA12	28 C3
Allen Av CT8	58 A4
Allen Ct ME12	37 A4
Allen Fld TN23	12 A6
Allen St ME14	35 C2
Allenby Av CT14	22 B3
Allens TN12	34 C5
Alley Way TN12	40 B3
Allington Dr ME2	52 A3
Allington Rd TN12	40 B3
Allnutt Mill Cl ME15	35 A6
Allotment La TN13	46 D3
Alma Pl, Ramsgate CT11	43 B3
Alma Pl, Rochester ME2	52 C4
Alma Rd, Margate CT9	36 C3
Alma Rd, Ramsgate CT11	43 B3
Alma Rd, Sheerness ME12	47 D3
Alma Rd, Swanscombe DA10	29 F2
Almeria Cl CT20	33 A3
Almon Pl ME1	44 D4
Almond Dr BR8	53 B2
Almond Tree Cl ME12	47 B5
Alpha Rd, Birchington CT7	14 D2
Alpha Rd, Ramsgate CT11	43 A4
Alsager Rd ME11	41 A3
Alston Cl ME12	37 C2
Amazon Ct DA12	28 D2
Ambrose Hill ME5	27 A6
Ames Rd DA12	29 E3
Amherst Cl CT9	19 C4
Amherst Hill ME7	18 C2
Amherst Rd, Rochester ME1	44 D6
Amherst Rd, Sevenoaks TN13	46 C3
Amherst Rd, Tunbridge Wells TN4	50 C6
Amherst Redoubt ME7	18 C3
Anchor Bsns Pk ME10	48 D1
Anchor La, Deal CT14	22 C2
Anchor La, Sheerness ME12	47 B1
Anchor Wharf ME4	18 B2
Andrew Broughton Way ME14	35 C3
Angel Centre TN9	55 B3
Angel Cl CT1	16 C3
Angel La TN9	55 C3
Angel Walk TN9	55 B3
Angley Rd TN17	20 A5
Angley Walk TN17	20 C3
Anna Pk CT7	14 C1
Anne Cl CT7	14 E2
Anne of Cleves Rd DA1	21 B1
Anne Roper Cl TN28	38 E3
Annes Rd CT10	15 D1
Annetts Hall TN15	13 C4
Annie Rd ME6	49 B4
Anns Rd CT11	43 B3
Anselm Cl ME10	48 C4
Anvil Cl CT7	14 D3
Apple Cl ME6	49 B5
Apple Ct TN12	40 B4
Apple Orch BR8	53 B5
Applecross Cl ME1	44 B5
Appledore Av ME12	47 C5
Appledore Cl CT9	19 B4
Appledore Rd, Ashford TN26	60 B3
Appledore Rd, Tenterden TN30	54 C5
Appleford Dr ME12	37 A2
Applegarth Dr DA1	21 C6
Appletons TN11	17 C6
Approach Rd, Broadstairs CT10	15 C4
Approach Rd, Margate CT9	36 D3
Apsley St TN23	12 C4
Archer Way BR8	53 E1
Archers Sq North CT14	22 C5
Archery Sq South CT14	22 C5
Archway Rd CT11	43 A4
Arden Bsns Pk ME2	18 A1
Arden Dr TN24	12 D3
Arden St ME7	27 A2
Ardenlee Dr ME14	35 D2
Ardent Av CT14	22 C4
Arethusa Pl DA9	29 B1
Argent Bsns Pk ME11	41 B3
Argles Cl DA9	29 A2
Argyle Av CT9	58 F2
Argyle Gdns CT9	58 F2
Argyle Rd, Sevenoaks TN13	46 C6
Argyle Rd, Tunbridge Wells TN4	50 D1
Argyle Rd, Whitstable CT5	59 A3
Argyll Dr CT11	43 B1
Ark La CT14	22 C1
Arkley Rd CT6	32 C2
Arklow Sq CT11	43 C3
Arlington TN23	12 A5
Arlington Gdns CT9	19 B6
Arlott Cl ME14	35 B1
Armada Way ME4	18 B5
Armoury Dr DA12	28 C3
Armstrong Rd ME15	35 C6
Arnold Rd, Gravesend DA12	28 D5
Arnold Rd, Margate CT9	36 C3
Arnolde Cl ME2	18 A1
Arthur Rd, Birchington CT7	14 B2
Arthur Rd, Deal CT14	22 A5
Arthur Rd, Gillingham ME8	27 C6
Arthur Rd, Hythe CT21	33 B5
Arthur Rd, Margate CT9	36 D2
Arthur Rd, Rochester ME1	44 D6
Arthur Salmon Cl ME13	25 B3
Arthur St, Sittingbourne ME10	48 A3
Arthur St West DA11	28 A3
Artillery Gdns CT1	16 D2
Artillery Rd CT1	16 D2
Artillery Row DA12	28 C3
Artillery St CT1	16 D2
Arundel Av ME10	48 B6
Arundel Cl TN9	55 A4
Arundel Rd, Dartford DA1	21 A1
Arundel Rd, Margate CT9	19 A4
Arundel Rd, Tunbridge Wells TN1	56 D5
Arundel St ME14	35 B1
Ascot Cl TN15	13 C5
Ascot Gdns CT8	58 B3
Ascot Rd DA12	28 B6
Ash Cl, Edenbridge TN8	24 B5
Ash Cl, Swanley BR8	53 B2
Ash Gro TN29	34 D1
Ash Rd, Dartford DA1	21 B5
Ash Rd, Rochester ME2	52 B5
Ash Rd, Sandwich CT13	45 B1
Ash Rd, Westerham TN16	57 D4
Ash Tree La ME5	27 B6
Ash Trees Cl TN9	32 D3
Ashbee Cl ME6	49 C3
Ashburnham Rd TN10	55 C1
Ashbys Cl TN8	24 C6
Ashbys Yd TN9	55 B3
Ashcombe Dr TN8	24 B2
Ashcroft Rd, Rochester ME3	52 D1
Ashcroft Rd, Tonbridge TN12	40 C5
Ashdown Cres TN28	38 B4
Ashen Tree La CT16	23 C1
Ashenden Cl ME2	52 D1
Ashes La TN11	17 A6
Ashford Rd, Ashford TN26	30 A4
Ashford Rd, Faversham ME13	25 C5
Ashford Rd, Harrietsham ME17	30 A2
Ashford Rd, Lenham ME17	30 A2
Ashford Rd, Maidstone ME14	35 C4
Ashford Rd, New Romney TN28	38 A2
Ashford Rd, Tenterden TN30	54 B5
Ashgrove TN25	12 A1
Ashleigh Gdns TN27	31 B4
Ashley Cl TN13	46 B4
Ashley Rd TN13	46 B4
Ashurst Rd ME14	35 D2
Aspdin Rd DA11	39 C6
Aspen Cl BR8	53 B1
Astley St ME14	35 C3
Astor Dr CT14	22 B3
Astrid Rd CT14	22 A6
Athelstan Rd, Chatham ME4	18 B6
Athelstan Rd, Faversham ME13	25 B3
Athelstan Rd, Margate CT9	36 D2
Athol Pl ME13	25 A2
Athol Rd CT9	59 C2
Athol Ter CT16	23 E1
Atlantic Cl DA10	29 E2
Atterbury Cl TN16	57 C5
Attlee Dr DA1	21 D2
Atwater Ct ME17	32 D5
Aubretia Walk ME10	48 C3
Audley Av CT9	58 E2
Augusta Cl ME7	27 A1
Augusta Rd CT11	43 C4
Augustine Rd, Gravesend DA12	28 D3
Augustine Rd, Sheerness ME12	37 B1
Austen Cl DA9	29 C2
Austen Gdns DA1	21 D1
Austens Orch TN30	54 A6
Austin Cl ME5	27 C6
Austin Rd DA11	28 A4
Avebury Av, Ramsgate CT11	43 C2
Avebury Av, Tonbridge TN9	55 B3
Avenue CT11	43 B1
Avenue Gdns CT9	19 B3
Avenue Le Puy TN9	55 C4
Avenue of Remembrance ME10	48 B3
Avenue Rd, Herne Bay CT6	32 A1
Avenue Rd, Ramsgate CT11	43 C3
Avenue Rd, Sevenoaks TN13	46 C4
Avereng Rd CT19	26 A1
Avery Cl ME15	35 B6
Avington Cl ME15	35 B6
Avon Cl DA12	28 D5
Avondale Cl CT5	59 D4
Avondale Rd ME1	27 B3
Avonmouth Rd DA1	21 B2
Aynsley Ct CT13	45 D1
Azalea Dr BR8	53 C3
Back La, Faversham ME13	25 D2
Back La, Sheerness ME12	37 D3
Back Rd West CT16	23 F1
Baddlesmere Rd CT5	59 D1
Badfields ME1	44 C4
Badsell Rd TN12	40 A4
Baffin Cl ME4	18 B6
Baileys Fld TN23	12 A5
Bairds Hill CT10	15 B2
Bairdsley Cl CT10	15 B2
Baker Cres DA1	21 A3
Baker St ME1	44 C5
Bakers Cross TN17	20 C5
Bakers Walk ME1	44 C3
Balcomb Cres CT9	19 B6
Baldwin Rd ME12	37 E3
Balfour Ct CT14	22 C6

Baliol Rd CT5 59 C2
Ballard Bsns Pk ME2 52 B6
Ballard CI TN12 34 B5
Ballard Way TN12 40 D3
Balliemoor Ct*, Argyll Dr CT10 43 B1
Balmer CI ME8 42 A3
Balmoral PI CT11 43 C4
Balmoral Rd, Gillingham ME7 27 A3
Balmoral Rd, Margate CT9 58 E3
Balmoral Ter ME10 48 A3
Baltic PI DA9 29 E2
Baltic Rd TN9 55 A5
Bambridge Ct ME14 35 A1
Bamford Way CT14 22 C4
Bank St, Ashford TN23 12 C4
Bank St, Chatham ME4 18 D5
Bank St, Cranbrook TN17 20 B4
Bank St, Faversham ME13 25 C3
Bank St, Maidstone ME14 35 B4
Bank St, Sevenoaks TN13 46 C6
Bank St, Tonbridge TN9 55 B2
Bankfields TN27 31 A4
Banks Rd ME2 52 D3
Bankside, Ashford TN26 30 B5
Bankside, Gravesend DA11 39 B2
Banky Fields CI ME8 42 D1
Banner Farm Rd TN2 56 D6
Banning St ME2 52 C2
Bardell Ter ME1 44 D4
Barden Park Rd TN9 55 A3
Barden Rd TN9 55 A3
Barfreston CI ME15 35 A6
Barge Ct DA9 29 C1
Barham Dr TN11 20 C4
Barker Rd ME16 35 B4
Barkers Ct ME10 48 A3
Barler PI ME11 41 B1
Barleycorn Dr ME8 42 A4
Barlow CI ME8 42 A6
Barn Cres CT9 58 E2
Barn Hawe TN8 24 C5
Barn Mdw TN12 51 B2
Barn Platt TN23 12 B6
Barnard Ct ME4 18 C6
Barnes Av CT9 58 E2
Barnes CI ME13 25 B1
Barnes Walk TN12 34 C5
Barnesende Ct CT13 45 D2
Barnett Fld TN23 12 A6
Barnfield, Gravesend DA11 28 A5
Barnfield, Tenterden TN30 54 C2
Barnfield Rd ME13 25 C1
Barnsole Rd ME7 27 B3
Baron CI ME7 27 C1
Barons Ct TN4 50 D6
Barrack Hill CT21 33 A3
Barrack Row DA11 28 B2
Barrel Arch CI TN12 34 A5
Barretts Rd TN18 31 B1
Barrier Rd ME4 18 B3
Barrington Cres CT7 14 E3
Barrow Gro ME10 48 A3
Barrow Hill TN23 12 B4
Barrow Hill Cotts TN23 12 B3
Barrow Hill PI TN23 12 B3
Barrow Hill Ter TN23 12 B3
Barrows CI CT7 14 D3
Bartholomew CI CT21 33 A2
Bartholomew La CT21 33 A3
Bartholomew St CT21 33 B3
Bartholomew Way BR8 59 D3
Bartlett Dr CT5 28 A4
Bartlett Rd, Gravesend DA11 28 A4
Bartlett Rd, Westerham TN16 57 C5
Bartletts CI ME12 41 D1
Barton Hill Dr ME4 37 A4
Barton Rd, Maidstone ME15 35 C5
Barton Rd, Strood ME2 52 C4
Basden Cotts TN18 31 C1
Basi CI ME2 52 D2
Basing CI ME15 35 D2
Baskerville TN24 12 C3
Basmere CI ME4 35 D2
Bassett CI CT21 33 D2
Bassett Rd ME10 48 A3
Bastion Rd CT17 23 B3

Bat & Ball Enterprise Centre TN14 46 C1
Bat & Ball Rd TN14 46 C2
Batchelor St ME4 18 C4
Bath Hard La ME1 44 D4
Bath PI CT9 36 C2
Bath Rd CT9 36 C2
Bath St DA11 28 B2
Bathurst CI TN12 51 B3
Bathurst Rd TN12 51 B3
Bay Hill CT15 41 C5
Bay Hill CI CT15 41 C6
Bay View Rd CT10 15 B6
Bayford Rd ME10 48 D3
Bayham Rd TN13 26 D4
Bayle CI ME15 26 D3
Bayle St CT20 26 D3
Bayly Rd DA1 21 D3
Bayswater Dr ME8 42 A6
Bayview Rd CT5 59 A5
Beach Av CT7 14 C2
Beach Rd, Dover CT15 41 C6
Beach Rd, Westgate-on-Sea CT8 58 C2
Beach Rise CT8 58 D2
Beach St, Deal CT14 22 D1
Beach St, Folkestone CT20 26 E3
Beach St, Herne Bay CT6 32 B1
Beach St, Sheerness ME12 47 C2
Beach Ter ME12 47 C2
Beach Walk CT5 59 B1
Beachy Path TN30 54 B4
Beacon CI ME8 42 A3
Beacon Heights CT5 59 C1
Beacon Hill CT6 32 D1
Beacon Oak Rd TN30 54 C4
Beacon Rd, Broadstairs CT10 15 A2
Beacon Rd, Herne Bay CT6 32 D2
Beacon Rd, Maidstone ME17 32 B6
Beacon Walk, Herne Bay CT6 32 D1
Beaconsfield Av ME7 27 B3
Beaconsfield Gdns CT10 15 B3
Beaconsfield Rd, Chatham ME4 18 B6
Beaconsfield Rd, Deal CT14 22 C3
Beaconsfield Rd, Maidstone ME15 35 A4
Beaconsfield Ter CT21 33 C4
Bean Rd DA9 29 B4
Beaton CI DA9 29 B1
Beatrice Gdns DA11 39 D5
Beatrice Rd CT9 36 B4
Beatty Av ME7 27 D5
Beauchamp Av CT14 22 A5
Beaufort CI ME2 18 A2
Beaufort Rd ME2 52 A2
Beaumanor CT6 32 C3
Beaumont Davey CI ME13 25 D3
Beaumont Ter ME13 25 D3
Beaver Rd TN23 12 C6
Becket Ct TN27 31 C5
Becket Mews CT2 31 C5
Beckett St ME13 25 C2
Bedford PI ME16 35 A4
Bedford Rd, Dartford DA1 21 D4
Bedford Rd, Gravesend DA11 28 A5
Bedford Rd, Tunbridge Wells TN4 50 C2
Bedford Ter TN1 56 B5
Bedson Walk ME8 42 D1
Beech Av BR8 53 E3
Beech Ct ME13 25 D3
Beech Ct CT1 16 D6
Beech Hurst CI ME15 35 C5
Beech Rd, Dartford DA1 21 B5
Beech Rd, Rochester ME2 52 A5
Beech Rd, Sevenoaks TN13 46 C6
Beech St TN1 56 D1
Beechcroft Gdns CT11 43 D1
Beechenlea La DA8 53 E4
Beecholme Dr TN24 12 C1
Beechwood Av, Chatham ME5 27 B6
Beechwood Av, Deal CT14 22 C3
Beechwood Av, Sittingbourne ME10 48 A1

Beechwood Ct CT14 22 C3
Beer Cart La CT1 16 B4
Beggars La TN13 57 D3
Belgrave CI CT11 43 A3
Belgrave Rd, Margate CT9 36 B3
Belgrave Rd, Tunbridge Wells TN1 56 C1
Belgrove TN1 56 C5
Bell Inn Rd CT21 33 C3
Bell La TN12 51 B4
Bell Rd ME10 48 B5
Belle Vue Rd CT6 32 D1
Bellevue Av CT11 43 B4
Bellevue Rd, Ramsgate CT11 43 C4
Bellevue Rd, Sheerness ME12 37 C3
Bellevue Rd, Whitstable CT5 59 C4
Bellevue St CT20 26 D2
Bells La TN15 43 A5
Bells CI TN30 54 B5
Bells La TN30 54 B5
Belmont Rd, Broadstairs CT10 15 C4
Belmont Rd, Faversham ME13 25 C4
Belmont Rd, Gillingham ME7 27 A4
Belmont Rd, Ramsgate CT11 43 A3
Belmont Rd, Sittingbourne ME10 48 A4
Belmont Rd, Westgate-on-Sea CT8 58 C3
Belmont Rd, Whitstable CT5 59 A3
Belmont St CT11 43 B3
Belmont Yd CT5 59 B3
Belmore Pk TN24 12 B3
Beltinge Rd CT6 32 C1
Belton CI CT5 59 B3
Beltring Rd TN4 50 C5
Belvedere CI ME12 28 C4
Belvedere Rd, Broadstairs CT10 15 C4
Belvedere Rd, Faversham ME13 25 D2
Benacre Rd CT5 59 A6
Bench St CT16 23 B1
Benden CI TN12 51 C2
Bennett Ho DA11 28 B2
Bennetts Mews TN30 54 A6
Bensted Gro ME13 25 A3
Bentham Hill TN3 50 A2
Bentley St DA12 28 C2
Berber Rd ME2 52 C3
Bere CI DA9 29 C1
Berengrave La ME8 42 A1
Beresford Gap CT7 14 D1
Beresford Gdns CT9 19 B2
Beresford Rd, Gillingham ME7 27 B4
Beresford Rd, Gravesend DA11 39 D3
Beresford Rd, Ramsgate CT11 43 A4
Beresford Rd, Whitstable CT5 59 B3
Berkeley Cres DA1 21 D4
Berkeley Rd, Birchington CT7 14 C1
Berkeley Rd, Tunbridge Wells TN1 56 B6
Berkley Rd DA12 28 B2
Bernard St DA12 28 C2
Berridge Rd ME12 47 D3
Berry St ME10 48 B3
Berwick Way TN14 46 C1
Best La CT1 16 B4
Best St ME4 18 B4
Bethel Rd TN13 46 D4
Bethersden Rd BR10 29 E3
Bettescombe Rd ME8 42 A3
Bevan PI BR8 53 D3
Bevans CI DA9 29 C3
Beverley CI ME8 42 B2
Beverly CI CT17 14 E2
Bexley St CT5 59 A2
Bickley Rd TN9 55 B4
Bickmore Way TN9 55 C1
Biddenden Rd TN27 31 D6
Bierce Ct CT7 14 C2
Biggin St CT16 23 B1
Bigglestons Link CT1 16 D4
Bill Street Rd ME2 52 D2
Bilton Sq CT9 36 B2
Bingham Rd ME2 52 D1
Bingley CI ME6 49 B2
Bingley Rd ME1 52 D1
Binnie Ct CT10 15 B6
Birch CI TN13 46 C4
Birch Hill Ct CT7 14 E3
Birch Rd, Tonbridge TN9 40 C4

Birch Rd, Whitstable CT5 59 D4
Birch Tree Way ME15 35 D5
Birchington CI ME14 35 D3
Birchwood Av TN4 50 B1
Birchwood Park Av BR8 53 D2
Birchwood Rd BR8 53 A1
Birchwood Rise CT17 33 A2
Birchwood Ter BR8 53 A1
Birdcage Walk TN1 56 C5
Birds Av CT9 58 E3
Birdwood Av CT14 22 A3
Birling Rd, Ashford TN24 12 D4
Birling Rd, Snodland ME6 49 B3
Birnam Sq ME16 35 A4
Bishops Av CT10 15 C2
Bishops Courtyard CT11 16 D4
Bishops Way ME15 35 B4
Black Bull Rd CT19 26 C1
Black Eagle CI TN16 57 B6
Black Griffin La CT1 16 A3
Black Horse Mews TN15 13 B6
Black Mill La TN27 31 A5
Blackberry Way TN12 40 D4
Blackdown Dr TN24 12 C2
Blackfriars St CT1 16 C2
Blackhorse Ct TN27 31 C5
Blackhouse Hill CT21 33 C3
Blackhouse Rise CT21 33 C2
Blackmans CI DA1 21 A5
Blackthorne Rd ME8 42 D2
Blair Dr TN13 46 C4
Blake Gdns DA1 21 D1
Blandford Gdns ME10 48 A6
Blatcher CI ME12 37 C4
Blaxland CI ME13 25 B1
Bleak Rd TN29 34 B2
Blendon Rd ME29 35 D2
Blenheim CI DA1 21 A3
Blenheim Gro DA12 28 C3
Blenheim Rd, Dartford DA1 21 A3
Blenheim Rd, Deal CT14 22 C2
Blenheim Rd, New Romney TN28 38 D3
Blenheim Rd, Sittingbourne ME10 48 D5
Bligh Rd DA11 28 B2
Blighs Ct*, Blighs Rd TN13 46 C6
Blighs Rd TN13 46 C6
Blighs Walk*, Blighs Rd TN13 46 C6
Bloomfield Ter TN16 57 D4
Blue Boar La ME1 44 D3
Blue Line La TN24 12 C3
Bluebell CI ME7 27 C2
Blueberry CI TN13 15 B6
Bluefield Mews CT5 59 A6
Bluett St ME14 35 C2
Bluewater Parkway DA9 29 A3
Bluewater Pk Retail Pk DA9 29 A3
Blythe Rd ME15 35 D4
Boat House Rd ME12 47 A1
Bodiam Ct ME16 35 A5
Bodle Av DA10 29 E3
Bogarde Dr ME3 52 D1
Bognor Dr CT6 32 A2
Boley Hill ME1 44 C3
Boleyn Av CT9 58 D2
Boleyn Way DA10 29 E4
Bolton Rd CT19 26 C1
Bolton St CT11 43 A3
Bond Rd, Ashford TN23 12 B6
Bond Rd, Gillingham ME8 42 A6
Bondfield CI TN4 50 D2
Bonetta CI ME12 47 C4
Bonham Dr ME10 48 D2
Bonney Way BR8 53 C2
Booth Rd ME4 18 B6
Bordyke TN9 55 C2
Boresisle TN30 54 B2
Borland CI DA9 29 A2
Borough Green Rd TN15 13 A5
Borough Rd, Gillingham ME7 27 B4
Borough Rd, Queenborough ME11 41 B2
Borstal Av CT5 59 A3
Borstal Hill CT5 59 A4
Borstal Rd ME1 44 A6
Boscastle Ct CT11 43 C2
Boscombe Rd CT19 26 B1
Bosville Av DN13 46 B4
Bosville Dr TN13 46 B4
Bosville Rd TN13 46 B4
Botany TN9 55 C3
Botany Ind Est TN9 55 C3
Boughton Av CT11 43 D1
Boulogne Ct CT20 26 E2

Boundary CI ME12 37 E4
Boundary Rd, Chatham ME4 18 A5
Boundary Rd, Hythe CT21 33 A4
Boundary Rd, Ramsgate CT11 43 A3
Bourne CI TN9 55 C1
Bourne Enterprise Centre TN15 13 B5
Bourne Grange La TN17 17 A6
Bourne La, Ashford TN26 30 B5
Bourne La, Tonbridge TN9 55 C1
Bourne Way BR8 53 B2
Bournemouth Gdns CT19 26 B1
Bournemouth CT19 26 B1
Bournes PI TN26 60 B1
Bournewood TN26 30 B5
Bouverie PI CT20 26 C3
Bouverie Rd West CT20 26 A3
Bouverie Sq CT20 26 C3
Bow Arrow La DA1 21 D3
Bowens Fld TN23 12 B5
Bower La ME16 35 A4
Bower PI ME16 35 A5
Bower Walk TN12 51 B3
Bowers Av CT9 58 D2
Bowes Rd ME2 52 D3
Bowl Rd TN27 17 C1
Bowles Lodge TN18 31 C2
Bowling Green La CT14 22 B4
Bowling Green Ter CT17 23 B3
Bowling St CT13 45 D1
Bowls PI TN12 40 C3
Boxley TN23 12 A6
Boxley CI ME2 47 C5
Boxley Rd ME14 35 C2
Boyne PI TN4 56 A2
Bracken Ct CT10 15 A3
Brackley CI ME4 35 D3
Brackwood CI ME8 42 A5
Bradbourne Park Rd TN13 46 B4
Bradbourne Rd TN13 46 B2
Bradbourne Vale Rd TN13 46 A2
Bradfield Rd TN24 12 C1
Bradford St TN9 55 B3
Bradley Dr ME10 48 A6
Bradstone Av CT19 26 C1
Bradstone New Rd CT20 26 C2
Bradstone Rd CT20 26 C1
Bradstow Way CT10 15 B2
Braeside Av TN13 46 A4
Braeside CI TN13 46 A4
Bramble CI TN25 60 B4
Bramble La TN25 60 A4
Brambledown CT19 26 B1
Bramblehill Rd ME13 25 C2
Bramley CI, Gillingham ME8 42 D2
Bramley CI, Swanley BR8 53 C4
Bramley Ct TN12 34 A5
Bramley Gdns TN12 40 B3
Bramley Rd ME6 49 C3
Bramley Rise ME2 52 A3
Bramleys TN23 31 C5
Bramston Rd ME12 37 D3
Brandon Rd DA11 21 D3
Brandon St DA11 28 B3
Brandon Way CT17 14 E3
Brasenose Rd ME7 27 B5
Brasier Ct ME12 37 A4
Brassey Av CT10 15 B5
Brasted Ct ME2 52 C2
Brasted Rd TN16 57 D5
Brattle TN26 60 B3
Breakneck Hill DA9 29 B2
Bream CI ME20 49 C6
Brecon Chase ME12 37 C3
Brecon Rise TN24 12 B2
Bredgar CI ME14 35 D2
Bredhurst CI ME12 47 C4
Breedon Av TN4 50 C2
Bremner CI BR8 53 E3
Brenchley CI ME1 18 A6
Brenchley Rd, Maidstone ME15 35 B6
Brenda Ter CM10 48 B5
Brendon Dr TN24 12 C2
Brent Hill ME13 25 C2
Brent La DA1 21 C4
Brent Rd ME13 25 C2
Brents Ind Est ME13 25 D1
Brewer St, Deal CT14 22 D2
Brewer St, Maidstone ME14 35 B3

Brewery La TN13 — 46 C6
Brewery Rd ME10 — 48 B1
Brian Cres TN4 — 50 D3
Briar Cl, Ashford TN25 — 60 B4
Briar Cl,
 Edenbridge TN8 — 24 C3
Briar Cl Ind Est TN25 — 60 B4
Briars Walk CT10 — 15 B5
Briary Clo CT9 — 58 D3
Brices Alley CT5 — 59 A2
Brickenden Rd TN17 — 20 C5
Brickmakers
 Bsns Centre ME10 — 48 D1
Brickworks Cl TN9 — 55 A6
Bridewell La TN30 — 54 B5
Bridewell Pk CT5 — 59 D3
Bridge Cl, Ashford TN26 — 60 B3
Bridge Cl, Hythe CT21 — 33 A3
Bridge Cl,
 Tonbridge TN9 — 55 C4
Bridge Rd,
 Ashford TN23 — 12 A4
Bridge Rd,
 Faversham ME13 — 25 D2
Bridge Rd,
 Gillingham ME7 — 27 A1
Bridge Rd, Margate CT9 — 58 E2
Bridge Rd,
 Rochester ME1 — 44 C6
Bridge Rd,
 Sheerness ME12 — 47 C2
Bridge St TN25 — 60 B5
Bridge Vw DA9 — 29 B1
Bridgeside CT14 — 22 C2
Bridgeside Mews ME15 — 35 A6
Bridgewater Rd ME12 — 47 C4
Brielle Way,
 Queenborough ME11 — 41 C1
Brielle Way,
 Sheerness ME12 — 47 A6
Bright Rd ME4 — 18 D6
Bright Ridge TN4 — 50 B3
Brightlingsea Rd CT13 — 45 C2
Brights Pl CT11 — 43 B3
Brindle Gro CT11 — 43 C2
Brindles Fld TN9 — 55 A5
Brionne Gdns TN9 — 55 D4
Brisbane Rd ME4 — 18 C5
Brissenden Cl TN28 — 38 C2
Bristol Rd DA12 — 28 D6
Briton Ct ME12 — 47 C4
Briton Rd ME13 — 25 C3
Brittains La TN13 — 46 A4
Britton St ME7 — 18 D3
Broad Rd DA10 — 29 E3
Broad St,
 Canterbury CT1 — 16 D2
Broad St, Deal CT14 — 22 D2
Broad St, Margate CT9 — 36 B2
Broad St,
 Ramsgate CT11 — 43 B4
Broad St,
 Sheerness ME12 — 47 C3
Broadcloth TN17 — 20 C6
Broadlands Av TN28 — 38 C2
Broadlands Cres TN28 — 38 C2
Bradley Av CT7 — 14 C4
Bradley Rd CT9 — 19 B6
Broadmead Rd CT19 — 26 B2
Broadstairs Rd CT10 — 15 A3
Broadview Av ME8 — 42 A2
Broadway,
 Gillingham ME8 — 27 D5
Broadway,
 Maidstone ME16 — 35 A4
Broadway,
 Sheerness ME12 — 47 D2
Broadway Shopping
 Centre ME16 — 35 A4
Brockenhurst Rd CT11 — 43 C3
Brockhill Rd CT21 — 33 A2
Brockley Rd CT9 — 36 D2
Brockman Rd CT20 — 26 B2
Brockway TN15 — 13 C6
Brogdale Pl ME13 — 25 B4
Brogdale Rd ME13 — 25 B5
Brompton Cl ME4 — 18 B2
Brompton Farm Rd
 ME2 — 52 A2
Brompton Hill ME4 — 18 B2
Brompton La ME2 — 52 A2
Brompton Rd ME7 — 18 D2
Bromstone Mews CT10 — 15 A4
Bromstone Rd CT10 — 15 A5
Bronte Gro DA1 — 21 D1
Bronte Vw DA12 — 28 C4
Brook Ct TN8 — 24 C3
Brook La,
 Snodland ME6 — 49 B5
Brook La,
 Tonbridge TN9 — 55 D2
Brook Rd,
 Aylesford ME20 — 49 A6
Brook Rd,
 Faversham ME13 — 25 D1
Brook Rd, Swanley BR8 — 53 B2

Brook St, Ashford TN26 — 60 B3
Brook St,
 Snodland ME6 — 49 D3
Brook Ter ME7 — 27 B2
Brooke Av CT9 — 58 F3
Brooke Rd TN24 — 12 C3
Brookfield Ct,
 Ashford TN23 — 12 A6
Brookfield Ct,
 Tunbridge Wells TN4 — 50 C2
Brookfield
 Ind Pk TN23 — 12 A4
Brookfield Rd TN23 — 12 A6
Brookfields TN11 — 17 B5
Brooklands,
 Ashford TN27 — 31 B4
Brooklands,
 Dartford DA1 — 21 B5
Brooklyn Pad ME7 — 27 B2
Brooklyn Villas TN12 — 34 A5
Brooks Pl ME14 — 35 C3
Brooks Way TN29 — 34 B3
Brookside TN17 — 20 C5
Broom Hill Rd ME2 — 52 A2
Broomfield Rd,
 Faversham ME13 — 25 C1
Broomfield Rd,
 Sevenoaks TN13 — 46 A3
Broomfield Rd,
 Swanscombe DA10 — 29 F3
Broomhill Park Rd TN4 — 50 B3
Broomhill Rd TN3 — 50 A5
Broomwaters TN11 — 17 B4
Brown St ME8 — 42 B1
Browning Rd DA1 — 21 D1
Brownings TN8 — 24 B2
Brownings Yd CT5 — 59 A2
Bruce Cl CT14 — 22 B4
Brunswick Rd CT7 — 14 D4
Brunswick Sq CT6 — 32 B1
Brunswick St,
 Maidstone ME15 — 35 B5
Brunswick St,
 Ramsgate CT11 — 43 B4
Brunswick St East ME15 — 35 C4
Brunswick Ter TN1 — 56 B6
Brunswick Walk DA12 — 28 D3
Bryant Rd ME2 — 52 C3
Bryant St ME4 — 18 C5
Buckham Thorns Rd
 TN16 — 57 C5
Buckhurst Av TN13 — 46 C6
Buckhurst La TN13 — 46 C6
Buckingham Rd,
 Broadstairs CT10 — 15 D4
Buckingham Rd,
 Gillingham ME7 — 27 B3
Buckingham Rd,
 Gravesend DA11 — 39 C3
Buckingham Rd,
 Margate CT9 — 36 B4
Buckingham Rd,
 Tunbridge Wells TN1 — 56 C5
Buckland Hill ME16 — 35 A3
Buckland Pl ME16 — 35 A3
Buckland Rd ME16 — 35 A2
Buckthorn Cl CT14 — 22 C1
Bull La ME1 — 44 C3
Buller Rd ME4 — 18 B6
Bullers Av CT6 — 32 A2
Bullfields ME6 — 49 C3
Bullfinch Cl TN12 — 40 C5
Bullion Cl TN12 — 40 B4
Bullivant Cl DA9 — 29 A2
Bulwark Rd CT14 — 22 D1
Bulwark St West CT17 — 23 B4
Bunkley Mdw TN26 — 30 B6
Burch Av CT13 — 45 C3
Burdens TN27 — 31 C5
Burgate Cl CT14 — 16 C3
Burgate La CT1 — 16 D4
Burgess Rd ME2 — 52 C4
Burgoyne Ct ME14 — 35 B1
Burleigh Rd TN27 — 17 B3
Burley Rd ME10 — 48 A3
Burlington Gdns CT9 — 58 F2
Burnaby Rd DA1 — 39 D3
Burnham Cres DA1 — 21 A1
Burnham Rd DA1 — 21 A1
Burnham
 Trading Est DA1 — 21 A1
Burns Cres TN9 — 55 A5
Burns Rd ME7 — 27 A1
Burnt Oak Ter ME7 — 27 A2
Burritt Mews ME1 — 44 C5
Burritt St ME1 — 44 D5
Burrow Rd CT19 — 26 F1
Burrstock Way ME8 — 42 D1
Busbridge Rd ME6 — 49 A4
Bushfield Walk DA10 — 29 E3
Butcher Cl TN12 — 40 B3
Butcher Walk DA10 — 29 E3
Butchery La CT1 — 16 C4
Buttercup Cl TN12 — 40 C5

Butterfly Av DA1 — 21 C6
Buttermere Cl ME7 — 27 D3
Bybrook Ct TN24 — 12 D2
Bybrook Rd TN24 — 12 D1
Bychurch Pl ME15 — 35 C5
Bycliffe Mews DA11 — 28 A3
Bycliffe Ter DA11 — 28 A3
Byron Av CT9 — 36 C3
Byron Rd ME7 — 27 A5
Bysing Wood Rd ME13 — 25 A1
Bythorne St ME8 — 42 D1

Cadogan Gdns TN1 — 56 C3
Caernarvon Dr ME15 — 35 B6
Caernarvon Gdns CT10 — 15 D4
Cairns Cl DA1 — 21 B1
Caistor Rd TN9 — 55 A3
Calcroft Av DA9 — 29 C2
Caldecote Cl ME8 — 42 D1
Caldew Gro ME10 — 48 A3
Caledon Ter CT1 — 16 C6
Caledonian Ct ME8 — 42 A2
Calehill Cl ME14 — 35 D1
Callis Court Rd CT10 — 15 C2
Calthorpe Mews ME2 — 52 D3
Calverley Park Cres TN1 — 56 D3
Calverley Park Gdns
 TN1 — 56 D3
Calverley Pk CT9 — 56 C2
Calverley St TN1 — 56 C2
Cambourne Av CT8 — 58 B3
Cambrian Gro DA11 — 28 B3
Cambridge Cl CT7 — 14 E3
Cambridge Gdns,
 Folkestone CT20 — 26 C2
Cambridge Gdns,
 Tunbridge Wells TN2 — 56 D5
Cambridge Rd,
 Deal CT14 — 22 C5
Cambridge Rd,
 Dover CT17 — 23 C3
Cambridge Rd,
 Faversham ME13 — 25 B3
Cambridge Rd,
 Sittingbourne ME10 — 48 D4
Cambridge Rd,
 Strood ME2 — 52 C3
Cambridge Ter,
 Chatham ME4 — 18 B4
Cambridge Ter,
 Dover CT16 — 23 C2
Cambridge Ter,
 Folkestone CT20 — 26 E2
Cambridge Villas TN1 — 55 B3
Camden Cl DA1 — 39 C4
Camden Cres CT16 — 23 C2
Camden Ct TN1 — 56 D1
Camden Hill TN1 — 56 D5
Camden Rd,
 Broadstairs CT10 — 19 D6
Camden Rd,
 Gillingham ME7 — 27 B1
Camden Rd,
 Ramsgate CT11 — 43 B4
Camden Rd,
 Sevenoaks TN13 — 46 C3
Camden Rd,
 Tunbridge Wells TN1 — 56 C2
Camden Sq CT11 — 43 B4
Camden St ME14 — 35 C2
Camelia Cl CT9 — 58 F2
Campbell Cl,
 Deal CT14 — 22 C5
Campbell Rd,
 Maidstone ME15 — 35 B5
Campbell Rd,
 Tunbridge Wells TN4 — 50 C5
Cample Shon Rd ME8 — 42 A5
Canada Rd CT14 — 22 C4
Canada Ter ME14 — 35 B1
Canadian Av ME7 — 27 C4
Canal Basin DA12 — 28 D2
Canal Rd,
 Gravesend DA12 — 28 C2
Canal Rd, Strood ME2 — 52 D4
Canal Rd
 Ind Pk DA12 — 28 D2
Canning St ME14 — 35 B1
Cannon
 Bridge Works TN9 — 55 D2
Cannon La TN9 — 55 C2
Cannon Rd CT11 — 43 A4
Cannon St, Deal CT14 — 22 C1
Cannon St, Dover CT16 — 23 C2
Cannon St,
 New Romney TN28 — 34 B2
Cannon St,
 Romney Marsh TN29 — 34 B2
Cannon Walk DA12 — 28 C3
Cannonbury Rd CT11 — 43 A5
Cannongate Av CT21 — 33 C3
Cannongate Cl CT21 — 33 D3
Cannongate Gdns CT21 — 33 D3
Cannongate Rd CT21 — 33 C3
Canon Cl ME10 — 44 C6

Canons Gate Rd CT16 — 23 D1
Canterbury La CT1 — 16 C4
Canterbury Rd,
 Ashford TN24 — 12 C3
Canterbury Rd,
 Birchington CT7 — 14 C4
Canterbury Rd,
 Faversham ME13 — 25 D4
Canterbury Rd,
 Gravesend DA12 — 28 C5
Canterbury Rd,
 Herne Bay CT6 — 32 C2
Canterbury Rd,
 Margate CT9 — 36 A3
Canterbury Rd,
 Sittingbourne ME10 — 48 D3
Canterbury Rd,
 Westgate-on-Sea CT8 — 58 A3
Canterbury Rd,
 Whitstable CT5 — 59 A4
Canterbury St ME7 — 27 A3
Canute Cl,
 Birchington CT7 — 14 A2
Canute Rd,
 Faversham ME13 — 25 C4
Capability Way DA9 — 29 C1
Capel Rd,
 Faversham ME13 — 25 B3
Capel Rd,
 Sittingbourne ME10 — 48 A4
Capstan Mews DA11 — 39 D3
Capstan Row CT14 — 22 D1
Cardinal Cl,
 Sheerness ME12 — 37 D3
Cardinal Cl,
 Tonbridge TN9 — 55 D5
Carey Cl TN28 — 38 C4
Carisbrooke Rd ME2 — 52 A2
Carlton Rd DA1 — 21 D4
Carlton Av,
 Broadstairs CT10 — 15 C2
Carlton Av,
 Gillingham ME7 — 27 B4
Carlton Av,
 Ramsgate CT11 — 43 A4
Carlton Av,
 Sheerness ME12 — 47 A6
Carlton Rd TN23 — 12 A3
Carlton Rd East CT8 — 58 B2
Carlton Rd West CT8 — 58 A3
Carlton Rise CT8 — 58 B3
Carmichael Rd DA9 — 29 C1
Caroline Cres CT10 — 15 A2
Caroline Sq CT9 — 36 C2
Carp Cl,
 Aylesford ME20 — 49 C6
Carp Cl, Chatham ME4 — 18 A6
Carpenters Cl ME1 — 18 A6
Carpenters La TN11 — 17 B5
Carriage Mews CT2 — 16 B1
Carrick Dr TN13 — 46 B4
Carriers Rd TN17 — 20 C4
Carrington Cl ME7 — 27 C2
Carrington Rd DA1 — 21 D3
Carroways Pl ME2 — 36 C2
Carsington Gdns DA1 — 21 B6
Carters Wood TN26 — 30 B5
Carton Cl ME1 — 44 D6
Carville Av TN4 — 50 C2
Casey Way DA10 — 29 E2
Castalia Cotts CT14 — 22 C5
Castle Av,
 Broadstairs CT10 — 15 C2
Castle Av, Hythe CT21 — 33 B3
Castle Av,
 Rochester ME1 — 44 C5
Castle Cres CT21 — 33 B2
Castle Flds TN9 — 55 B2
Castle Hill ME1 — 44 C3
Castle Hill Av CT20 — 26 A2
Castle Hill Pass CT20 — 26 B2
Castle Hill Rd CT16 — 23 B1
Castle Rd,
 Chatham ME4 — 18 C6
Castle Rd, Hythe CT21 — 33 B1
Castle Rd,
 Sittingbourne ME10 — 48 D3
Castle Rd,
 Swanscombe DA10 — 29 F3
Castle Rd,
 Tonbridge Wells TN4 — 56 A3
Castle Rd,
 Whitstable CT5 — 59 C1
Castle Rd Bsns
 Precinct ME10 — 48 D1
Castle Rd Technology
 Centre ME10 — 48 D1
Castle Row ME1 — 16 B5
Castle St,
 Canterbury CT1 — 16 A5
Castle St, Dover CT16 — 23 C2
Castle St,
 Greenhithe DA9 — 29 A2
Castle St,
 Queenborough ME11 — 41 B1

Castle St,
 Southborough TN4 — 50 C1
Castle St,
 Swanscombe DA10 — 29 F3
Castle St, Tonbridge TN9 — 55 B2
Castle St,
 Tunbridge Wells TN1 — 56 C5
Castle Ter TN11 — 17 B6
Castle View Rd ME2 — 52 B4
Castle Vw
 Bsns Centre ME1 — 44 D3
Castleacres
 Ind Est ME10 — 48 D1
Castlemaine Av ME7 — 27 C2
Castlemere Av ME11 — 41 B1
Castlemount Rd CT16 — 23 C1
Catherine Pl TN1 — 56 D3
Catherine St ME1 — 44 D6
Catherine Way CT10 — 15 B2
Cattle Market CT13 — 45 D2
Causton Rd TN17 — 20 B4
Cavalry Ct CT14 — 22 C5
Cave Hill ME15 — 35 A6
Cavenagh Rd CT15 — 41 D5
Cavendish Av,
 Gillingham ME7 — 27 C2
Cavendish Av,
 Sevenoaks TN13 — 46 A3
Cavendish Ct,
 Herne Bay CT6 — 32 C1
Cavendish Ct,
 Tonbridge TN9 — 55 D2
Cavendish Dr TN2 — 56 D6
Cavendish Rd,
 Herne Bay CT6 — 32 C2
Cavendish Rd,
 Rochester ME1 — 44 D6
Cavendish St CT11 — 43 B4
Caversham Cl ME8 — 42 C1
Cavour Rd,
 Faversham ME13 — 25 C3
Cavour Rd,
 Sheerness ME12 — 47 D3
Caxton Cl TN30 — 54 A6
Caxton La TN11 — 17 B5
Caxton Rd CT9 — 58 F3
Cazeneuve St ME1 — 44 D4
Cecil Av,
 Sheerness ME12 — 47 C4
Cecil Av, Strood ME2 — 52 C3
Cecil Ct, Ashford TN24 — 12 C3
Cecil Ct, Herne Bay CT6 — 32 D2
Cecil Pk CT6 — 32 C2
Cecil Rd,
 Gravesend DA11 — 28 A4
Cecil Rd,
 Rochester ME1 — 44 C5
Cecil Sq CT9 — 36 B2
Cecil St CT9 — 36 C2
Cecilia Gro CT10 — 15 A2
Cecilia Rd CT11 — 43 B2
Cedar Cl,
 Birchington CT7 — 14 E3
Cedar Cl,
 Broadstairs CT10 — 15 B1
Cedar Cl, Margate CT9 — 19 B4
Cedar Cl,
 Sittingbourne ME10 — 48 D4
Cedar Cl, Swanley BR8 — 53 A2
Cedar Ct TN4 — 50 C6
Cedar Dr TN8 — 24 B4
Cedar Rd, Dartford DA1 — 21 B5
Cedar Rd, Strood ME2 — 52 A5
Cedar St*,
 Burgess Row TN30 — 54 A6
Cedar Ter Rd TN13 — 46 C3
Cedric Rd CT8 — 58 B2
Celtic Rd CT14 — 22 A5
Cemetery La,
 Ashford TN24 — 12 D2
Cemetery La,
 Tonbridge TN24 — 17 C4
Cemetery Rd ME6 — 49 B2
Centenary CT27 — 17 B2
Central Av,
 Gravesend DA12 — 28 B5
Central Av,
 Sittingbourne ME10 — 48 B3
Central Bsns Pk ME2 — 18 A1
Central Par TN14 — 32 A1
Central Park Gdns ME4 — 18 A6
Central Rd,
 Dartford DA1 — 21 C1
Central Rd,
 Ramsgate CT11 — 43 A2
Central Rd, Strood ME2 — 52 B4
Century Rd ME8 — 42 A2
Century Walk CT14 — 22 C2
Chada Av ME7 — 27 B5
Chadwick Cl DA11 — 39 D6
Chaffinch Way TN12 — 40 C5
Chalk Av TN30 — 54 B2
Chalk Pit Hill ME4 — 18 C5
Chalk Rd ME11 — 41 B1
Chalkwell Rd ME10 — 48 B4
Challenger Cl TN12 — 40 B4

63

Chamberlain Rd ME4 18 D6
Chambers Cl DA9 29 A2
Chancellor Way TN13 46 B3
Chancery Ct DA1 21 D4
Chancery La ME15 35 C4
Chandlers Mews DA9 29 C1
Chandos Rd CT10 15 C4
Chandos Sq CT10 15 D4
Channel View Rd CT17 23 B4
Channel Vw CT20 26 E2
Chantlers Hill TN12 40 C6
Chantry Ct CT1 16 C2
Chantry Pl TN12 34 B5
Chantry Rd TN12 34 B5
Chapel Ct DA10 29 E3
Chapel Hill Cl CT9 36 D6
Chapel La, Dover CT16 23 C2
Chapel La, St Margarets at Cliffe CT15 41 B4
Chapel La, Tonbridge TN12 51 C4
Chapel Pl, Birchington CT7 14 E3
Chapel Pl, Dover CT17 23 C2
Chapel Pl, Ramsgate CT11 43 A4
Chapel Pl, Tunbridge Wells TN1 56 B6
Chapel Place La CT11 43 A4
Chapel Rd ME6 49 C3
Chapel Row TN9 34 C2
Chapel St, Deal CT14 22 D2
Chapel St, Faversham ME13 25 D3
Chapel St, Herne Bay CT6 32 C1
Chapel St, Hythe CT21 33 B4
Chapel St, Minster ME12 37 E3
Chapel St, Sheerness ME12 47 B2
Chaplin Dr TN27 31 C5
Chapman Ho CT14 22 B5
Chappell Way ME10 48 A1
Chapter Rd ME2 52 A4
Charing Cres CT8 58 A3
Charing Grn TN27 17 B3
Charing Hill TN27 17 C2
Charles Cl ME6 49 C3
Charles Ho CT14 22 B5
Charles Rd, Deal CT14 22 B4
Charles Rd, Ramsgate CT11 43 B2
Charles St, Chatham ME4 18 A5
Charles St, Greenhithe DA9 29 A1
Charles St, Herne Bay CT6 32 C1
Charles St, Maidstone ME16 35 A5
Charles St, Sheerness ME12 47 B2
Charles St, Strood ME2 52 C4
Charles St, Tunbridge Wells TN4 50 C3
Charlesworth Dr CT7 14 E3
Charlotte Sq CT20 36 C3
Charlotte St, Folkestone CT20 26 D2
Charlotte St, Sittingbourne ME10 48 A2
Charlton Ter TN9 55 C2
Charnock BR8 53 C3
Chart Cl ME13 28 B5
Chart Rd TN23 12 A3
Charter House Dr TN13 46 B4
Charter St, Chatham ME4 18 B6
Charter St, Gillingham ME7 27 A1
Chartway TN13 46 C5
Chartwell Cl ME2 52 D2
Chater Ct CT14 22 C4
Chatham Hill, Chatham ME5 18 D5
Chatham Hill, Gillingham ME7 27 A5
Chatham Hill Rd TN14 46 C2
Chatham Pl CT11 43 A3
Chatham St ME1 44 D5
Chatsworth Dr ME2 52 D2
Chatsworth Rd, Dartford DA1 21 A1
Chatsworth Rd, Gillingham ME7 27 A2
Chattenden Ct ME14 35 C1
Chaucer Pk DA1 21 C4
Chaucer Rd, Broadstairs CT10 15 B5
Chaucer Rd, Gillingham ME7 27 A5
Chaucer Rd, Gravesend DA11 39 C2

Chaucer Rd, Sittingbourne ME10 48 A4
Cheddar Cl TN24 12 C2
Cheeselands TN27 13 B2
Chegworth Gdns ME10 48 A6
Chelmar Rd ME4 18 C5
Chequers Centre ME15 35 C4
Chequers Cl ME2 52 B2
Chequers Pk TN25 60 C6
Chequers Rd ME12 37 F3
Cheriton Gdns CT20 26 B2
Cheriton Pl, Deal CT14 22 C4
Cheriton Pl, Folkestone CT20 26 C3
Cheriton Rd, Deal CT14 22 C4
Cheriton Rd, Folkestone CT19 26 A2
Cherry Amber Cl ME8 42 B2
Cherry Av BR8 53 B3
Cherry Cl, Ashford TN26 30 B6
Cherry Cl, Maidstone ME17 32 B5
Cherry Cl, Sittingbourne ME10 48 A1
Cherry Garden Cres TN25 60 C5
Cherry Garden La TN25 60 C5
Cherry Gdns, Herne Bay CT6 32 B3
Cherry Gdns, New Romney TN28 38 E3
Cherry Orch, Ashford TN26 60 A1
Cherry Orch, Tenterden TN30 54 A6
Cherry Tree Cl ME12 47 B5
Cherry Tree Ct CT5 59 D1
Cherry Tree Rd ME8 42 B2
Cherrywood Rise TN25 12 A2
Chesfield Cl TN11 17 C5
Chesham Dr ME8 42 A4
Chester Rd, Gillingham ME7 27 B6
Chester Rd, Westgate-on-Sea CT8 58 C2
Chestnut Av, Greenhithe DA9 29 A4
Chestnut Av, Tonbridge TN12 51 B2
Chestnut Av, Tunbridge Wells TN4 50 D3
Chestnut Cl, Edenbridge TN8 24 B4
Chestnut Cl, Tenterden TN30 54 C3
Chestnut Cl, Tunbridge Wells TN4 50 D3
Chestnut La TN13 46 B4
Chestnut Rd DA1 21 B4
Cheviot Ct CT10 15 D3
Cheviot Ho DA11 39 C2
Cheviot Way ME7 12 C2
Chicago Av ME7 27 C3
Chichester Cl, Ashford TN23 12 B5
Chichester Cl, Gillingham ME8 42 C2
Chichester Dr TN13 46 A6
Chichester Rd TN9 55 A4
Chiddingfold Cl ME2 37 D3
Chiffinch Gdns DA11 39 D6
Childs Cres DA10 29 D3
Chilham Av CT8 58 A3
Chilham Cl, Chatham ME4 18 A5
Chilham Cl, Sheerness ME12 47 C5
Chillington St ME14 35 B1
Chilston Rd, Maidstone ME17 32 C5
Chilston Rd, Tunbridge Wells TN4 50 D6
Chiltenhurst TN8 24 A3
Chiltern End TN24 12 B3
Chiltern Rd DA1 39 D6
Chiltern Way TN9 55 C1
Chilton Av ME10 48 D3
Chilton Ct ME8 42 A1
Chippendayle Dr ME17 30 B2
Christ Church Rd CT20 26 B3
Christchurch Av TN1 56 C5
Christchurch Cres DA12 28 C3
Christchurch Ct CT17 23 B2
Christchurch Rd, Ashford TN23 12 B5
Christchurch Rd, Gravesend DA12 28 C4
Christmas St ME7 27 C1
Christopher Rd ME4 18 C6
Chulkhurst TN27 13 B2
Church App TN28 38 B3
Church Cotts TN17 20 B4
Church Cres ME17 30 D2

Church Fld, Dartford DA2 21 B6
Church Fld, Edenbridge TN8 24 C5
Church Fld, Snodland ME6 49 D1
Church Flds CT9 36 C3
Church Grn, Staplehurst TN12 51 B4
Church Grn, Tonbridge TN12 34 B5
Church Hill, Chatham ME5 27 A6
Church Hill, Dartford DA2 21 B6
Church Hill, Hythe CT21 33 B3
Church Hill, Ramsgate CT11 43 B4
Church La, Chatham ME4 18 B1
Church La, Deal CT14 22 A3
Church La, Maidstone ME17 30 C2
Church La, New Romney TN28 38 B3
Church La, Canterbury CT1 16 A5
Church La, Canterbury CT1 16 C2
Church La, Tonbridge TN9 55 C2
Church Mdws CT14 22 A2
Church Mews ME8 42 B2
Church Path, Chatham ME7 18 D2
Church Path, Deal CT14 22 A4
Church Path, Gillingham ME7 27 B5
Church Path, Gravesend DA11 39 C2
Church Path, Strood ME2 52 C4
Church Path, Tenterden TN30 54 A5
Church Rd, Ashford TN23 12 C4
Church Rd, Broadstairs CT10 15 D4
Church Rd, Faversham ME13 25 D2
Church Rd, Harrietsham ME17 30 C2
Church Rd, Hythe CT21 33 B3
Church Rd, Maidstone ME15 35 A6
Church Rd, Margate CT9 36 A6
Church Rd, New Romney TN28 38 A4
Church Rd, Ramsgate CT11 43 B4
Church Rd, Romney Marsh TN29 34 C2
Church Rd, Sittingbourne ME10 48 D3
Church Rd, Southborough TN4 50 B1
Church Rd, Swanscombe DA10 29 F2
Church Rd, Tenterden TN30 54 B5
Church Rd, Tonbridge TN12 40 C3
Church Rd, Tunbridge Wells TN1 56 A3
Church Rise TN21 33 B3
Church St Marys ME17 45 D1
Church Sq, Broadstairs CT10 15 D4
Church Sq, Maidstone ME17 32 D6
Church St, Ashford TN25 60 C5
Church St, Broadstairs CT10 15 A3
Church St, Canterbury CT1 16 D4
Church St, Chatham ME4 18 C4
Church St, Dover CT16 23 C2
Church St, Gillingham ME7 27 C2
Church St, Sittingbourne ME10 48 A3
Church St, Edenbridge TN8 24 C5
Church St, Faversham ME13 25 D2
Church St, Folkestone CT20 26 D3
Church St, Gillingham ME7 27 C2
Church St, Gravesend DA11 28 B2
Church St, Hadlow TN11 17 C6

Church St, Maidstone ME14 35 B3
Church St, Margate CT9 36 C3
Church St, Rochester ME1 44 D4
Church St, Tonbridge TN9 55 C2
Church St, Tovil ME15 35 A6
Church St, Whitstable CT5 59 C3
Church Ter, Chatham ME5 27 A6
Church Ter, Sheerness ME12 37 D3
Church Vw, Ashford TN27 13 B2
Church Vw, Swanley BR8 53 B2
Church Walk, Ashford TN27 31 B5
Church Walk, Cranbrook TN18 31 C2
Church Walk, Dartford DA2 21 B6
Church Walk, Gravesend DA12 28 D4
Church Walk, Northfleet DA11 39 B2
Churchfield Pl CT9 36 C3
Churchfield Way TN25 60 B5
Churchfields CT10 15 B1
Churchill Ho CT14 22 B6
Churchill Bsns Centre TN16 57 D5
Churchill Cl CT15 41 B5
Churchill Ct, Hythe CT21 33 A4
Churchill Rd, Gravesend DA11 28 A4
Churchill Rd, Sheerness ME12 37 E3
Churchill Way ME13 25 B1
Cinque Ports Av CT21 33 A5
Cinque Ports Rd TN28 38 C4
Citadel Cres CT17 23 A4
Citadel Rd CT17 23 A4
City Way ME1 44 D5
Civic Way TN1 56 C3
Claire Ct CT10 15 C3
Clanricarde Gdns TN1 56 B3
Clanricarde Rd TN1 56 B3
Clanwilliam Rd CT14 22 D3
Clapper La TN12 51 A2
Clare Rd CT5 59 B1
Claremont Gdns TN2 56 D6
Claremont Pl CT1 16 A6
Claremont Rd, Deal CT14 22 B3
Claremont Rd, Folkestone CT20 26 D2
Claremont Rd, Maidstone ME4 35 D3
Claremont Rd, Tunbridge Wells TN1 56 C5
Claremont Way ME4 18 B4
Clarence Av, Margate CT9 19 C3
Clarence Av, Rochester ME1 44 D5
Clarence Pl, Deal CT14 22 C1
Clarence Pl, Dover CT17 23 C4
Clarence Rd, Gravesend DA12 28 B3
Clarence Rd, Chatham ME4 18 D6
Clarence Rd, Deal CT14 22 D6
Clarence Rd, Herne Bay CT6 32 A2
Clarence Rd, Sheerness ME12 47 D2
Clarence Rd, Tunbridge Wells TN1 56 B3
Clarence Row, Gravesend DA12 28 B3
Clarence Row, Sheerness ME12 47 D2
Clarence Row, Tunbridge Wells TN1 56 B3
Clarence St, Folkestone CT20 26 D2
Clarence St, Herne Bay CT6 32 B1
Clarendon Cl ME10 48 B6
Clarendon Dr ME2 52 C2
Clarendon Gdns CT11 43 A4
Clarendon Mews, Broadstairs CT10 15 B4
Clarendon Mews, New Romney TN28 38 C1
Clarendon Pl CT17 23 A3
Clarendon Rd, Broadstairs CT10 15 C4
Clarendon Rd, Dover CT17 23 A2

Clarendon Rd, Gravesend DA12 28 C2
Clarendon Rd, Margate CT9 36 D2
Clarendon Rd, Sevenoaks TN13 46 B5
Clarendon St CT17 23 A3
Claridge Mews CT21 33 B4
Clavadal Rd TN12 40 C3
Clearmount Dr TN27 17 C2
Clearmount Pk TN27 17 C2
Cleave Rd ME7 27 B6
Cleaver La CT11 43 B4
Clerks Fld TN27 31 B5
Cleveland Ho DA11 39 C2
Cleveland Rd ME7 27 B2
Cliff Cl CT21 33 C2
Cliff Fld CT8 58 A2
Cliff Gdns ME12 37 E3
Cliff Prom CT10 15 D1
Cliff Rd, Birchington CT7 14 B1
Cliff Rd, Broadstairs CT10 15 D1
Cliff Rd, Hythe CT21 33 C2
Cliff Rd, Strood ME2 52 C3
Cliff Rd, Whitstable CT5 59 C1
Cliff St CT11 43 B4
Cliff Ter CT9 36 C1
Cliffe Av CT9 58 F1
Cliffe Rd ME2 52 C1
Clifford Gdns CT14 22 A6
Clifford Rd CT5 59 C4
Cliffside Dr CT10 43 C1
Clifton Cl, Maidstone ME14 35 D2
Clifton Cl, Rochester ME2 52 A4
Clifton Cres CT20 26 A4
Clifton Gdns CT9 36 D2
Clifton Gro DA11 28 B3
Clifton Marine Par DA11 28 A2
Clifton Mews CT9 36 D1
Clifton Pl, Margate CT9 36 D2
Clifton Pl, Tunbridge Wells TN2 56 C6
Clifton Rd, Folkestone CT20 26 A4
Clifton Rd, Gillingham ME7 27 A1
Clifton Rd, Gravesend DA11 28 B2
Clifton Rd, Margate CT9 36 D2
Clifton Rd, Whitstable CT5 59 A3
Clifton St CT9 36 C3
Cliftonville Av CT9 19 A3
Clinton Bsns Centre TN12 51 B1
Clipper Cl ME2 18 A1
Clipper Ct ME2 18 A1
Clive Rd, Gravesend DA11 28 B2
Clive Rd, Rochester ME1 44 C5
Cliveden Pl CT10 15 A3
Clock Tower Mews ME6 49 C1
Clockhouse La TN13 46 B3
Cloth Hall Gdns TN27 13 C2
Clovelly Dr ME12 37 B2
Clovelly Rd CT5 59 A5
Clover Ct ME10 48 D2
Clover St ME4 18 B4
Clover Walk TN8 24 C3
Clover Way TN12 40 C4
Coast Rd ME8 38 F4
Coastguard Cotts CT21 33 B5
Coats Av ME12 47 B5
Cobay Cl CT21 33 C4
Cobb Walk ME13 25 B2
Cobbets Way TN8 24 B6
Cobblers Bridge Rd CT6 32 A3
Cobbs Cl TN12 40 B4
Cobbs Mews CT20 26 B3
Cobbs Pas CT21 33 B4
Cobbs Pl CT9 36 C2
Cobbs Wood Ind Est TN23 12 A4
Cobden Pl CT1 16 C2
Cobden Rd, Chatham ME4 18 D6
Cobden Rd, Hythe CT21 33 B5
Cobden Rd, Sevenoaks TN13 46 C3
Cobham Av ME10 48 A6
Cobham Chase ME13 25 B2
Cobham Cl, Greenhithe DA9 29 B3
Cobham Cl, Maidstone ME16 35 A3
Cobham Cl, Rochester ME2 52 A4
Cobham Rise ME7 27 C3
Cobham St DA11 28 B3
Cobham Ter TN23 29 B3

Cock La TN26 30 B6
Cockreed La TN28 38 A3
Codrington Rd CT11 43 A4
Cogate Rd TN12 40 B4
Colburn Rd CT10 43 D1
Coldharbour La TN25 60 D5
Coldharbour Rd DA11 39 D5
Cole Ter ME17 32 B6
Coleman Stairs CT7 14 D1
Colemans St CT29 34 C2
Colemans Stairs Rd CT7 14 D1
Coll Yd ME1 44 C3
Collard Cl CT6 32 D3
College Av, Gillingham ME7 18 D4
College Av, Maidstone ME15 35 B5
College Av, Tonbridge TN9 55 A5
College Cotts ME15 35 B5
College Ct TN23 12 C4
College Pl DA9 29 C1
College Rd, Chatham ME4 18 C1
College Rd, Deal CT14 22 C1
College Rd, Gravesend DA11 39 A1
College Rd, Maidstone ME15 35 B5
College Rd, Margate CT9 36 B5
College Rd, Sittingbourne ME10 48 A4
College Walk ME15 35 B5
Collet Walk ME8
Collingwood CT10 15 A4
Collingwood Cl CT8 58 A4
Collingwood Ho DA9 29 C2
Collingwood Rd CT5 59 A3
Collins Rd TN28 38 C4
Collis St ME2 52 C2
Collison Pl TN30 54 D5
Colney Rd DA11 21 C3
Colonel Stephens Way TN30 54 B3
Colonels Way TN4 50 D1
Colyer Rd DA11 39 C5
Commerce Way TN8 24 B3
Commercial Pl DA12 28 C2
Commercial Rd, Paddock Wood TN12 40 B4
Commercial Rd, Strood ME2 52 C3
Commercial Rd, Tonbridge TN9 55 B4
Commissioners Rd ME2 52 D3
Commodore Rd ME14 35 D2
Common Rd TN11 17 B4
Commonwealth Cl ME10 48 D4
Concord Cl TN12 40 B3
Conduit St ME15 25 D2
Conifer Way BR8 53 A1
Coniston Av TN4 50 B6
Coniston Cl ME7 27 D2
Conn Rd ME7 27 A3
Connaught Gdns CT9 36 C4
Connaught Rd, Chatham ME4 18 D6
Connaught Rd, Folkestone CT20 26 C2
Connaught Rd, Margate CT9 36 C4
Connaught Rd, Sittingbourne ME10 48 A4
Connaught Way TN4 50 B6
Consort Cl ME14 35 D3
Constable Rd, Birchington CT7 14 D1
Constable Rd, Gravesend DA11 39 D6
Constables Rd CT16 23 D1
Constancia Ct CT20 26 B2
Constitution Rd, Chatham ME5 18 D5
Constitution Hill, Gravesend DA12 28 C4
Constitution Hill, Snodland ME6
Constitution Hill Rd TN4 50 B2
Constitution Rd ME5 18 D5
Convent Cl CT15 41 C5
Conway Cl, Birchington CT7 14 B2
Conway Cl, Rochester ME2 52 A2
Conway Mews ME7 18 C2
Conyerd Rd TN15 13 A6
Cookham Hill ME1 44 B6
Cooks La ME10 48 B1
Cooling Rd ME2 52 D1
Coolinge Rd CT20 26 B2
Coomb Fld TN8 24 B5
Coombe Av TN14 46 C1

Coombe Cl ME6 49 C4
Coombe La TN30 54 A5
Coombe Rd, Gravesend DA12 28 C5
Coombe Rd, Maidstone ME15 35 B6
Cooper Rd ME6 49 B5
Copenhagen Rd ME7 27 A4
Copland Av ME12 37 C4
Copper Beech Cl DA12 28 D3
Copper Beech Vw TN9 55 A4
Copper La TN12 34 C6
Copperas Ct CT5 59 D1
Copperfields TN29 34 B2
Copperwood TN24 12 D2
Coppin St CT14 22 D1
Copthall Av TN18 31 B2
Copthall Gdns CT20 26 C2
Cordelia Cres ME1 44 C6
Cork La TN11 51 A6
Corkwell St ME4 18 A5
Corner Farm Rd TN12 51 B2
Cornford Rd CT7 14 E3
Cornforth Cl TN12 51 C3
Cornhill CT11 43 A5
Cornwall Av CT11 43 C2
Cornwall Gdns CT9 19 B3
Cornwall Rd, Deal CT14 22 C5
Cornwall Rd, Gillingham ME7 27 A2
Cornwall Rd, Rochester ME1 44 C5
Cornwallis Av ME7 27 D4
Cornwallis Circle CT5 59 A3
Cornwallis Gdns CT10 15 C2
Cornwall Av DA12 28 C6
Corona Ter ME6 49 B5
Coronation Cl CT10 15 A1
Coronation Cres, Margate CT9 58 E3
Coronation Cres, Queenborough ME11 41 A1
Coronation Par CT19 26 F2
Coronation Rd, Chatham ME5 27 A6
Coronation Rd, Ramsgate CT11 43 A4
Coronation Sq TN29 34 B2
Corporation Rd ME7 27 B2
Corporation St ME1 44 C2
Corral Cl ME5 27 B6
Correnden Rd TN10 55 A1
Cortland Cl ME1 48 A1
Corunna Cl CT21 33 A3
Corys Rd ME1 44 C2
Cossack St ME1 44 C5
Cossington Rd CT1 16 D5
Costells Mdw TN16 57 D5
Cotswold Cl TN24 12 C2
Cotswold Rd DA11 39 D6
Cottage Rd, Chatham ME4 18 B2
Cottage Rd, Ramsgate CT11 43 B4
Cottage Row CT13 45 D1
Cottall Av ME4 18 B6
Cotton Hill Walk TN26 30 B6
Couchman Green La TN12 51 C1
Coulman St ME7 27 B3
Coulter Ho DA9 29 C2
Coulton Av DA11 39 D3
Council Rd DA11 39 B2
County Rd ME14 35 B3
Court App CT20 26 B3
Court Cres BR8 53 C4
Court Hall ME11 41 A1
Court La TN11 17 C6
Court Lane Pl TN11 17 C6
Court Lodge La ME17 30 C1
Court Lodge Rd ME7 27 D2
Court Rd CT14 22 A6
Court St ME13 25 D2
Courtenay Rd ME14 35 B3
Courthope TN12 40 C4
Courtlands, Herne Bay CT6 32 D3
Courtlands, Tonbridge TN10 55 A1
Courtlands Way CT8 58 C2
Courtwood Dr TN13 46 A4
Courtyard Mews DA9 29 A3
Coventry Gdns CT14 22 C4
Covey Hall Rd ME6 49 C2
Cowdray Rd CT14 22 A5
Cowdray Sq CT14 22 A5
Cowgate Hill CT17 23 C2
Cowley Av DA9 29 A2
Cowley Rise CT9 19 B6
Cowper Rd, Deal CT14 22 B3
Cowper Rd, Gillingham ME7 27 A5
Cowper Rd, Margate CT9 36 C3
Cowper Rd, Sittingbourne ME10 48 D3

Cox Gdns ME8 27 D6
Coxs Cl ME6 49 B2
Cozenton Cl ME8 42 A1
Cradducks La TN12 51 D2
Cragie Walk ME8 42 A6
Cramptons Rd TN14 46 C1
Cranbourne Cl CT11 43 C2
Cranbrook Dr ME10 48 A6
Cranbrook Rd, Cranbrook TN18 31 B1
Cranbrook Rd, Tonbridge TN12 51 C5
Crane House Gdns TN18 31 B1
Crane La TN17 20 C5
Cranford Cl ME8 42 A1
Cranford Rd DA1 21 B4
Cranham Sq TN12 34 B5
Cranleigh Dr BR8 53 C4
Cranleigh Gdns CT5 59 B4
Cranmere Ct ME2 52 D3
Crates Yd TN4 50 C6
Cravel Walk CT1 16 C4
Craven Cl CT9 58 F3
Crawford Gdns CT9 19 A3
Crawford Rd CT10 15 B3
Crawshay Cl TN13 46 A3
Crayford Cl ME4 35 D2
Craylands La DA10 29 D2
Craylands Sq DA10 29 D2
Craythorne TN30 54 C4
Craythorne Cl TN28 38 C2
Craythorne La TN28 38 B3
Cremer Pl ME13 25 B2
Cremers Rd ME10 48 D2
Crendon Pk TN4 50 C3
Crescent Gdns BR8 53 A1
Crescent Rd, Birchington CT7 14 D2
Crescent Rd, Faversham ME13 25 D2
Crescent Rd, Margate CT9 36 A3
Crescent Rd, Ramsgate CT11 43 A4
Crescent Rd, Tunbridge Wells TN1 56 C3
Crescent St ME10 48 B3
Cress Way ME13 25 B3
Cressey Ct ME4 18 A4
Cressfield TN23 12 A5
Crest Ind Est TN12 34 B4
Crest Vw DA9 29 A1
Crete Hall Rd DA11 39 C2
Cricketers Ct ME17 30 B2
Crinan Ct*, Argyll Dr CT10 43 B1
Cripps La CT15 41 B5
Crispin Cl ME13 25 D1
Croft Ct TN8 24 C5
Croft Gdns ME17 32 C6
Croft La TN8 24 C5
Croft Rd, Ashford TN24 12 D4
Croft Rd, Westerham TN16 57 B5
Crofton Rd CT8 58 C4
Cromer Rd ME4 52 C3
Cromer St TN1 55 A3
Crompton Gdns ME15 35 C4
Cromwell Rd, Maidstone ME14 35 C3
Cromwell Rd, Sheerness ME12 47 B5
Cromwell Rd, Whitstable CT5 59 B1
Cromwell Ter ME4 18 C5
Crooked La DA12 28 B2
Crosley Rd ME7 27 B6
Cross La, Faversham ME13 25 C3
Cross La, Sittingbourne ME10 48 B1
Cross La East DA12 28 B5
Cross La West DA12 28 B5
Cross Rd, Birchington CT7 14 E2
Cross Rd, Deal CT14 22 A6
Cross Rd, Chatham ME4 18 C4
Cross St, Gillingham ME7 27 A2
Cross St, Gravesend DA12 28 C2
Cross St, Herne Bay CT6 32 A3
Cross St, Maidstone ME14 35 B1
Cross St, Strood ME2 52 C3
Cross Way ME10 44 C6
Crossways ME10 48 B6
Crossways Blvd DA9 29 A1
Crouch House Cotts TN8 24 A4
Crouch House Rd TN8 24 A2
Crouch La TN15 13 C5
Crow Hill, Broadstairs CT10 15 C3

Crow Hill, Sevenoaks TN15 13 C5
Crow Hill Rd, Margate CT9 58 E3
Crow Hill Rd, Sevenoaks TN15 13 C5
Crow La ME1 20 B4
Crowhurst Rd TN15 13 B6
Crown Ct TN17 20 B4
Crown Quay La ME10 48 C3
Crown Rd, Edenbridge TN8 24 D2
Crown Rd, Sittingbourne ME10 48 A1
Crown St ME7 27 A2
Crownfields TN13 46 B6
Crowther Cl TN12 51 B3
Croydon Rd TN16 57 A4
Crundwell Rd TN4 50 B2
Crusader Ct DA1 21 D1
Crystal Bsns Centre CT13 45 F1
Cudham Gdns CT9 19 D3
Cullet Dr ME11 41 A2
Culverden Av TN4 50 C5
Culverden Down TN4 50 B6
Culverden Park Rd TN4 50 C6
Culverden Pk TN4 50 C6
Culverden Sq TN4 56 B1
Culverden St TN1 56 B1
Culvers La TN29 34 C3
Culvers Cl TN1 56 B6
Cumber Ld Rd CT11 43 A4
Cumberland Av, Broadstairs CT10 15 C3
Cumberland Av, Gravesend DA12 28 C3
Cumberland Ct TN10 55 A1
Cumberland Dr DA1 21 D4
Cumberland Gdns TN1 56 B6
Cumberland Mews TN1 56 B6
Cumberland Rd, Gillingham ME7 27 A1
Cumberland Rd, Margate CT9 58 E3
Cumberland Walk TN1 19 A3
Cumberland Yd TN1 56 B6
Cunningham Cl TN4 50 D4
Cunningham Cres CT7 14 C2
Cunningham Rd TN4 50 D4
Currie Rd TN30 54 B4
Curtis Way ME13 25 C2
Curzon Cl CT14 22 C5
Curzon Rd, Chatham ME4 18 B5
Curzon Rd, Maidstone ME14 35 C1
Cutbush Cl ME17 30 B2
Cutbush Ct ME14 35 D3
Cuthbert Rd CT8 58 B2
Cutmore St DA11 28 B3
Cutty Sark Cl DA9 29 A2
Cuxton Rd ME2 52 B6
Cyclamen Rd BR8 53 B3
Cygnet Gdns DA11 28 A5
Cylinder Rd CT21 33 A2
Cypress Ct ME7 27 D2
Daglish Cl TN28 38 C3
Dagmar Rd ME4 18 D6
Dahlia Dr BR8 53 E2
Dalby Rd CT9 36 D2
Dalby Sq CT9 36 D2
Dale Ct CT11 43 C2
Dale Rd, Rochester ME1 44 C6
Dale Rd, Swanley BR8 53 A2
Dale St, Chatham ME4 18 A6
Dale St, Tunbridge Wells TN1 56 D1
Dalewood Ml ME10 48 D5
Dallinger Rd CT7 14 C1
Dalmaney Cl CT10 15 D3
Dalmeny Av CT9 19 C4
Dalton St ME7 27 A2
Damson Ct BR8 53 B3
Dan Dr ME13 25 A1
Dane Cres CT11 43 B2
Dane End Rd CT8 58 A2
Dane Gdns CT9 19 B6
Dane Hill CT9 36 C2
Dane Hill Row CT9 36 C2
Dane John Cotts CT1 16 B6
Dane John Mews CT1 16 B5
Dane Mt CT9 19 B6
Dane Park Rd, Margate CT9 36 C2
Dane Park Rd, Ramsgate CT11 43 B2
Dane Pk CT9 36 D3
Dane Rd, Birchington CT7 14 A2
Dane Rd, Margate CT9 36 C2
Dane Rd, Ramsgate CT11 43 B3
Dane Valley Rd CT9 19 A5
Danedale Av ME12 37 F3

Danemoor TN30 54 C
Danes Cl DA11 39 B
Danes Hill ME7 27 D
Danes Mead Ter CT9 36 C
Danvers Rd TN9 55 B
Darby Pl CT20 26 C
Darby Rd CT20 26 C
Darcy Sq TN28 38 E
Darenth Gdns TN16 57 5
Darenth Rd DA11 21 C
Dark Hill ME13 21 C
Dark La CT21 33 A
Darland Av ME7 27 C
Darlington Dr ME12 37 A
Darlington St CT20 26 C
Darnley Cl CT10 15 B
Darnley Rd, Gravesend DA11 28 A
Darnley Rd, Strood ME2 52 A
Darnley St DA11 28 B
Darracott Cl CT14 22 B
Darren Gdns CT10 15 B
Dart Cl ME2 52 A
Dartford Rd, Dartford DA1 21 A3
Dartford Rd, Sevenoaks TN13 46 C5
Darwin Ct ME1 44 D
Darwin Rd CT7 14 C
Dashwood Rd DA11 39 B
Davenport Av ME7 27 B
David Av CT9 19 C
Davids Cl CT10 15 C
Davie Cl ME12 47 C
Davington Hill ME13 25 C
Davis Av, Deal CT14 22 A
Davis Av, Gravesend DA11 39 D
Davis Cl TN13 46 C
Dawes St ME7 27 A
Dawks Mdw TN27 31 B
Dawson Rd CT19 26 D
De Burgh St CT17 23 A
De Mere Cl ME8 42 A
De Warren Ho DA11 39 C
Deacon Cl ME2 52 A
Deacon Ct TN4 50 D
Deacons Trading Est TN9 55 D3
Deakin Leas TN9 55 B
Deal Castle Rd CT14 22 D
Deal Rd CT13 45 D
Dean Ct CT1 16 D
Dean Rd, Rochester ME2 52 A
Dean Rd, Sittingbourne ME10 48 A
Deane Cl CT5 59 B
Deanwood Dr ME8 42 A
Deborah Cl CT5 59 C
Deedes Cl CT21 33 C
Delagarde Rd TN16 57 C
Delmark Rd ME12 47 D
Delamere Gdns ME6 49 C
Delamere Rd ME6 49 C
Delane Rd CT14 22 A
Delce Rd ME1 44 D
Delf St CT13 45 D
Delfside CT13 45 D
Dence La CT6 32 D
Dence Pk CT6 32 D
Dencorra Way TN23 12 A
Dene Holm Rd DA11 39 C
Dene Lodge CT15 41 C
Dene Rd DA1 21 C
Dene Walk CT9 36 C
Dengemarsh Rd TN29 34 C
Denington Ct TN4 50 C
Denmark Rd CT11 43 B
Dennes La TN29 34 B
Dennes Mill Cl TN25 60 B
Dennis Rd DA11 28 B
Dental St CT21 33 B
Dent-de-Lion Ct CT9 58 D
Dent-de-Lion Rd, Margate CT9 58 E3
Dent-de-Lion Rd, Westgate-on-Sea CT8 58 B2
Denton Way CT9 19 B4
Derby Cl ME10 48 A1
Dering Rd CT6 32 B2
Derwent Dr TN4 50 B6
D'Este Rd CT11 43 C4
Detling Av CT10 43 C1
Detling Cl ME12 47 C5
Detling Rd DA11 39 D4
Devon Av CT14 22 C5
Devon Cl ME8 42 B1
Devon Gdns CT7 14 C1
Devon Rd CT19 26 C1
Devonshire Gdns CT9 19 B3
Devonshire Rd, Gillingham ME7 27 A1
Devonshire Rd, Gravesend DA12 28 B4

ial Cl, Gillingham ME7 27 D2
ial Cl, Greenhithe DA9 29 D2
ial Rd ME7 27 D2
iamond Ct ME12 47 C4
iamond Ho CT5 59 B2
iamond Rd CT5 59 B2
iana Gdns CT14 22 A3
iana Rd ME4 18 C6
ibden Rd CT14 22 D1
ickens Rd, Broadstairs CT10 15 D3
ickens Rd, Rochester ME1 44 C6
ickens Way TN18 31 C2
ickley La ME17 32 A4
ickson Ct ME10 48 D3
ickson Rd CT17 23 A1
ieu Stone La CT16 23 C1
ignals Cl ME8 42 B1
illywood La ME2 52 A1
immock Cl TN12 40 D3
ixon Cl ME15 35 B5
obwells TN17 20 C5
ock Rd ME4 18 B3
oddington Ct ME16 35 A3
oes Alley ME10 48 B3
oggerel Acre CT5 59 C5
oggets Cl TN8 24 B6
oggetts Sq ME2 52 D4
ola Av CT14 22 B2
olphin Ct CT6 32 B1
olphin Dr ME8 42 A6
olphin La CT16 23 C2
olphin Pk ME10 48 D2
olphin Pl CT16 23 C2
olphin Rd, Romney Marsh TN29 34 C2
olphin Rd, Sittingbourne ME10 48 D2
Dolphin St, Deal CT14 22 D1
Dolphin St, Herne Bay CT6 32 B1
Dombey Cl ME1 44 C6
Dominic Ct CT10 15 A3
Domneva Rd CT8 58 B2
Dongola Rd ME2 52 C2
Donnithorne Ho CT6 32 B1
Doon Brae TN4 50 C1
Dorcas Gdns CT10 15 C2
Dorchester Cl DA1 21 D4
Dorchester Rd DA12 28 D6
Doric Av TN4 50 B2
Doric Cl TN4 50 B2
Dorothy Av TN17 20 C6
Dorset CT14 22 B6
Dorset Ct CT14 22 C6
Dorset Gdns, Birchington CT7 14 C3
Dorset Gdns, Deal CT14 22 B6
Dorset Pl ME13 25 C3
Dorset Rd ME12 47 B4
Dorset Rd Ind Est ME12 47 B4
Dorset St TN13 46 C6
Dossett Ct CT14 22 A6
Douglas Alms Houses ME17 32 C5
Douglas Av, Hythe CT21 33 C3
Douglas Av, Whitstable CT5 59 B3
Douglas Cl CT10 15 A3
Douglas Rd, Deal CT14 22 A5
Douglas Rd, Herne Bay CT6 32 C3
Douglas Rd, Lenham ME17 32 C5
Douglas Rd, Maidstone ME16 35 A5
Douglas Rd, Tonbridge TN9 55 A4
Douglas Ter CT14 22 C3
Dour St CT16 23 B1
Douro Pl CT16 23 D2
Doust Way ME1 18 A4
Dovedale Ct, Ashford TN24 12 B3
Dovedale Ct, Birchington CT7 14 E3
Dover Pl TN23 12 C5
Dover Rd, Deal CT14 22 C6
Dover Rd, Dover CT15 41 A4
Dover Rd, Folkestone CT20 26 D2
Dover Rd, Gravesend DA11 39 C2
Dover Rd, Sandwich CT13 45 C4
Dover Rd East DA11 39 D3
Dover St, Canterbury CT1 16 D4
Dover St, Sittingbourne ME10 48 B3
Dowding Walk DA11 39 D6
Dowell Mews CT14 22 C5
Dowgate Cl TN9 55 D5
Dowling Cl ME6 49 A3
Downland Ct TN24 12 B3
Downlands ME17 30 D2
Downs Av, Dartford DA1 21 D4
Downs Av, Whitstable CT5 59 B3
Downs Cl, Charing TN27 17 B2
Downs Cl, Headcorn TN27 31 D5
Downs Pk CT6 32 D2
Downs Rd CT14 22 B6
Downs Way TN27 17 B2
Downside, Dover CT15 41 C5
Downside, Strood ME2 52 B4
Downsview Cl BR8 53 D2
Dr Hopes Rd TN17 20 C5
Drake Av ME12 37 D4
Drakes Av ME2 52 B3
Draper St TN4 50 C1
Drapers Av CT9 36 C4
Drapers Cl CT9 36 D5
Dray Ct TN11 17 B6
Drayton Rd TN9 55 C5
Dreadnought Av ME12 37 B4
Drew La CT14 22 C4
Drop Redoubt Rd CT17 23 B3
Droveway Gdns CT15 41 C5
Drum La TN24 12 C4
Drum Major Dr CT14 22 A5
Drury Rd TN30 54 B4
Dry Bank Ct TN10 55 B1
Dry Bank Rd TN10 55 B1
Dry Hill Park Cres TN10 55 B1
Dry Hill Park Rd TN10 55 B1
Dry Hill Rd TN10 55 B1
Dryland Rd, Sevenoaks TN15 13 B6
Dryland Rd, Snodland ME6 49 B3
Drywall ME10 48 D1
Duck La CT1 16 C2
Dudley Av CT8 14 F1
Dudley Rd, Folkestone CT19 26 E1
Dudley Rd, Gravesend DA11 39 D3
Dudley Rd, Tunbridge Wells TN1 56 B2
Duke St, Deal CT14 22 C1
Duke St, Margate CT9 36 B2
Dukes Mdw TN26 30 B5
Dumergue Av ME11 41 B1
Dumpton Gap Rd CT10 15 C6
Dumpton La CT11 43 B2
Dumpton Park Dr, Broadstairs CT10 15 C6
Dumpton Park Dr, Ramsgate CT11 43 C3
Dumpton Park Rd CT11 43 B2
Dumpton Pk CT11 43 B1
Duncan Cl CT5 59 A5
Duncan Dr CT7 14 C2
Duncan Rd, Gillingham ME7 27 A3
Duncan Rd, Ramsgate CT11 43 A4
Duncan Rd, Whitstable CT5 59 A4
Duncannon Pl DA9 29 C1
Dunera Dr ME14 35 B1
Dungeness Rd TN29 34 C2
Dunkery Rise TN24 12 B2
Dunkin Rd DA1 21 D1
Dunlop Ct TN18 31 C1
Dunnings La ME1 44 C4
Dunoon Ct*, Argyll Dr CT10 43 B1
Dunstan Av CT8 58 A4
Dunstan Gro TN4 50 D6
Dunstan Rd TN4 50 D5
Durban Rd CT9 36 D4
Durham Cl CT17 23 B2
Durham Hill CT17 23 B2
Durling Ct ME8 42 D1
Durrant Way DA10 29 E4
Dyke Rd CT19 26 E2
Dymchurch Rd, Hythe CT21 33 A4
Dymchurch Rd, New Romney TN28 38 C2

Eagle Hill CT11 43 A3
Eagle Way DA11 39 A1
Eagles Rd DA9 29 A1
Eaglestone Cl TN15 13 C4
Eardley Rd TN13 46 B5
Earl Rd DA11 39 D5
Earl St ME14 35 B3
Earls Av CT20 26 A4
Earlsfield Rd CT21 33 C3
Eason Villas TN12 34 B5
East Cliff, Dover CT16 23 E2
East Cliff, Folkestone CT19 26 E2
East Cliff Gdns CT19 26 E2
East Cliff Par CT6 32 D1
East Cliff Prom CT10 15 D2
East Cliff Rd TN4 50 C5
East Crescent Rd DA12 28 C2
East Cross TN30 54 B5
East Ct ME15 35 C6
East Hill, Ashford TN24 12 D4
East Hill, Dartford DA1 21 C3
East Hill, Tenterden TN30 54 C5
East Hill Dr DA1 21 C4
East Kent Av DA11 39 B2
East La ME12 47 B2
East Lodge Rd TN23 12 A3
East Mill DA11 28 A2
East Milton Rd DA12 28 D3
East Rd ME4 18 B1
East Roman Ditch CT16 23 E1
East Row ME1 44 C4
East St, Ashford TN23 12 B4
East St, Chatham ME4 18 C5
East St, Dover CT17 23 A1
East St, Faversham ME13 25 D3
East St, Folkestone CT19 26 E2
East St, Gillingham ME7 27 B2
East St, Herne Bay CT6 32 C1
East St, Hythe CT21 33 C3
East St, Maidstone ME17 30 B2
East St, Sittingbourne ME10 48 C3
East St, Snodland ME6 49 D3
East St, Tonbridge TN9 55 C2
East Ter DA12 28 C2
East Weald Dr TN30 54 C4
Eastbrook Pl CT16 23 C1
Eastchurch Rd CT9 19 D3
Eastern Av, Ashford TN23 12 B4
Eastern Av, Queenborough ME11 41 B2
Eastern Esp, Broadstairs CT10 15 D2
Eastern Esp, Margate CT9 19 A2
Eastern Rd, Gillingham ME7 27 D2
Eastern Rd, Romney Marsh TN29 34 C2
Eastfield Rd CT7 14 D3
Eastfields CT19 26 D1
Eastgate ME1 44 D3
Eastgate Ct ME1 44 D4
Eastgate Rd TN30 54 C4
Eastgate Terr ME1 44 C4
Eastlands Est TN12 40 B2
Eastling Rd ME13 25 A6
Eastmead Av TN23 12 C6
Eastwell Barn Mews TN30 54 B4
Eastwell Cl, Maidstone ME14 35 D2
Eastwell Cl, Tonbridge TN12 40 B3
Eastwell Mdws TN30 54 B5
Eastwood Rd ME10 48 A2
Eaton Hill CT9 36 B3
Eaton Rd CT9 36 B3
Eaves Ct ME10 48 D1
Ebbsfield Ind Est DA11 39 A1
Ebbsfleet Walk DA11 39 A2
Eccleston Rd ME15 35 A5
Echo Sq DA12 28 C5
Echo Walk ME12 37 E4
Eddington Bsns Pk CT6 32 B3
Eddington La CT6 32 A3
Eden Ct, Cranbrook TN18 31 B1
Eden Ct, Herne Bay CT6 32 A2
Eden Pl DA12 28 B3
Eden Rd TN1 56 B6
Edenbridge Dr ME12 47 C5
Edenbridge Trading Centre TN8 24 C6
Edenfield CT7 14 E3
Edgar Cl BR8 53 D2
Edgar Ho CT14 22 B5
Edgar Rd CT9 36 D1
Edge End Rd CT10 15 B4
Edgeler Ct ME6 49 B4
Edinburgh Rd, Ashford TN24 12 C4
Edinburgh Rd, Chatham ME4 27 A6
Edinburgh Rd, Gillingham ME7 27 A3
Edinburgh Rd, Margate CT9 58 E3
Edith Rd, Faversham ME13 25 C4
Edith Rd, Westgate-on-Sea CT8 58 C2
Edmanson Av CT9 58 D2
Edred Rd CT17 23 A1
Edward Dr CT7 14 F2
Edward Rd ME11 41 B1
Edward St, Chatham ME4 18 C5
Edward St, Strood ME2 52 C4
Edward St, Tunbridge Wells TN4 50 C2
Edwards Gdns BR8 53 B3
Edwards Rd CT16 23 C1
Edwin St DA12 28 B3
Edwina Av ME12 37 B3
Effingham Cres CT17 23 B1
Effingham St, Dover CT17 23 B1
Effingham St, Ramsgate CT11 43 B4
Egbert Rd, Birchington CT7 14 B2
Egbert Rd, Faversham ME13 25 C4
Egbert Rd, Westgate-on-Sea CT8 58 C2
Egdean Walk TN13 46 C4
Eglinton Rd DA10 29 F3
Elaine Av ME2 52 A4
Eldon St ME4 18 C4
Eldon Way TN12 40 B2
Eldon Way Ind Est TN12 40 B2
Elfrida Cl CT9 19 C5
Elgar Bretts Ct CT1 16 A6
Elham Way CT10 15 C6
Eliza Cook Cl DA9 29 B1
Elizabeth Ct, Broadstairs CT10 15 D1
Elizabeth Ct, Gravesend DA11 28 A2
Elizabeth Garlick Ct TN1 56 D1
Elizabeth Gdns CT21 33 B4
Elizabeth Huggins Cotts DA11 28 B5
Elizabeth Rd CT11 43 C4
Elizabeth St CT17 23 B4
Elizabeth Way CT6 32 D3
Ellen Av CT11 43 B1
Ellerslie DA12 28 D3
Ellesmere Mews TN28 38 C1
Ellington Av CT9 58 E3
Ellington Rd CT11 43 A4
Elliott St DA12 28 D3
Elliotts Pl ME13 25 D3
Ellis Cl BR8 53 B3
Ellis Dr TN28 38 C1
Ellis Way DA1 21 D6
Elm Cl DA1 21 A5
Elm Cotts TN8 24 B2
Elm Dr BR8 53 B1
Elm Gdns CT21 33 D3
Elm Gro, Maidstone ME15 35 C5
Elm Gro, Westgate-on-Sea CT8 58 B3
Elm La, Sheerness ME12 37 D4
Elm La, Tonbridge TN10 55 C1
Elm Pass CT21 33 B3
Elm Rd, Dartford DA1 21 A5
Elm Rd, Gillingham ME7 27 C2
Elm Rd, Gravesend DA12 28 C6
Elm Rd, Tunbridge Wells TN4 50 C2
Elm Rd, Westerham TN16 57 D4
Elmfield TN30 54 B5
Elmfield Cl DA11 28 B4
Elmfield Ct TN30 54 B5
Elmhurst Gdns ME4 18 A5
Elmley Way CT9 36 C6
Elms Av CT11 43 A4
Elmstead Pl CT20 26 E2
Elmstone Gdns CT9 19 D4
Elmstone Rd, Gillingham ME8 42 A3
Elmstone Rd, Ramsgate CT11 43 A3
Elmwood Cl CT10 15 B1
Elwick La TN23 12 C4
Elwick Rd TN23 12 C4
Ely Ct TN1 56 C2
Emily Jackson Cl TN13 46 B5
Empire Ter CT9 36 B5
Empire Walk DA9 29 C1
Engine Alley TN26 60 B2
Engineers Ct TN23 12 B4
Enterprise Way TN8 24 B3
Enticott Cl CT5 59 D3
Epple Bay Av CT7 14 E1
Epple Bay Rd CT7 14 D2
Epple Cotts CT7 14 F2
Epple Rd CT7 14 E2
Epps Rd ME10 48 A3
Erica Ct BR8 53 C3
Eridge Rd TN4 56 A6
Ernest Rd ME4 18 C5
Esplanade, Dover CT17 23 C3
Esplanade, Rochester ME1 52 D5
Esplanade, Sheerness ME12 47 C2
Esplanade, Strood ME2 44 B2
Esplanade, Westgate-on-Sea CT8 58 C1
Essex Gdns CT7 14 C3
Essex Rd, Dartford DA1 21 B3
Essex Rd, Gravesend DA11 28 A4
Essex Rd, Westgate-on-Sea CT8 58 C2
Essex St CT5 59 A4
Estuary Rd ME12 47 C4
Ethel Rd CT10 15 B3
Ethelbert Cres CT9 36 D1
Ethelbert Gdns CT9 36 C1
Ethelbert Rd, Birchington CT7 14 A2
Ethelbert Rd, Dover CT17 23 A1
Ethelbert Rd, Faversham ME13 25 B4
Ethelbert Rd, Margate CT9 36 D2
Ethelbert Rd, Ramsgate CT11 43 A4
Ethelbert Rd, Rochester ME1 44 C5
Ethelbert Sq CT8 58 C2
Ethelbert Ter, Margate CT9 36 D1
Ethelbert Ter, Westgate-on-Sea CT8 58 C2
Ethelred Ct ME13 25 C4
Ethelred Rd CT8 58 C2
Eton Way DA1 21 A1
Eureka Leisure Pk TN24 12 C1
Eurogate Bsns Pk TN24 12 B1
Eurolink Ind Est ME10 48 C2
Eurolink Way ME10 48 B2
Eva Rd ME7 27 B5
Evans Cl DA9 29 A2
Evelyn Cl ME2 52 D3
Everard Way ME13 25 B1
Everest La ME2 52 C2
Everest Pl BR8 53 C3
Eversleigh Rise CT5 59 C5
Evesham Rd DA12 28 D5
Ewins Cl TN12 40 C4
Exchange St CT14 22 D1
Exeter Rd DA12 28 D6
Exmoor Rise TN24 12 C2
Exmouth Rd ME7 27 A1
Eynsford Rd DA9 29 C2

Factory Rd DA11 39 B2
Fair St CT10 15 A4
Fairacre CT10 15 A4
Fairbourne La ME17 30 A3
Fairfield Cl TN28 38 B3
Fairfield Cres TN9 55 C5
Fairfield Ct TN15 13 B5
Fairfield Pk CT10 15 A4
Fairfield Rd, Broadstairs CT10 15 A4
Fairfield Rd, New Romney TN28 38 B3
Fairfield Rd, Ramsgate CT11 43 A1
Fairfield Rd, Sevenoaks TN15 13 B4
Fairfield Ter TN26 30 B6
Fairlight Cl TN4 50 D1
Fairlight Rd CT21 33 A3
Fairmead Rd TN8 24 B1
Fairmeadow ME14 35 B2
Fairview TN18 31 B2
Fairview Cl TN9 55 B6
Fairview Gdns CT14 22 A6
Fairview Rd ME10 48 C3
Fairwood Ind Est TN23 12 A5
Falcon Cl DA1 21 D2
Falcon Ct ME10 48 C5
Falcon Gdns ME12 37 D3
Falcon Mews DA11 39 D5
Falconers Ct TN8 24 B3
Fallowfield ME10 48 D5
Farleigh Hill ME15 35 A6
Farley Cft TN16 57 B5
Farley La TN16 57 B5
Farley Nursery TN16 57 C5
Farley Rd CT9 36 C6
Farlow Cl DA11 28 A6
Farm Av BR8 53 A2
Farm Cres ME10 48 C5

Farm Hill Av ME2 52 B2
Farm House Cl CT5 59 C4
Farm La CT16 23 C2
Farm Rd, Ashford TN26 30 B6
Farm Rd,
  Sevenoaks TN14 46 D1
Farmcombe CT2 56 D6
Farmcombe La TN2 56 C5
Farmcombe Rd TN2 56 D6
Farmcroft DA11 28 A5
Farmdale Av ME1 44 B6
Farmer Cl CT21 33 D2
Farmground Cl TN9 55 D4
Farmstead Dr TN8 24 C3
Farnaby Dr TN13 46 A6
Farnham Cl ME8 42 D2
Farnol Rd DA1 21 D1
Farrar Rd CT7 14 E3
Farrier Cl TN23 12 A1
Farrier St CT14 22 D1
Farthing Cl DA1 21 C1
Faversham Rd ME13 25 D3
Faversham Rd ME17 32 D5
Faversham Reach ME13 25 D1
Fawkes Av TN24 21 C6
Fawley Cl ME14 35 A1
Fay Cl ME1 44 B6
Fennel Cl ME1 44 B5
Fenoulhet Way CT6 32 C1
Fenton Ct CT14 22 A2
Fern Cl CT10 15 D3
Ferndale TN13 46 D3
Ferndale Ct CT7 14 D3
Ferndale Rd,
  Gillingham ME7 27 B3
Ferndale Rd,
  Gravesend DA12 28 B5
Fernhurst Cres TN4 50 C1
Fernlea Av CT8 32 A2
Fernleigh Ter ME10 48 A5
Ferrier Cl ME8 41 A3
Ferry Vw ME11 41 A3
Fiddlers Cl DA9 39 B1
Field Dr TN8 24 C3
Fielding St ME13 31 C2
Fieldways TN18 31 C2
Fieldworks Rd ME7 14 B1
Fifth Av CT9 19 B2
Fig Tree Rd CT10 15 D4
Finch Mews CT14 22 C4
Findlay Cl ME8 42 A5

**Fine Line
  Ind Est ME2 44 D1**
Finlay Cl ME13 25 B2
Finsbury Rd CT11 43 B3
Fintonagh Dr ME14 35 C1
Fir Tree Cl TN12 51 C4
Firbank Gdns CT9 36 B5
Firbanks CT5 59 D4
Fircroft Way TN8 24 B3
Firethorne Cl ME7 27 C2
Fisgard Ct DA12 28 D2
First Av, Chatham ME4 27 A6
First Av,
  Gillingham ME7 27 C6
First Av,
  Gravesend DA11 39 D4
First Av, Margate CT9 19 A2
First Av,
  Queenborough ME11 41 A2
First Av,
  Sheerness ME12 47 D3
Fisher Cl CT21 33 C4
Fisher St,
  Maidstone ME14 35 B2
Fisher St,
  Sandwich CT13 59 C3
Fishermens Hill DA11 39 B1
Fishers Cl TN12 51 C1
Fishers Oak TN14 46 D2
Fishers Rd TN12 51 C1
Fitzmary Av CT9 58 E2
Fitzroy Av CT9 19 A4
Fitzroy Rd CT5 59 D1
Five Bells La ME1 44 C4
Five Oak La TN12 51 A5
Five Wents BR8 53 E1
Flaxmans Ct ME7 18 C2
Flaxmore Pl TN4 50 D1
Fleet Av TN24 47 C4
Fleet Rd DA11 39 B6
Fleetwood Av CT6 32 A2
Fleetwood Cl ME12 37 B4
Fletcher Rd TN12 51 B3
Fletchers Way CT14 22 A2
Flint Gro CT10 15 A3
Flood La ME13 25 C2
Flora Rd CT11 43 B3
Florence Rd ME16 35 A5
Florence St ME2 52 C3
Florin Dr ME1 44 B5
Flower Rise ME14 35 B1
Floyd Cl CT14 50 C4
Flying Horse La CT16 23 C2
Foley St ME14 35 C2
Folkestone CT20 26 D4

Folkestone Rd CT17 23 A2
Folly Rd CT20 26 E1
Foord Rd,
  Folkestone CT19 26 C1
Foord Rd,
  Maidstone ME17 32 C5
Foord St ME1 44 D4
Forbes Rd ME13 25 C4
Force Green La TN16 57 C3
Ford Rd DA11 39 B1
Ford Way TN23 12 A5
Fordoun Rd CT20 15 B3
Fordwich Dr ME2 52 C1
Fordwich Gro CT14 50 C5
Fordwich Pl CT13 45 C2
Foreland Av CT9 19 C3
Foreland Ct CT15 41 C6
Foreland Heights CT10 15 D1
Foreland Rd CT15 41 C6
Forelands Sq CT14 22 B6
Foremans Walk TN27 31 B5
Forest Hill ME15 35 B6
Forest Rd TN12 40 C4
Foresters Way CT20 26 C2
Forge Cft TN8 24 C5
Forge Cl ME13 25 D4
Forge La, Ashford TN23 12 B4
Forge La,
  Gillingham ME7 27 B2
Forge La,
  Headcorn TN27 31 B4
Forge La,
  Whitstable CT5 59 A4
Forge Mdw ME17 30 B2
Forge Mdws TN27 31 B5
Forge Rd,
  Sittingbourne ME10 48 A1
Forge Rd,
  Tunbridge Wells TN4 50 C3
Forge Way TN12 40 C3
Forson Cl TN30 54 B4
Fort Cres CT9 36 C1
Fort Hill CT9 36 B2
Fort Pitt Hill ME1 18 A4
Fort Pitt St ME4 18 A5
Fort Prom CT9 36 C1
Fort Rd,
  Broadstairs CT10 15 D4
Fort Rd, Hythe CT21 33 A4
Fort Rd, Margate CT9 36 C2
Fort St ME1 44 D5
Fortrye Cl DA11 39 D5
Fortuna Ct CT11 43 A3
Fosse Bank Cl TN9 55 A5
Fosse Rd TN9 55 B2
Fostall Rd ME13 25 C1
Fosten La TN27 13 A2
Foster Clark Est ME15 35 D5
Foster St ME15 35 B4
Foster Way CT14 22 B3
Fosters Av CT10 15 A1
Fougeres Way TN24 12 B2
Fountain Rd ME2 52 A2
Fountain St ME10 48 B3
Four Elms Rd TN8 24 C3
Fox Av ME7 27 C4
Fox Lea TN15 13 B5
Fox St ME7 27 A2
Foxglove Cl TN8 24 C3
Foxglove Rise ME14 35 A1
Foxgrove Rd CT5 59 D2
Foxley Rd ME11 41 A1
Foxwood Gro DA11 39 D4
Foys Pass CT21 33 C3
Frampton Rd CT21 33 A4
Frances Gdns CT11 43 C3
Francis La,
  Ashford TN23 12 B6
Francis Rd,
  Broadstairs CT10 15 C1
Francis Rd,
  Dartford DA1 21 A2
Franciscan Way CT1 16 B3
Franklin Rd ME7 27 B3
Frant Fld TN8 24 C5
Frant Rd TN2 56 B6
Freda Cl CT10 43 C1
Frederick Rd, Deal CT14 22 A5
Frederick Rd,
  Gillingham ME7 27 A4
Frederick St ME10 48 A3
Freelands Rd ME6 49 A3
Freemens Way CT14 22 B5
Freesia Cl ME7 27 C2
Freight La TN17 31 C5

**Fremlin Walk Shopping
  Centre ME15 35 B3**
Frensham Cl TN6 49 C4
Freshfield La CT21 33 A2
Friars Cl CT5 59 C2
Friary Pl ME2 52 C4
Friendly Cl CT9 19 C4
Friends Av CT9 19 D4
Friends Gap CT9 19 D2
Frindsbury Rd ME2 52 D3
Frittenden Rd TN12 51 C4

Frobisher Way DA9 29 B1
Frog La TN1 56 B5
Frogmore Walk ME17 32 B5
Front Brents ME13 25 D2
Front Rd TN26 60 A2
Frythe Cl TN17 20 C5
Frythe Cres TN17 20 C5
Frythe Walk TN17 20 C5
Frythe Way TN17 20 C5
Fuggles Cl TN12 40 B4
Fulham Av CT9 58 F3
Fullers Dr CT9 36 C3
Fullers Hill TN16 57 C5
Fulsam Pl CT9 36 A3
Fulston Pl ME10 48 C4
Fulwich Rd DA1 21 C3
Furrells Rd ME1 44 D4
Further Fld TN12 51 B2

Gabriels Hill ME15 35 B3
Gads Hill ME7 27 D1
Gagetown Ter ME14 35 B6
Gainsborough Av CT9 19 C5
Gainsborough Cl ME8 42 A4
Gainsborough Dr DA11 39 C6
Gainsborough Rd CT7 14 D2
Galahad Av ME2 52 A5
Galbri Dr ME2 52 B5
Galley Hill Rd DA10 29 F2

**Galley Hill
  Trading Est DA10 29 E2**
Galliard St CT13 45 D2
Galloways ME12 34 B3
Gallwey Av CT7 14 B2
Galway Rd ME12 47 D3
Gann Rd CT5 59 C2
Gaol La CT16 23 C2
Garden Cl CT12 51 B5
Garden Ct TN13 46 D3
Garden Rd,
  Sevenoaks TN13 46 D2
Garden Rd,
  Tonbridge TN9 55 C2
Garden Rd,
  Tunbridge Wells TN1 56 D2
Garden St,
  Gillingham ME7 18 C2
Garden St,
  Tunbridge Wells TN1 56 D2
Gardenia Cl ME2 52 D1
Gardens ME12 47 D4
Gardiner St ME7 27 A2
Gardyne Mews TN9 55 B4
Garfield Rd,
  Gillingham ME7 27 B2
Garfield Rd,
  Margate CT9 36 A3
Garlinge Rd TN4 50 C2
Garrard Av CT9 58 F2
Garraton Rd ME12 47 B1
Garrison Cl BR8 53 C2
Garrolds Cl BR8 53 C2
Gas House Rd ME1 44 C2
Gas Pass CT1 16 A5
Gas Rd ME10 48 B1
Gas St CT1 16 A5
Gasson Rd DA10 29 F3
Gassons Rd ME6 49 A3
Gasworks La TN23 12 B4
Gatefield La ME13 25 D3
Gatekeeper Chase ME8 42 B2
Gatwick Rd DA12 28 B6
Gaunts Cl CT14 22 A4
Gaze Hill Av ME10 48 B4
Gdn St TN1 56 D2
George Hill Rd CT10 19 D4
George La,
  Folkestone CT20 26 D3
George La,
  New Romney TN28 38 B3
George Pk CT9 58 F2
George Rd TN12 51 B3
George St,
  Ashford TN23 12 C5
George St, Deal CT14 22 C1
George St,
  Maidstone ME15 35 C5
George St,
  Ramsgate CT11 43 B4
George St,
  Sittingbourne ME10 48 D3
George St,
  Staplehurst TN12 51 B1
George St,
  Tonbridge TN9 55 B4
George V Av CT9 36 A4
George Wood TN29 34 C2
Georges Lees CT13 45 D2
Georgian Cl ME11 41 B3
Gerald Av ME4 18 B6
Gerrards Dr ME10 48 B5
Gibbs Hill TN27 31 C5
Gibraltar Av CT14 18 C1
Gibraltar Hill ME4 18 B4
Gibson St ME14 48 A3
Gilbert Cl DA10 29 D3
Gilbert Rd CT11 43 A3

Gilbert Ter ME14 35 B1
Giles Gdns CT9 36 C4
Gilford Rd CT14 22 C3
Gilham Gro CT14 25 D2
Gill Cres DA11 28 A6
Gillett Rd TN29 34 C1
Gillingham Grn ME7 27 C2
Gillingham Rd ME7 27 A4
Gills Cotts ME1 18 A4
Ginsbury Cl ME2 18 A2
Giraud Dr ME13 25 B1
Gladstone Rd,
  Broadstairs CT10 15 B5
Gladstone Rd,
  Chatham ME4 18 A6
Gladstone Rd,
  Dartford DA1 21 C3
Gladstone Rd,
  Deal CT14 22 C5
Gladstone Rd,
  Maidstone ME14 35 B6
Gladstone Rd,
  Margate CT9 36 C4
Gladstone Rd,
  Tonbridge TN9 55 A4
Gladstone Rd,
  Whitstable CT5 59 A2
Glanville Rd,
  Gillingham ME7 27 B3
Glanville Rd,
  Strood ME2 52 C4
Gleanings Mews ME1 44 D4
Glebe Cl CT15 41 B5
Glebe Gdns,
  Maidstone ME17 32 D6
Glebe Gdns,
  Margate CT9 58 E3
Glebe La ME10 48 D5
Glebe Rd,
  Margate CT9 58 E3
Glebe Way CT5 59 A4
Gleblands TN27 13 B2
Glen Vw DA12 28 C4
Glencoe Rd,
  Chatham ME4 18 B6
Glencoe Rd,
  Margate CT9 36 D3
Glendale BR8 53 D4
Glendale Rd ME12 37 C2
Glenside CT5 59 B4
Glenwood Cl TN30 54 B1
Glenwood Dr ME12 37 C3
Glistening Glade ME8 42 A4
Globe La ME4 18 B3
Gloucester Av,
  Broadstairs CT10 15 A5
Gloucester Av,
  Margate CT9 19 C3
Gloucester Cl ME8 42 C2
Gloucester Mews TN28 38 C1
Gloucester Pl CT20 26 C1
Gloucester Rd CT5 59 C2
Glovers Cres ME10 48 B4
Glovers Mill ME1 44 D5
Glynne Cl ME8 42 A5

**Goblands Fm
  Ind Est TN11 17 D6**
Goddards Cl TN17 20 A5
Godden Rd ME6 49 B3
Goddings Dr ME1 44 B6
Goddington La ME17 30 A1
Goddington Rd ME2 52 B2
Godfrey Cl ME2 52 B2
Godfrey Walk TN12 12 C6
Godinton Rd,
  Ashford TN23 12 B4
Godinton Rd,
  Ashford TN23 12 C4
Godinton Way TN23 12 B4

**Godinton Way
  Ind Est TN23 12 B4**
Godwin Rd,
  Dover CT16 23 D1
Godwin Rd,
  Margate CT9 19 A3
Godwyne Cl CT16 23 C1
Godwyne Rd CT16 23 C1
Golden Acre La CT8 58 A3
Golden Cl CT8 58 A3
Golden Hill CT5 59 C5
Golden Sq TN30 54 C4
Golden St CT14 22 D1
Goldfinch Cl,
  Faversham ME13 25 C1
Goldfinch Cl,
  Tonbridge TN12 40 C5
Golding Rd TN13 46 C2
Goldings TN12 40 B5
Goldsel Rd BR8 53 B4
Goldsmid Rd TN4 56 B4
Goldsmith Ct TN30 54 C4
Goldsmith Rd ME8 42 A6
Goldsworth Dr ME2 52 C2
Goldthorne Cl ME14 35 D3
Golf Rd CT14 22 C1

Golford Rd TN17 20 D
Goodall Cl ME8 42 A
Goodfellow Way CT16 23 B
Goodnestone Rd ME10 48 D
Goods Station Rd TN1 56 C

**Goods Station Rd
  Trading Est TN1 56 C**
Goodwin Cl TN8 24 A
Goodwin Rd CT15 41 C
Gooseneck La TN27 31 B
Gordon Av ME1 41 B
Gordon Gro CT8 58 B
Gordon Henry Ho TN8 24 C
Gordon Pl DA12 28 C
Gordon Prom DA12 28 C
Gordon Prom East
  DA12 28 D
Gordon Rd,
  Canterbury CT1 16 A
Gordon Rd,
  Chatham ME4 18 C
Gordon Rd,
  Dartford DA1 21 B
Gordon Rd,
  Gillingham ME8 18 C
Gordon Rd,
  Gillingham ME7 27 B
Gordon Rd,
  Gravesend DA11 39 D
Gordon Rd,
  Herne Bay CT6 32 C
Gordon Rd,
  Margate CT9 36 D
Gordon Rd,
  Ramsgate CT11 43 A
Gordon Rd,
  Sevenoaks TN13 46 B
Gordon Rd,
  Strood ME2 52 B
Gordon Rd,
  Whitstable CT5 59 A
Gordon Sq CT7 14 C
Gordon Rd,
  Rochester ME1 44 C
Gordon Ter,
  Romney Marsh TN29 34 C
Gore Court Rd ME10 48 A
Gore End Cl CT7 14 C
Gorham Cl ME8 49 B
Gorham Dr TN9 55 D
Gorrell Ct CT5 59 B
Gorrell Rd CT5 59 B
Gorse Mead TN23 12 A
Gorse Rd ME2 52 B
Gorst St ME7 27 A
Gosfield Rd CT6 32 C
Gosselin St CT5 59 B
Goudhurst Cl ME16 35 A
Goudhurst Rd,
  Cranbrook TN17 20 A
Goudhurst Rd,
  Marden TN12 34 A
Goudhurst Rd,
  Tonbridge TN12 51 A
Gouge Av TN14 39 D
Grace Cl CT20 26 D
Grace Hill CT20 26 C
Grace Rd ME8 47 B
Grace Walk CT14 22 A
Grafton Rd ME10 48 B
Grafton Way ME10 48 C
Graham Cl ME7 18 C
Grampion Cl TN24 12 C
Granary Cl TN12 40 D
Granary Cl ME8 42 B
Granary Pl CT5 59 A
Granby Rd DA11 39 C
Grand Par TN28 38 F
Grange Cl,
  Edenbridge TN8 24 C
Grange Cl,
  Westerham TN16 57 D
Grange Cres TN30 54 B
Grange Ct CT20 26 D
Grange Hill ME5 18 D
Grange Rd,
  Broadstairs CT10 15 A
Grange Rd, Deal CT14 22 B
Grange Rd,
  Gillingham ME7 27 B
Grange Rd,
  Gravesend DA11 28 A
Grange Rd, Hythe CT21 33 A
Grange Rd,
  Ramsgate CT11 43 A
Grange Rd,
  Sevenoaks TN15 13 D
Grange Rd,
  Strood ME2 52 D
Grange Rd,
  Tenterden TN30 54 A
Grange Way,
  Broadstairs CT10 15 A
Grange Way,
  Rochester ME1 44 C
Grant Cl CT10 15 A

rantham Av CT14 22 A3
rantley Cl TN1 56 B5
ranville Av CT10 15 C5
ranville Cl ME13 25 C2
ranville Farm Mews CT11 43 C3
ranville Pl ME12 47 D3
ranville Rd, Broadstairs CT10 15 C5
ranville Rd, Deal CT14 22 C6
ranville Rd, Dover CT15 41 C5
ranville Rd, Gillingham ME7 27 C3
ranville Rd, Gravesend DA11 28 A4
ranville Rd, Maidstone ME14 35 B1
ranville Rd, Sevenoaks TN13 46 B5
ranville Rd, Sheerness ME12 47 C3
ranville Rd, Westerham TN16 57 B5
ranville St CT14 22 C3
rasmere Gro ME2 52 D1
rasmere Rd CT5 59 D3
ravel Walk, Ashford TN23 12 B3
ravel Walk, Rochester ME1 44 D4
ravesend Rd ME2 52 A2
raylen Cl CT14 22 B1
rayshott Cl ME10 48 C4
raystone Rd CT5 59 D1
reat Basin Rd ME12 47 B2
reat Elms TN11 17 B5
reat Hall Arcade TN1 56 C4
reat Lines ME7 18 C3
reat Mead TN8 24 B3
reat Queen St DA1 21 C3
reatness La TN14 46 C2
reatness Rd TN14 46 D2
recian Rd TN1 56 C5
recian St ME14 35 C2
reen Court Rd BR8 53 B4
reen Ct TN12 51 B4
reen La, Ashford TN26 60 B2
reen La, Broadstairs CT10 15 A3
reen La, Hythe CT21 33 A3
reen La, Margate CT9 19 D5
reen La, Tonbridge TN12 40 C5
reen La, Whitstable CT5 59 A4
Green Manor Way DA11 29 F1
Green Rd CT7 14 C2
Green St ME7 27 A3
Green Way TN29 34 B3
Greenacre Cl BR8 53 C4
Greenbanks DA1 21 B6
Greenfield TN8 24 C4
Greenfield Cotts CT1 16 A6
Greenfield Rd ME7 27 B2
Greenhill TN12 51 B2
Greenhithe, Greenhithe DA9 29 A2
Greenhithe, Maidstone ME15 35 B5
Greenlands TN15 13 D5
Greenly Way TN28 38 C3
Greenside, Maidstone ME15 35 C4
Greenside, Swanley BR8 53 B2
Greenview Walk ME7 27 D4
Greenway, Cranbrook TN17 20 A5
Greenway, Faversham ME13 25 B2
Greenways ME10 48 D4
Greenwood Way TN13 46 A5
Gregory Cl ME8 42 A6
Gregory Ct TN25 60 C5
Grenham Bay Av CT7 14 B2
Grenham Rd CT7 14 C2
Grenville Gdns CT7 14 C2
Grenville Way CT10 15 A4
Gresham Av CT9 58 E2
Gresham Cl ME8 42 B1
Greshams Way TN8 24 A3
Griffin St CT14 22 C1
Grigg La TN27 31 C5
Griggs Way TN15 13 C5
Grimshill Rd CT5 59 B4
Grimthorpe Av CT5 59 A5
Grisbrook Farm Cl TN29 34 C2
Grisbrook Rd TN29 34 C2
Groom Way ME17 32 D6
Grosvenor Av ME4 18 A5
Grosvenor Cres DA1 21 A2
Grosvenor Gdns CT9 36 C3
Grosvenor Hill CT9 36 B3
Grosvenor Pk TN1 56 B1
Grosvenor Rd, Broadstairs CT10 15 B4
Grosvenor Rd, Tunbridge Wells TN1 56 B1
Grosvenor Rd, Whitstable CT5 59 A5
Grosvenor Walk TN1 56 C1
Grotto Gdns CT9 36 D2
Grotto Hill CT9 36 C2
Grotto Rd CT9 36 D2
Grove Av TN1 56 C5
Grove Cl ME13 25 A3
Grove Hill Gdns TN1 56 D5
Grove Hill Rd TN1 56 C4
Grove Pl ME13 25 A3
Grove Rd, Chatham ME4 18 D6
Grove Rd, Deal CT14 22 C5
Grove Rd, Folkestone CT20 26 D1
Grove Rd, Gillingham ME7 27 D2
Grove Rd, Gravesend DA11 39 A1
Grove Rd, Ramsgate CT11 43 A4
Grove Rd, Sevenoaks TN14 46 D2
Grove Rd, Strood ME2 52 D3
Grove Ter CT1 16 A6
Grovelands ME17 32 D5
Grover St TN1 56 D2
Grundys Hill CT11 43 B4
Guardian Ind Est TN12 34 B4
Guildcourt La CT13 45 D1
Guildford Av CT8 58 B3
Guildford Ct CT14 22 D6
Guildford Lawn CT11 43 A4
Guildford Rd TN1 56 C5
Guildhall St, Canterbury CT1 16 C3
Guildhall St, Folkestone CT20 26 C2
Guiness Dr ME3 52 D1
Gun La ME2 52 C4
Gun Tower Mews ME1 44 H4
Gundulph Rd ME1 18 A4
Gunn Rd DA10 29 E3
Guston Rd ME14 35 D2
Guy Cl CT10 15 C1
Gwynn Rd DA11 39 C5
Gybbon Rise TN12 51 B3

Hackfield TN23 12 A5
Hadleigh Gdns CT6 32 D1
Hadley Ct TN4 50 C5
Hadlow Pk TN11 17 C5
Hadlow Rd, Maidstone ME14 35 D2
Hadlow Rd, Tonbridge TN9 55 C2
Haffenden Cl TN12 34 B5
Haffenden Mdw TN27 17 B2
Haffenden Rd TN30 54 B4
Hafod Pass CT21 33 C3
Haig Av, Chatham ME4 18 C6
Haig Av, Gillingham ME7 27 C4
Haig Gdns DA12 28 C3
Hailstone Cl TN11 17 B6
Haldane Gdns DA11 39 B4
Hales Cl TN30 54 B5
Halfmile Ride CT9 36 B6
Hall Cl ME10 48 B1
Hall Rd, Dartford DA1 21 C1
Hall Rd, Gravesend DA11 39 B6
Halland Ct TN8 24 B5
Hallford Way DA1 21 A2
Halliday Ct CT21 33 A3
Halliday Dr CT14 22 C5
Hallwards TN12 51 B5
Halstatt Rd CT14 22 A6
Halstow Way TN23 12 A6
Ham La ME17 32 B5
Ham Rd ME13 25 C1
Ham Shades La CT5 59 D3
Hamerton Rd DA11 39 A1
Hamilton Ct TN4 50 D6
Hamilton Rd, Deal CT14 22 B4
Hamilton Rd, Gillingham ME7 27 B1
Hamilton Rd, Romney Marsh TN29 34 C3
Hamilton Rd, Whitstable CT5 59 B2
Hammonds TN18 31 C1
Hammonds Sq ME6 49 C3
Hamond Hill ME4 18 A4
Hampton Rd ME14 35 D1
Hamstreet Rd, Ashford TN26 60 C3
Hamstreet Rd, Hamstreet TN26 30 C6
Hancock Cl ME2 52 C2
Hancocks Fld CT14 22 A3
Hanmer Way TN12 51 B4
Hannah Cl ME4 18 C6
Hanover Cl, Ashford TN23 12 A4
Hanover Cl, Deal CT14 22 D6
Hanover Cl, Margate CT9 19 D3
Hanover Cl, Sittingbourne ME10 48 B4
Hanover Ct CT10 15 B4
Hanover Rd TN1 56 B2
Hanover Sq CT6 32 C1
Hanover St CT6 32 B1
Hanway ME8 27 D6
Harbledown Gdns CT9 19 D2
Harbour Approach Rd CT20 26 E3
Harbour Par CT11 43 B4
Harbour St, Broadstairs CT10 15 D4
Harbour St, Folkestone CT20 26 E2
Harbour St, Ramsgate CT11 43 B4
Harbour St, Whitstable CT5 59 A2
Harbour Way CT20 26 E2
Harbourne La TN30 54 D1
Harcourt Gdns ME8 42 A6
Harden Rd, Gravesend DA11 28 A5
Harden Rd, Romney Marsh TN29 34 C2
Hardinge Rd TN24 12 C3
Hardres Rd CT11 43 B3
Hardres St CT11 43 B4
Hards Town ME4 18 C4
Hardy Av DA11 39 D5
Hardy St ME14 35 B2
Hare St, Chatham ME4 18 D5
Hare St, Sheerness ME12 47 D2
Harebrook CT11 43 C2
Harkness Ct ME10 48 D3
Harlech Cl ME2 52 A2
Harmer Ct TN4 50 C2
Harmer Rd DA10 29 F3
Harmer St DA12 28 C2
Harmsworth Gdns CT10 15 C2
Harnet St CT13 45 D1
Harold Av, Gillingham ME7 27 C4
Harold Av, Westgate-on-Sea CT8 58 C2
Harold Ct ME13 25 C4
Harold Pass CT16 23 D1
Harold Rd, Birchington CT7 14 B1
Harold Rd, Margate CT9 19 A3
Harold Rd, Sittingbourne ME10 48 D3
Harold St, Dover CT16 23 C1
Harold St, Queenborough ME11 41 B2
Harolds Rd CT16 23 D1
Harper Rd TN23 12 A6
Harps Av ME12 37 C3
Harpswood La CT21 33 A2
Harrier Dr ME10 48 C4
Harriet Dr ME1 44 B6
Harris Ct ME7 27 C6
Harris Rd ME12 47 D3
Harrison Dr ME17 30 C2
Harrison Rd, Ramsgate CT11 43 A5
Harrison Rd, Sevenoaks TN15 13 B6
Harrison Way TN13 46 B3
Harrow Cl TN8 24 C3
Harrow Dene CT10 15 A3
Harrowber Dr ME15 35 D5
Harrowby Gdns DA11 39 D5
Hart Dyke Cres BR8 53 B2
Hart Dyke Rd BR8 53 B2
Hart St ME16 35 A5
Hart St Commercial Centre ME16 35 A5
Hartfield Pl DA11 39 C3
Hartington St ME4 18 C5
Hartley Rd, Cranbrook TN17 20 A6
Hartley Rd, Westerham TN16 57 D4
Hartlip Cl ME12 47 C6
Hartnokes TN18 31 C1
Hartsdown Rd CT9 36 A3
Hartshill Rd DA11 28 A5
Hartslands Rd TN13 46 D4
Harvel Av ME2 52 A4
Harvesters Cl ME8 42 A4
Harvey Av CT14 22 C5
Harvey Dr ME10 48 C5
Harvey Pl CT20 26 E2
Harvey Rd ME8 42 A2
Harvey St CT20 26 D2
Harville Rd TN25 60 A6
Harwich St CT5 59 A4
Harwick Dr TN28 38 C2
Harwood Rd ME8 42 D1
Hasted Cl DA9 29 C3
Hastings Av CT9 19 A4
Hastings Pl CT13 45 D2
Hastings Rd ME15 35 C4
Hatch Rd ME17 32 B6
Hatch St ME13 25 C2
Hatfield Rd, Margate CT9 36 A3
Hatfield Rd, Ramsgate CT11 43 A4
Hatfield Rd, Rochester ME2 52 C3
Hathaway Ct ME1 44 B4
Hatherall Rd ME14 35 C2
Hatton Cl DA11 39 D6
Hatton Mews DA9 29 C1
Havelock Rd, Deal CT14 22 B5
Havelock Rd, Tonbridge TN9 55 B2
Havelock St CT1 16 D3
Haven Cl BR8 53 D2
Haventhorpe TN24 12 C3
Hawden Rd TN9 55 B2
Hawkenbury Rise ME2 52 C1
Hawkesbury St CT17 23 B4
Hawkhurst Cl CT7 14 E2
Hawkhurst Way CT10 15 C6
Hawkins Cl ME7 18 C2
Hawks La CT1 16 B4
Hawkwood Cl ME1 44 D4
Hawley Rd DA1 21 B6
Hawley Sq CT9 36 C2
Hawley St CT9 36 C2
Hawthorn Av ME12 47 B5
Hawthorn Cl, Edenbridge TN8 24 B4
Hawthorn Cl, Ramsgate CT11 43 A1
Hawthorn Rd, Dartford DA1 21 A5
Hawthorn Rd, Sittingbourne ME10 48 A2
Hawthorn Rd, Strood ME2 52 A5
Haydens Mews TN9 55 C1
Hayle Rd ME15 35 B5
Haymen St ME4 18 A5
Haynes Rd DA11 28 A6
Hays Rd ME6 49 A4
Haysel ME10 48 C5
Haywain Cl TN12 40 C5
Hayward Av ME2 52 C3
Hayward Dr DA1 21 C6
Haywards Cl, Deal CT14 22 A4
Haywards Cl, New Romney TN28 38 C3
Hazebrouck Rd ME13 25 A2
Hazel End BR8 53 C4
Hazel Gro ME12 37 B1
Hazel Rd DA1 21 B6
Hazelwood Mdw CT13 45 D3
Hazlemere Dr ME7 27 D3
Headcorn Gdns CT9 19 D3
Headcorn Rd, Maidstone ME17 32 C6
Headcorn Rd, Tonbridge TN12 51 C2
Headley Ct TN8 24 C4
Heard Way ME10 48 D2
Heartenoak Rd TN18 31 C1
Heath Cl BR8 53 C2
Heath Ct CT15 41 B5
Heath Gdns DA1 21 A4
Heath La DA1 21 A4
Heath St DA1 21 B4
Heather Bank TN12 40 D4
Heather Cl, Margate CT9 36 A4
Heather Cl, Sittingbourne ME10 48 C3
Heather Dr, Maidstone ME15 35 C6
Heather Dr, Tenterden TN30 54 B1
Heather End BR8 53 B4
Heathfield Cl ME14 35 D1
Heathfield Rd, Ashford TN24 12 C3
Heathfield Rd, Maidstone ME14 35 D1
Heathfield Ter BR8 53 B1
Heathorn St ME14 35 C2
Heathview TN4 50 B1
Heathwood Dr CT11 43 B1
Heathwood Gdns BR8 53 A1
Hectorage Rd TN9 55 C4
Hedge Place Rd DA9 29 A3
Hedley St ME14 35 C3
Heights Ter CT17 23 A3
Helena Av CT9 36 C4
Hellyar Ct ME1 44 D5
Hendley Dr TN17 20 B4
Hendy Rd ME6 49 D2
Hengist Av CT9 19 A4
Hengist Rd, Birchington CT7 14 A2
Hengist Rd, Deal CT14 22 C1
Hengist Rd, Westgate-on-Sea CT8 58 A2
Henley Cl, Gillingham ME8 42 A2
Henley Cl, Tenterden TN30 54 B2
Henley Flds TN30 54 B3
Henley Mdws TN30 54 B2
Henley Rd TN12 40 C3
Henley Vw TN30 54 C2
Henry Ct CT1 16 B6
Henry St, Chatham ME4 18 D5
Henry St, Gillingham ME8 42 C1
Henshill La TN18 31 A3
Herald Walk DA1 21 D2
Herbert Rd, Chatham ME4 18 C5
Herbert Rd, Gillingham ME8 42 A2
Herbert Rd, Swanscombe DA10 29 F3
Hereford Gdns CT7 14 D3
Hereson Rd CT11 43 B3
Hereward Av CT7 14 B1
Heritage Gdns CT16 23 D1
Herman Ter ME4 18 C5
Hermitage Cl CT21 33 A4
Hermitage Ct TN9 55 C2
Herne Av CT6 32 D3
Herneville Gdns CT6 32 D2
Heron Cl TN8 24 C3
Heron Dr ME12 37 C4
Herschell Rd CT7 14 C2
Herschell Rd East CT14 22 C5
Herschell Rd West CT14 22 C5
Herschell Sq CT14 22 C5
Hertford Pl CT11 43 A5
Hertford Rd CT9 19 B5
Hertford St CT11 43 A4
Hertsfield Av ME2 52 C1
Hever Cft ME2 52 B6
Hever Gdns ME16 35 A5
Hever Rd TN8 24 C6
Hewett Pl BR8 53 B3
Hewitt Cl ME7 27 D2
Hewitt Rd CT16 23 B1
Hibbs Cl BR8 53 B2
Hibernia St CT11 43 B4
Higgins La ME4 18 B3
High Dewar Rd ME8 42 C2
High Elms ME8 42 A1
High Firs BR8 53 C4
High Halden Rd TN27 13 C3
High St, Ashford TN24 12 C4
High St, Biddenden TN27 13 C2
High St, Blue Town ME12 47 B2
High St, Borough Green TN15 13 B5
High St, Broadstairs CT10 15 A3
High St, Broadstairs CT10 15 C4
High St, Canterbury CT1 16 B3
High St, Canterbury CT1 16 D2
High St, Catham ME7 18 C2
High St, Chatham ME4 18 B4
High St, Cranbrook TN17 20 A5
High St, Dartford DA1 21 B3
High St, Deal CT14 22 C1
High St, Dover CT17 23 B1
High St, Edenbridge TN8 24 C5
High St, Frindsbury ME2 52 C4
High St, Garlinge CT9 58 E3
High St, Gillingham ME7 27 A3
High St, Gravesend DA11 28 B2
High St, Greenhithe DA9 29 A1
High St, Hadlow TN11 17 B6
High St, Hawkhurst TN18 31 A1
High St, Headcorn TN27 31 B5
High St, Herne Bay CT6 32 B1
High St, Hythe CT21 33 B4
High St, Lenham ME17 32 C6
High St, Maidstone ME14 35 B4
High St, Marden TN12 34 B5
High St, Margate CT9 36 B2
High St, Minster ME12 37 D3
High St, New Romney TN28 38 B3
High St, Northfleet DA11 39 A2

Entry	Ref
High St, Queenborough ME11	41 A1
High St, Rainham ME8	42 B2
High St, Ramsgate CT11	43 A3
High St, Rochester ME1	44 C3
High St, Romney Marsh TN29	34 B3
High St, Sandwich CT13	45 D2
High St, Sevenoaks TN13	46 C5
High St, Sheerness ME12	47 D2
High St, Sittingbourne ME10	48 B1
High St, Sittingbourne ME10	48 B3
High St, Snodland ME6	49 C2
High St, St Margarets at Cliffe CT15	41 B4
High St, Staplehurst TN12	51 C3
High St, Swanley BR8	53 D3
High St, Swanscombe DA10	29 F2
High St, Tenterden TN30	54 A5
High St, Tonbridge TN9	55 B4
High St, Tunbridge Wells TN1	56 B5
High St, Westerham TN16	57 B6
High St, Whitstable CT5	59 A2
High St, Wye TN25	60 C5
High Street Chatham ME1	18 A4
High Street Rochester ME1	18 A4
Highbury La TN30	18 A4
Highfield CI, Cranbrook TN18	31 B2
Highfield CI, Hythe CT21	33 A2
Highfield Gdns CT9	36 A4
Highfield Rd DA1	21 B4
Highfield Rd North DA1	21 B3
Highfield Rd South DA1	21 B4
Highfields Rd TN23	24 B1
Highgate Hill TN18	31 B3
Highlands Hill BR8	53 E1
Highlands Row TN26	60 B1
Highsted Rd ME10	48 B4
Highview Rd ME12	37 D3
Hilda May Av BR8	53 C2
Hilda Rd ME4	18 C5
Hildenfields TN10	55 A1
Hilders CI TN8	24 A2
Hilders La TN8	24 A2
Hildersham Ct CT10	15 A2
Hill Cres ME17	32 D5
Hill Crest, Sevenoaks TN13	46 A3
Hill Crest, Tunbridge Wells TN4	50 D3
Hill Rd DA2	21 B6
Hill St TN1	56 C1
Hill Top TN9	55 B5
Hill Top Rd CT6	32 D1
Hill View TN24	12 D3
Hill View CI TN15	13 B5
Hillary Av DA11	39 D6
Hillary Rd ME14	35 B1
Hillbrow La TN23	12 A5
Hillbrow Rd, Ashford TN23	12 A6
Hillbrow Rd, Ramsgate CT11	43 A2
Hillcrest, Greenhithe DA9	29 A2
Hillcrest, Tunbridge Wells TN4	50 D3
Hillcrest Dr DA9	29 B2
Hillcrest Rd, Chatham ME4	18 B6
Hillcrest Rd, Edenbridge TN8	24 B1
Hillcrest Rd, Hythe CT21	33 A3
Hiller CI CT10	15 B2
Hillgarth TN4	50 D2
Hillingdon Av TN13	46 C2
Hillingdon Rd DA11	28 B5
Hillingdon Rise TN13	46 D2
Hills Ter ME4	18 B5
Hillside TN9	55 A5
Hillside Av, Gravesend DA12	28 D5
Hillside Av, Queenborough ME11	41 A3
Hillside Av, Rochester ME2	52 D3
Hillside Ct BR8	53 E3
Hillside Dr DA12	28 D5
Hillside Rd, Chatham ME4	18 C4
Hillside Rd, Sevenoaks TN13	46 D4
Hillside Rd, Sheerness ME12	37 B2
Hillside Rd, Whitstable CT5	59 D3
Hillside St CT21	33 B3
Hilltop CT5	59 A5
Hilltop Gdns DA1	21 D2
Hilltop Rd, Rochester ME2	52 D2
Hillview Rd CT5	59 A4
Hillyfield ME2	52 B2
Hillyfield Rd TN23	12 A5
Hillyfields Rise TN23	12 A5
Hilton CI ME13	25 D4
Hilton Rd TN23	12 A3
Hinchliffe Way CT9	19 C5
Hitchen Hatch La TN13	46 B4
Hither Fld TN27	17 B3
Hive La DA11	39 B2
Hockenden La BR8	53 A1
Hockeredge Gdns CT18	58 D2
Hodges Gap CT9	19 B2
Hodgson Cres ME6	49 C2
Hog La DA11	39 C6
Hogs Cnr CT13	45 E2
Holborough Rd ME6	49 C2
Holcombe CI TN16	57 C5
Holcombe Rd, Chatham ME4	18 B6
Holcombe Rd, Rochester ME1	44 C6
Holden Corner TN4	50 B2
Holden Park Rd TN4	50 C3
Holden Rd TN4	50 B2
Holding St ME8	42 B2
Holford St TN9	55 B3
Holland CI ME12	37 D2
Holland Rd ME14	35 C2
Hollicondane Rd CT11	43 A3
Hollington PI TN24	12 C3
Hollingworth Way TN16	57 D5
Hollow La ME6	49 A4
Holly Bush La TN13	46 C3
Holly CI, Gillingham ME7	27 C2
Holly CI, Hythe CT21	33 C3
Holly Cotts TN4	50 A4
Holly Gdns, Maidstone ME14	35 D1
Holly Gdns, Margate CT9	19 C4
Holly La CT9	19 B3
Holly Rd, Dartford DA1	21 A4
Holly Rd, Ramsgate CT11	43 B2
Holly Rd, Rochester ME2	52 A5
Hollybush CI TN13	46 D4
Hollybush Ct TN13	46 D5
Hollybush Rd DA12	28 C5
Hollytree Av BR8	53 C2
Hollywood La ME2	52 D1
Holm Oak Gdns CT10	15 B4
Holmesdale Rd TN13	46 D4
Holmleigh Av DA1	21 A1
Holmside ME7	27 C6
Holton CI CT7	14 E4
Holtye Cres ME15	35 D1
Holyoake Ter TN13	46 B5
Holyrood Dr ME12	37 A4
Home Gdns DA1	21 B3
Home Mead CI DA12	28 B3
Home Vw ME10	48 D3
Homefield Ct ME14	22 B2
Homefield CI BR8	53 D2
Homestead CT9	36 C4
Homestead Ct CT14	22 A4
Homestead Rd TN8	24 B1
Homewood Av ME10	48 A4
Homewood Rd TN30	54 C3
Honduras Ter ME4	35 C1
Hone St ME2	52 C3
Honeybee Glade ME8	42 A5
Honeycrest Ind Est TN12	51 B1
Honeypot CI ME2	52 D3
Honeysuckle CI CT9	36 A5
Honeysuckle Rd CT11	43 C3
Honfleur Rd CT13	45 C2
Honywood Rd ME17	32 B6
Hook La, Ashford TN27	17 C7
Hook La, Maidstone ME14	30 A2
Hook Rd ME8	49 B2
Hookfields DA11	39 D6
Hoopers PI ME1	44 C4
Hoopers Rd ME1	44 C4
Hop Pocket La TN12	40 C2
Hope Av TN11	17 B5
Hope La TN28	38 A1
Hope Rd, Deal CT14	22 C3
Hope Rd, Swanscombe DA10	29 F2
Hope St, Chatham ME4	18 C5
Hope St, Maidstone ME14	35 B2
Hope St, Sheerness ME12	47 C3
Hope Ter TN4	50 C6
Hopgarden CI TN8	24 C3
Hopsons PI ME12	37 A3
Hopwood Gdns TN4	50 D5
Hornbeam CI, Ashford TN23	12 A3
Hornbeam CI, Tonbridge TN12	40 B5
Horsa Rd CT7	14 A2
Horse Wash La ME1	44 C2
Horsebridge Rd CT5	59 A2
Horsford Walk ME13	25 B1
Horsley Rd ME1	44 C5
Horton PI TN16	57 D4
Hortons Way TN16	57 C4
Hoser Gdns CT7	14 E2
Hosey Hill TN16	57 D5
Hospital, Canterbury CT1	16 B4
Hospital La, Rochester ME1	18 A4
Hospital Rd TN13	46 C2
Hotel Rd, Dover CT15	41 D5
Hotel Rd, Gillingham ME8	27 D6
Hothfield Rd ME8	42 B1
Houselands Rd TN9	55 B2
Howard Av, Rochester ME1	44 D5
Howard Av, Sittingbourne ME10	48 A1
Howard CI ME12	37 D2
Howard Rd CT10	15 B5
Howland Rd TN12	34 B5
Hubert Pas CT16	23 D2
Hubert Way CT10	15 A2
Hugh PI ME13	25 D2
Hugin Av CT10	15 A1
Hulkes La ME1	18 A4
Humber Cres ME2	52 B4
Humber Rd DA1	21 B2
Hundreds CI CT8	58 A3
Hunsdon Dr TN13	46 C2
Hunters Chase CT5	59 B5
Hunters Walk CT14	22 A2
Hunting Gate CT7	14 C2
Huntingdon CI TN17	20 C5
Huntley Av DA11	39 B2
Huntleys Pk TN4	50 B6
Hunts Farm CI TN15	13 C5
Huntsman La ME14	35 D3
Hurst CI TN12	51 C2
Hurst PI ME8	42 B2
Hutsons CI CT17	31 B1
Hyde CI CT17	23 A2
Hydes Orch TN27	31 C5
Hyndford Cres DA9	29 C2
Hyperion Dr ME2	52 B2
Hythe CI TN14	50 C2
Hythe PI CT13	45 D3
Hythe Rd ME10	48 A1
Hythe St DA1	21 B3
Hyton Dr CT14	22 A2
Iden Cres TN12	51 B4
Iden Rd ME2	52 D1
Imber CI TN17	20 C5
Imbert CI TN28	38 C4
Impala Gdns TN4	50 D5
Imperial Av ME12	37 A4
Imperial Bsns Pk DA11	**28 A2**
Imperial Rd ME7	27 A5
Imperial Retail Pk DA11	**28 A2**
Industrial Distribution Centre ME6	**49 B4**
Ingle CI CT7	14 E2
Ingle Rd ME4	18 C5
Ingleden Park Rd TN30	54 C3
Ingles La CT20	26 C2
Ingles Mews CT20	26 B3
Ingles Rd CT20	26 B3
Inglewood BR8	53 C1
Ingoldsby Rd CT7	14 B2
Ingram Rd, Dartford DA1	21 B5
Ingram Rd, Gillingham ME7	27 C2
Ingress Gdns DA9	29 D2
Ingress Park Av DA9	29 C1
Inner London Rd TN1	56 B4
Institute Rd, Chatham ME4	18 C5
Institute Rd, Faversham ME13	25 D3
Instone Rd TN4	50 B5
Inverness Ter CT10	15 C5
Invicta Rd, Margate CT9	19 B5
Invicta Rd, Sheerness ME12	47 D3
Invicta Rd, Whitstable CT5	59 C3
Irchester St CT11	43 C4
Iron Bar La CT1	16 C4
Irvine CI CT9	19 C5
Irving Walk DA10	29 E4
Irving Way BR8	53 B1
Island Wall CT5	59 A2
Ivanhoe Rd, Herne Bay CT6	32 D3
Ivanhoe Rd, Westgate-on-Sea CT8	58 B2
Ivens Way ME17	30 B2
Ivory CI ME13	25 A1
Ivy Bower CI DA9	29 A1
Ivy CI DA12	28 D6
Ivy House Rd CT5	59 C3
Ivy La, Canterbury CT1	16 D4
Ivy La, Ramsgate CT11	43 A5
Ivy PI, Canterbury CT1	16 A6
Ivy PI, Deal CT14	22 C1
Ivy St ME8	42 B2
Ivy Villas DA9	29 A2
Jaarlen Rd TN29	34 A3
Jackson CI DA9	29 A2
Jacksons La TN30	54 B5
Jacob CI CT9	36 B5
Jaffa CI CT5	59 A3
Jaggard Way TN12	51 B4
James CI TN11	17 C5
James Hall Gdns CT14	22 B5
James St, Ashford TN23	12 B4
James St, Chatham ME4	18 B4
James St, Gillingham ME7	27 A2
James St, Maidstone ME14	35 C2
James St, Ramsgate CT11	43 A5
James St, Rochester ME1	44 D4
James Whatman Way ME14	35 B2
Jarmans Fld TN25	60 D6
Jarvis PI TN30	54 B2
Jasper Av ME1	44 D6
Jeffery St ME7	27 A2
Jeffrey CI TN12	51 B2
Jeffrey St ME14	35 C3
Jellicoe Av DA12	28 C6
Jellicoe Av West DA12	28 C6
Jemmett Rd TN23	12 B6
Jempsons TN17	20 B4
Jenkins Dale ME4	18 B5
Jenner Rd ME1	44 D5
Jennifer Gdns CT9	19 C6
Jersey Rd ME2	52 B5
Jesmond St CT19	26 C1
Jessamine Ter BR8	53 A1
Jetty Rd ME12	47 A2
Jewell Gro TN12	34 C5
Jewell Rd ME12	47 A2
Jewry La CT1	16 B3
Jeyes Rd ME7	27 A4
Jezreels Rd ME7	27 B6
Jockey La TN17	20 C5
John St, Broadstairs CT10	15 D4
John St, Maidstone ME14	35 B1
John St, Rochester ME1	44 C4
John St, Tunbridge Wells TN4	50 C6
Johns Grn CT13	45 B4
Johnson Av ME4	18 D1
Johnson CI DA11	39 C6
Johnson CI ME13	25 B1
Johnson Rd ME10	48 A3
Johnson Way ME12	37 B3
Johnsons Way DA9	29 C3
Joiners St ME4	18 B4
Jointon Rd CT20	26 A3
Joseph Wilson Ind Est CT5	**59 D5**
Joy La CT5	59 A4
Joy Rd DA12	28 C4
Joyce CI TN17	20 B5
Joyce Green La DA1	21 C1
Joyce Green Walk DA1	21 C1
Jubilee CI DA9	29 C2
Jubilee Ct CT5	59 D1
Jubilee Dr CT14	22 C5
Jubilee Rd CT13	45 C2
Jubilee St ME10	48 A2
Jubilee Ter ME7	27 A2
Jubilee Way CT16	23 F1
Judd CI ME4	18 C5
Judd Rd, Faversham ME13	25 A3
Judd Rd, Tonbridge TN9	55 B3
Julie CI CT10	15 B1
Junction Rd, Dartford DA1	21 B3
Junction Rd, Gillingham ME7	27 A4
Juniper CI CT5	59 C3
Juniper Walk BR8	53 C4
Jurys Gap Rd TN29	34 A4
Karloff Way ME3	52 D4
Katherine Rd DA11	24 C4
Keary Rd DA10	29 F4
Keating Ct ME1	44 B5
Keel Gdns TN4	50 B5
Keeley Mews ME7	27 C5
Kelly Dr ME7	27 A6
Kelvedon Rd CT14	22 C5
Kempes PI TN25	60 C6
Kemsley CI DA9	29 B2
Kendal CI TN9	55 C4
Kendal CI TN9	55 C4
Kendal Pk TN4	50 A5
Kendal Rise CT10	15 B5
Kenilworth Ct CT15	41 C1
Kenilworth Dr ME8	42 A1
Kennedy CI ME13	25 D1
Kennedy Dr CT14	22 B6
Kennedy Gdns TN13	46 D3
Kennet Dr CT14	22 A4
Kent Av, Ashford TN24	12 B5
Kent Av, Sheerness ME12	37 B2
Kent Av, Sittingbourne ME10	48 A4
Kent CI TN12	40 C3
Kent Gdns CT12	14 C2
Kent Ho TN18	31 C1
Kent Kraft Ind Est DA11	**29 F1**
Kent PI CT11	43 C4
Kent Rd, Dartford DA1	21 B3
Kent Rd, Gravesend DA11	28 A4
Kent Rd, Margate CT9	19 B5
Kent Rd, Sheerness ME12	47 C3
Kent Rd, Snodland ME6	49 C4
Kent Rd, Tunbridge Wells TN4	50 C5
Kent St, Sheerness ME12	47 B2
Kent St, Whitstable CT5	59 A4
Kentish Ct ME16	35 A4
Kenward Ct TN11	17 B6
Kenwyn Rd DA1	21 B2
Kenya Ter ME14	35 B1
Kerry Hill Way ME14	35 A1
Keston Ct ME8	27 D6
Kestrel CI, Edenbridge TN8	24 C3
Kestrel CI, Sittingbourne ME10	48 C4
Kestrel Ct CT5	59 D1
Keswick CI TN9	55 C2
Kettlewell Ct BR8	53 D2
Keyes Av ME4	18 B6
Keyes Rd DA1	21 D1
Keyworth CI TN12	40 B3
Khalsa Av DA12	28 C3
Khartoum PI DA12	28 C2
Khartoum Rd ME7	18 B3
Khyber Rd ME4	18 D1
Kibbles La TN4	50 B2
Kilbride Ct*, Argyll PI DA11	43 B1
Kiln CI ME10	48 C4
Kiln CI ME13	25 A2
Kiln Fld TN30	54 C5
Kiln Way TN12	40 C5
Kilndown Gdns CT19	19 D3
Kimberley Rd ME7	27 A5
Kincraig Dr TN13	46 B4
King Arthurs Dr ME2	52 B2
King Edward Av, Broadstairs CT10	15 C4
King Edward Av, Dartford DA1	21 A3
King Edward Rd, Birchington CT7	14 C4
King Edward Rd, Chatham ME4	18 B6
King Edward Rd, Gillingham ME7	27 D2
King Edward Rd, Greenhithe DA9	29 A2
King Edward Rd, Maidstone ME15	35 B6
King Edward Rd, Rochester ME1	44 C4
King Edward St CT5	59 A4
King Fisher Walk CT10	15 A3
King St, Canterbury CT1	16 C3
King St, Chatham ME4	18 C4
King St, Deal CT14	22 C5
King St, Dover CT17	23 C2
King St, Gillingham ME7	27 A2
King St, Gravesend DA12	28 B2
King St, Maidstone ME14	35 B3
King St, Margate CT9	36 B2

Name	Ref
ing St, Ramsgate CT11	43 B4
ing St, Rochester ME1	44 C4
ing St, Sandwich CT13	45 D2
ing St, Sheerness ME12	47 B2
ing St, Sittingbourne ME10	48 A3
ing St, Walmer CT14	22 D2
ing William Rd ME7	29 A2
ingfisher Cl CT9	58 E3
ingfisher Ct CT6	32 A2
ingfisher Dr DA9	29 A2
ingfisher Mdws ME16	35 B5
ings Av, Ashford TN23	12 B4
ings Av, Birchington CT7	14 A2
ings Av, Broadstairs CT10	15 C3
ings Av, Rochester ME1	44 C5
ings Av, Whitstable CT5	59 C3
ings Bastion ME7	18 C3
ings Bri CT1	16 B3
ings Dr DA12	28 B6
ings Head Alley ME12	47 B2
ings Head La CT21	33 C3
ings Mews CT1	16 D1
ings Mill Cl ME10	48 A1
ings Orch ME1	44 C3
ings Rd, Ashford TN27	31 B5
ings Rd, Birchington CT7	14 D4
ings Rd, Faversham ME13	25 C3
ings Rd, Herne Bay CT6	32 B2
ings Rd, Ramsgate CT11	43 A3
ings Rd, Sheerness ME12	37 D3
ings Rd, Tonbridge TN9	55 C5
Kings Row ME15	35 C6
Kings Wlk ME14	35 C3
Kingsbridge Ct CT20	26 E2
Kingsdale Ct DA10	29 E2
Kingsdown Cl ME16	35 A3
Kingsdown Pk CT5	59 C1
Kingsdown Rd, Deal CT14	22 D6
Kingsdown Rd, Dover CT15	41 B4
Kingsland Gro TN27	31 C5
Kingsley Rd, Maidstone ME15	35 C4
Kingsley Rd, Whitstable CT5	59 B4
Kingsmead Rd CT1	16 D1
Kingsnorth Gdns CT20	26 A2
Kingsnorth Rd ME13	25 C4
Kingsnorth Rd Gdns DA1	21 A3
Kingston Av CT9	58 F3
Kingston Ct DA11	39 A1
Kingswear Gdns ME2	52 D4
Kingswood TN24	12 D1
Kingswood Av, Chatham ME4	18 B6
Kingswood Av, Swanley BR8	53 D3
Kingswood Cl DA1	21 A2
Kingswood Rd ME7	27 B3
Kinnings Row TN9	55 C2
Kipling Rd TN23	12 B4
Kippington Cl TN13	46 A5
Kippington Rd TN13	46 A4
Kirby Cl TN17	20 C5
Kirbys Heights CT2	16 A1
Kirbys La CT2	16 A2
Kirk Ct TN13	46 B4
Kirkdale Rd TN1	56 D1
Kirkman Ct TN12	15 B4
Kirkwood Av TN26	60 B2
Kitchener Av DA12	28 C6
Kitchener Rd ME2	52 C2
Kitewell La TN29	34 C1
Klondyke Ind Est ME11	41 A2
Knaves Acre TN27	31 C5
Knight Av ME7	27 B2
Knight Rd ME2	52 B6
Knightrider Ct ME15	35 C4
Knightrider St, Maidstone ME15	35 B4
Knightrider St, Sandwich CT13	45 E2
Knights Av CT10	15 C2
Knights Manor Way TN24	21 C2
Knights Rd CT16	23 A2
Knights Templars CT17	23 A3
Knights Way TN27	31 C5
Knightsbridge Ct TN4	50 B6
Knockhall Chase DA9	29 B2
Knockhall Rd DA9	29 C3
Knockwood Rd TN30	29 C3
Knold Pk CT9	36 B5
Knole Rd TN13	46 D4
Knole Way TN13	46 C6
Knott Cl ME14	35 B1
Knotts La, Canterbury CT1	16 C2
Knotts La, Dover CT15	41 B4
Knotts Pl TN13	46 B5
Knowle Rd ME14	35 C1
Knowles Gdns TN27	31 C5
Knowles La TN12	51 B1
Knowles Wlk TN12	51 C2
La Tene CT14	22 A6
Laburnum Av, Dartford DA1	21 A5
Laburnum Av, Sandwich CT13	45 C2
Laburnum Av, Swanley BR8	53 B3
Laburnum Gro DA11	39 C3
Laburnum Pl ME10	48 A2
Laburnum Rd ME2	52 A6
Ladds La ME6	49 C1
Ladds Way BR8	53 B3
Ladies Walk CT21	33 C4
Lady Woottons Grn CT1	16 D3
Ladys Gift Rd TN4	50 B3
Ladywell CT16	23 B1
Lagonda Way DA1	21 A1
Lake View Rd TN13	46 A3
Lake Wlk ME20	49 C6
Lakelands ME7	30 C2
Lakeside ME7	49 B5
Lakeside Cl ME2	18 A1
Lakeside Pk ME2	18 A1
Lakeview Cl ME6	49 C5
Laking Av CT10	15 C1
Laleham Gdns CT9	19 B4
Laleham Rd CT9	19 B4
Laleham Walk CT9	19 A5
Lambarde Dr TN13	46 B3
Lambarde Rd TN13	46 A3
Lambert Ho CT14	22 B5
Lambert Mews ME6	49 C2
Lambs Bank TN9	55 A6
Lambs Way CT9	59 A6
Laming Rd CT7	14 E3
Lammas Dr ME10	48 A1
Lammas Gate ME12	25 D1
Lamorna Av DA12	28 D5
Lamplighters Cl TN26	21 C3
Lancaster Cl ME7	30 B5
Lancaster Ct DA2	21 D2
Lancaster Gdns CT7	14 C3
Lancaster Rd CT17	23 B2
Lancelot Av ME2	52 A4
Lancelot Cl ME14	22 A5
Landale Gdns DA1	21 A4
Landbury Walk TN25	12 A2
Landseer Av DA11	39 C6
Lane Av DA9	29 C2
Lane End CT6	32 A1
Lanes Av DA11	28 A6
Langdon Cl CT15	41 B5
Langdon Rd ME1	44 C5
Langham Cl CT9	58 E2
Langhorne Gdns CT20	26 B4
Langley Gdns CT9	19 D2
Langport Rd TN28	38 D3
Langton Cl ME14	35 D3
Langton Gdns*, Whitefriars St CT1	16 C4
Lansbury Cres DA1	21 D2
Lansdown Rd CT1	16 C6
Lansdowne Rd, Chatham ME4	18 A6
Lansdowne Rd, Sevenoaks TN13	46 D3
Lansdowne Rd, Tonbridge TN9	55 B2
Lansdowne Rd, Tunbridge Wells TN1	56 D3
Lansdowne Sq TN1	56 D2
Lanthorne Mews TN1	56 C3
Lanthorne Rd CT10	15 B1
Lapwing Cl ME12	37 C4
Larch Gro TN12	40 C4
Larch Rd DA1	21 B5
Larch Ter ME12	47 B5
Larch Walk BR8	53 B1
Larkfield Av, Gillingham ME7	27 C4
Larkfield Av, Sittingbourne ME10	48 A1
Larkfields DA11	39 D6
Larkin Ct DA12	52 D1
Larksfield Rd ME13	25 C1
Larkstore Pk TN12	51 B1
Laser Quay ME2	44 D2
Latimer Pl ME7	27 A3
Laureate Cl CT14	19 B4
Laurel Av DA12	28 C5
Laurel Bk TN4	50 D4
Laurel Cl ME4	21 B4
Laurel Rd ME7	27 A1
Laurel Walk ME8	42 A4
Laureston Pl CT16	23 D1
Lauriston Mount CT10	15 B3
Lausanne Rd CT9	36 C3
Lavender Cl CT9	36 A4
Lavender Ct ME10	48 C4
Lavender Hill, Swanley BR8	53 B2
Lavender Hill, Tonbridge TN9	55 C5
Lavender Mews CT1	16 A4
Lavinia Rd DA1	21 C3
Lawford Gdns DA1	21 A2
Lawn Cl, Chatham ME4	18 D6
Lawn Cl, Swanley BR8	53 A1
Lawn Rd, Broadstairs CT10	15 C3
Lawn Rd, Gravesend DA11	39 B1
Lawn Rd, Tonbridge TN9	55 B4
Lawrance Sq DA11	28 A6
Lawrence Hill Rd DA1	21 A2
Lawrence St ME7	27 A3
Lawson Gdns DA1	21 B1
Lawson Rd DA1	21 A1
Laxton Gdns TN12	40 B3
Laxton Way ME10	48 A1
Layfield Rd ME7	27 C1
Le Temple Rd TN13	40 D3
Lea Cl CT21	33 A2
Leacon Rd TN23	12 A4
Leas Rd CT14	22 B4
Leather Cl TN8	24 B6
Leathermarket TN8	24 C5
Leatt Cl CT14	15 A4
Lee Rd ME6	49 B2
Leechcroft Av BR8	53 D3
Leet Cl ME7	27 C2
Leewood Pl BR8	53 B3
Leicester Av CT9	19 C3
Leigh Ct ME12	37 A4
Leigh Rd DA11	28 B5
Leighton Cl TN4	50 C4
Leighville Dr CT6	32 A2
Leitch Row ME7	18 C1
Leith Park Rd DA12	28 B4
Leivers Rd CT14	22 A5
Lendon Rd TN15	18 C2
Lendrim Cl ME7	35 D3
Lenfield Av ME14	15 B6
Lenham Cl CT10	15 B6
Lenham Gdns CT9	58 E3
Lenham Rd TN27	31 B4
Lenhead ME17	30 A2
Lennard Ct CT20	26 E1
Lennard Rd CT20	26 E1
Lennox Av DA11	28 A2
Lennox Rd East DA11	28 A2
Lennox Row ME4	18 C1
Leonard Av DA10	29 E4
Leonard Rd ME4	18 D6
Leonards Av CT11	43 B2
Leopold Rd, Chatham ME4	18 C5
Leopold Rd, Ramsgate CT11	43 B2
Leopold St CT11	43 B4
Lesley Cl BR8	53 B2
Lesley Pl ME16	35 A3
Leslie Av CT9	58 E3
Leslie Cres TN30	54 B2
Leslie Rd, Birchington CT7	14 D2
Leslie Rd, Gillingham ME7	25 C2
Leslie Smith Dr ME13	25 C2
Lester Rd ME4	18 C5
Lewis Cl ME13	25 A2
Lewis Cres TN9	19 A2
Lewis Mews ME6	49 B4
Lewis Rd DA10	29 E3
Leybourn Rd CT10	15 C6
Leybourne Dr CT9	58 E3
Leybourne Rd ME2	52 A3
Leybourne Way ME20	49 A6
Leyburn Rd CT16	23 C1
Leyburne Rd CT16	23 C1
Leyhill Cl BR8	53 C1
Libya Ter ME14	35 B1
Lightermans Mews DA11	39 D3
Lightermans Way DA9	29 D3
Lighthouse Rd CT15	41 C6
Lilac Gdns BR8	53 B3
Lilac Rd ME2	52 A6
Lillian Rd CT11	43 B3
Lime Av DA11	39 C3
Lime Cl TN12	34 B5
Lime Gro ME10	48 C3
Lime Hill Rd TN1	56 B6
Lime Kiln Rd CT1	16 B6
Lime Tree Av DA9	29 A4
Lime Tree Cl TN9	55 C2
Lime Tree Walk TN13	46 C6
Lime Trees TN12	51 B2
Limekiln St CT17	23 B4
Limes Cl TN30	54 D5
Limetree Ter ME17	32 D4
Limited TN30	54 B2
Lincoln Gdns CT7	14 C3
Lincoln Rd ME7	27 B1
Linden Av, Broadstairs CT10	15 C3
Linden Av, Dartford DA1	21 A5
Linden Av, Herne Bay CT6	32 A3
Linden Av, Whitstable CT5	59 C3
Linden Chase C2	21 A3
Linden Chase Rd TN13	46 B3
Linden Cl, Sittingbourne ME10	48 A4
Linden Cl, Tonbridge TN12	40 C4
Linden Cl, Tunbridge Wells TN4	56 A4
Linden Cl, Westgate-on-Sea CT8	47 B5
Linden Dr ME12	16 A2
Linden Gro CT20	26 A6
Linden Park Rd TN4	56 A5
Linden Rd, Gillingham ME7	27 B3
Linden Rd, Westgate-on-Sea CT8	58 C3
Lindenborough Rd CT10	15 B2
Lindfield Cotts ME13	25 A3
Lindisfarne Gdns ME16	35 A5
Lindridge La TN12	51 A1
Lines Ter ME4	18 C4
Lingfield Cl, Edenbridge TN8	24 A6
Lingfield Rd, Gravesend DA12	28 B5
Lingfield Rd, Sevenoaks TN15	13 C5
Lingley Dr ME2	52 D1
Linington Rd CT7	14 E3
Link La CT1	16 C4
Links Way TN28	38 E3
Linksfield Rd CT8	58 A4
Linnet Av CT14	15 A1
Lion Fld ME13	25 A3
Lion Yd ME13	25 A3
Lionel Rd TN9	55 A4
Lions Rd TN28	38 B4
Lister Cl CT14	22 B3
Lister Rd CT9	36 C3
Listmas Rd ME4	18 D5
Little Charles St*, Ruskins Vw CT1	32 C1
Little Chequers TN26	60 B6
Little Court Rd TN13	46 A4
Little Fld TN12	51 B2
Little Glovers ME10	48 B4
Little Knoll TN20	43 B2
Little Mount Sion TN1	56 B5
Little Queen St DA1	21 C3
Littlebrook CT23	12 B3
Littlebrook Manor Way DA1	21 D2
Littlestone Rd TN28	38 D3
Littlewood TN13	46 D2
Liverpool Lawn CT11	43 B5
Liverpool Rd CT14	22 C6
Liverymen Walk DA9	29 C1
Livingstone Circus ME7	27 B3
Livingstone Rd, Broadstairs CT10	15 A2
Livingstone Rd, Gillingham ME7	27 A3
Lloyd Rd CT10	15 C3
Loam Ct DA1	21 B5
Loampits Cl TN9	55 D1
Lobelia Cl ME7	27 C2
Lock St, Chatham ME7	18 D3
Lock St, Gillingham ME7	27 A3
Lockington Gr ME1	44 C4
Lockside TN9	55 C2
Loder Cl CT14	32 B5
Lodge Av DA1	21 A3
Lodge La CT16	57 C5
Lodge Oak Rd TN9	55 D5
Lodge Rd, Staplehurst TN12	51 B1
Lodge Rd, Tonbridge TN9	55 B2
London Rd, Deal CT14	22 A4
London Rd, Dover CT17	23 A1
London Rd, Faversham ME13	25 B4
London Rd, Gravesend DA11	39 C2
London Rd, Greenhithe DA9	29 A4
London Rd, Maidstone ME16	35 A3
London Rd, Rochester ME2	52 B4
London Rd, Sevenoaks TN13	46 A4
London Rd, Sevenoaks TN13	46 C5
London Rd, Sittingbourne ME10	48 A3
London Rd, Southborough TN4	50 B1
London Rd, Swanley BR8	53 A1
London Rd, Tonbridge TN16	55 A1
London Rd, Tunbridge Wells TN1	56 A3
London Rd, Westerham TN16	57 B2
London Rd Trading Est ME10	**48 A3**
Lonewood Way TN11	26 E2
Long Mill La TN15	17 C4
Long Port CT1	13 D5
Long Reach Cl CT5	16 D4
Long Steps CT15	59 A6
Longfellow Rd, Chatham ME4	41 D5
Longfellow Rd, Gillingham ME7	18 D5
Longfield TN30	27 A5
Longfield CM8	54 A6
Longford Cl ME8	42 C2
Longford Ter CT20	26 C3
Longford Way CT20	26 C3
Longhill Av ME5	18 D5
Longley Rd, Gillingham ME8	42 B2
Longley Rd, Rochester ME1	44 C5
Longmarket CT1	16 C4
Longridge ME10	48 D5
Longs Acre TN25	60 C6
Lonsdale Dr TN9	19 B2
Lonsdale Dr ME8	42 B3
Lonsdale Gdns TN1	56 B4
Lookers La CT21	33 B2
Loop Court Mews CT13	45 C1
Loop St CT13	45 C1
Loose Rd ME15	35 C5
Lord St DA12	28 B3
Lord Warden Sq CT17	23 C4
Lorenden Pk TN18	31 B2
Louisville Av ME7	27 B4
Love La, Canterbury CT1	16 D4
Love La, Gravesend DA12	28 C3
Love La, Margate CT9	36 C2
Love La, Rochester ME1	44 C4
Love La, Sheerness ME12	37 D2
Lovell Rd ME12	37 A4
Lovers La DA9	29 D1
Lovers Wlk TN9	55 C1
Low Cl DA9	29 A2
Lower Blackhouse Hill CT21	33 C3
Lower Boxley Rd ME14	35 B2
Lower Bridge St CT1	16 D4
Lower Cft BR8	53 D3
Lower Denmark Rd TN23	12 C6
Lower Northdown Av CT9	19 A4
Lower Rd, Ashford TN26	60 B3
Lower Rd, Faversham ME13	25 A3
Lower Rd, Gravesend DA11	29 F1
Lower Rd, Maidstone ME15	35 A3
Lower Rochester Rd ME2	52 C1
Lower Sandgate Rd CT20	26 B4
Lower Stone St ME15	35 C4
Lower Twell TN15	35 A6
Lower Woodlands Rd ME7	27 D2
Lowfield St DA1	21 B5
Lucas Cres DA1	29 C1
Lucas Rd ME6	49 A3
Lucerne St ME14	35 C3
Lucilina Dr TN8	24 B6
Luckhurst Gdns CT9	19 D3
Luckley Ho TN25	60 B5
Lucknow Rd TN12	40 C2
Lucks La TN12	40 C1
Lucks Way TN12	34 A5
Lucys Hill CT21	33 B3
Lucys Walk CT21	33 C4
Lullingstone Av BR8	53 D2
Lumsden Ter ME4	18 A4
Lunsford La ME20	49 B6
Luton Av CT10	15 B5
Luton Cl CT10	15 B5

Luton High St ME5 27 A6
Luton Rd, Chatham ME4 18 C5
Luton Rd,
Gillingham ME4 27 A6
Lyall Way ME8 42 A6
Lychfield Dr ME2 52 C2
Lydd Rd TN28 38 A3
Lydia Rd CT14 22 A6
Lyell Cl CT21 33 A4
Lyell Rd CT7 14 C2
Lyle Cl ME2 52 C2
Lyle Pk TN13 46 C3
Lyminge Way CT9 19 B4
Lymington Cl CT18 58 B3
Lymington Rd CT8 58 B3
Lynden Way ME8 53 A3
Lyndhurst Av CT9 19 A3
Lyndhurst Gro ME10 48 A5
Lyndhurst Rd,
Broadstairs CT10 15 C2
Lyndhurst Rd,
Ramsgate CT11 43 C3
Lynette Av ME2 52 B1
Lyngate Cl CT9 19 D3
Lynmead Cl TN8 24 B2
Lynmouth Dr ME12 37 D2
Lynors Av ME2 52 C1
Lynton Rd,
Gravesend DA11 28 B4
Lynton Rd, Hythe CT21 33 B4
Lynton Rd South DA11 33 A4
Lyons Cres TN9 55 C3

Mableden Cl TN28 38 B3
Mableden Rd TN9 55 A4
Mac Mews ME12 37 B4
MacDonald Ct TN12 40 C4
MacDonald Rd ME7 27 B2
Mace Ind Est TN24 12 D3
Mace La TN24 12 D4
Macmillan Gdns DA1 21 D1
Madan Cl TN16 57 D3
Madan Rd TN16 57 D4
Madden Cl DA10 29 E3
Madeira Cl CT20 26 A4
Madeira Pk TN2 56 C6
Madeira Rd,
Margate CT9 36 D2
Madeira Rd,
New Romney TN28 38 F4
Madeira Walk CT11 43 B4
Madison Way TN13 46 A3
Magazine Rd TN24 12 B3
Magdala Rd CT10 15 A2
Magdalen Ct CT10 15 C2
Magness Rd CT14 22 A6
Magnolia Av CT9 19 C3
Magnolia Cl TN9 55 C5
Magpie Ct ME12 37 B3
Magpie Grn TN8 24 C3
Magpie Hall Rd ME4 18 C5
Magwitch Cl ME1 44 B5
Maida Rd ME4 18 D6
Maidstone
Ind Centre ME16 35 A3
Maidstone Rd,
Ashford TN24 12 A1
Maidstone Rd,
Ashford TN27 31 A4
Maidstone Rd,
Charing TN27 17 A1
Maidstone Rd,
Chatham ME4 18 B6
Maidstone Rd,
Gillingham ME8 42 A3
Maidstone Rd,
Hadlow TN11 17 C6
Maidstone Rd,
Maidstone ME17 32 C5
Maidstone Rd,
Marden TN12 34 B5
Maidstone Rd,
Paddock Wood TN12 40 B4
Maidstone Rd,
Rochester ME1 44 C6
Maidstone Rd,
Sevenoaks TN15 13 B5
Maidstone Rd,
Swanley BR8 53 A1
Maidstone Rd,
Tonbridge TN12 40 A2
Main Gate Rd ME4 18 B2
Main Rd,
Edenbridge TN8 24 B1
Main Rd,
Queenborough ME11 41 B1
Main Rd,
Sheerness ME12 37 A5
Main Rd, Swanley BR8 53 E1
Maison Dieu Pl CT16 23 B1
Maison Dieu Rd CT16 23 B1
Maitland Ct ME8 25 B1
Major Yorks Rd TN4 56 A6
Makenade Av ME13 25 D4
Malham Dr CT9 36 D4
Mallard Cl DA1 21 D2

Mallard Ct ME12 37 B3
Mallard Way TN8 24 C3
Malling Rd ME6 49 B5
Malt Ho La TN30 54 A5
Malt Mews ME1 44 C3
Malta Ter ME4 35 B1
Malthouse Cl ME17 32 C6
Malthouse Hill CT21 33 B3
Maltings Cl TN11 17 B6
Malvern Ho DA11 39 C2
Malvern Rd,
Ashford TN24 12 C2
Malvern Rd, Dover CT17 23 A2
Malvern Rd,
Gillingham ME7 27 B6
Malvina Av DA12 28 C5
Man Sq TN9 55 D5
Manor Av CT14 22 A4
Manor Cl, Deal CT14 22 A4
Manor Cl,
Queenborough ME11 41 A3
Manor Ct CT1 16 B6
Manor Ct CT7 14 D3
Manor Gro,
Sittingbourne ME10 48 A4
Manor Gro,
Tonbridge TN9 55 C1
Manor House Gdns TN8 24 B5
Manor La ME1 44 A6
Manor Mews ME4 18 B4
Manor Rd,
Broadstairs CT10 15 B4
Manor Rd,
Chatham ME4 18 B4
Manor Rd, Deal CT14 22 A4
Manor Rd,
Edenbridge TN8 24 B5
Manor Rd,
Folkestone CT20 26 B3
Manor Rd,
Gravesend DA12 28 B2
Manor Rd,
Queenborough ME11 41 A3
Manor Rd,
Romney Marsh TN29 34 C3
Manor Rd,
Swanscombe DA10 29 D3
Manor Rd,
Tunbridge Wells TN4 50 B2
Manor Rd,
Whitstable CT5 59 D1
Manor St ME7 18 C2
Manor Way,
Ashford TN23 12 A3
Manor Way,
Swanscombe DA10 29 E1
Manse Par BR8 53 E4
Manse Way BR8 53 E4
Mansell Dr ME1 44 A6
Mansion House Cl TN27 13 C1
Mansion Row ME7 18 C2
Manston Rd CT9 19 C2
Manwood Cl ME10 48 B5
Manwood Rd CT13 45 E2
Maple Av ME7 27 C3
Maple Cl BR8 53 C1
Maple Cl, Dartford DA1 21 A5
Maple Rd,
Rochester ME2 52 A5
Maple St ME12 37 D4
Maplins Cl ME8 42 B2
Marathon Pad ME7 27 B4
Marcet Rd DA1 21 A2
Marconi Rd DA11 39 C6
Mardale Cl ME8 42 C2
Marden Rd,
Rochester ME2 52 D1
Marden Rd,
Tonbridge TN9 51 A2
Mardol Rd TN24 12 D1
Margaret St CT20 26 D2
Margate Rd
Gillingham ME7 27 C2
Margate Rd CT11 43 A2
Marian Av ME12 37 A3
Marian Sq TN12 51 C3
Marilyn Cres CT7 14 F2
Marina Dr, Dartford DA1 21 D4
Marina Dr,
Sheerness ME12 37 B3
Marina Esp CT11 43 C4
Marina Rd CT11 43 C4
Marina Cres CT20 26 D3
Marine Cl CT16 23 D2
Marine Dr CT9 36 B2
Marine Gap CT5 59 A2
Marine Gdns CT9 36 B2
Marine Heights CT8 58 C2
Marine Par, Dover CT16 23 D2
Marine Par,
Folkestone CT20 26 D4
Marine Par, Hythe CT21 33 C5
Marine Par,
New Romney TN28 38 F4
Marine Par,
Whitstable CT5 59 C1

Marine Parade Mews
CT20 26 D3
Marine Prom CT20 26 D4
Marine Rd CT14 22 D4
Marine Ter,
Folkestone CT20 26 E3
Marine Ter, Margate CT9 36 B3
Marine Walk St CT21 33 B3
Mariners Ct,
Greenhithe DA9 29 A1
Mariners Ct,
Whitstable CT5 59 A3
Mariners Lee CT5 59 B1
Mariners Vw ME7 27 D1
Mariners Way DA11 39 D3
Maritime Cl DA9 29 B2
Maritime Gate DA11 39 D3
Maritime Pl*,
Bulwark Rd CT14 22 D1
Mark St ME4 18 C6
Mark Way BR8 53 E4
Market Bldgs ME14 35 B3
Market Hill CT21 33 B3
Market Pl, Ashford TN27 17 B2
Market Pl, Dartford DA1 21 C3
Market Pl,
Faversham ME13 25 D2
Market Pl,
Folkestone CT20 26 D3
Market Pl,
Sevenoaks TN13 46 C6
Market Pl,
Tunbridge Wells TN2 56 A6
Market Sq, Dover CT16 23 C2
Market Sq,
Tunbridge Wells TN1 56 D2
Market Sq,
Westerham TN16 57 C5
Market St, Dartford DA1 21 B3
Market St, Deal CT14 22 D2
Market St, Dover CT16 23 C2
Market St,
Faversham ME13 25 D3
Market St,
Herne Bay CT6 32 B1
Market St, Margate CT9 36 B2
Market St,
Sandwich CT13 45 D1
Market St,
Tonbridge TN12 51 C1
Market St,
Tunbridge Wells TN2 56 A6
Market Way TN16 57 D5
Marl Hill TN4 50 B2
Marlborough Cl,
Broadstairs CT10 15 A5
Marlborough Cl,
New Romney TN28 38 D3
Marlborough Ct*,
Croydon Rd TN16 57 C5
Marlborough Rd,
Gillingham ME7 18 D4
Marlborough Rd,
Margate CT9 36 B4
Marlborough Rd,
Ramsgate CT11 43 A4
Marley Rd ME17 30 C1
Marlfield TN12 51 B2
Marlham TN8 24 B2
Marlowe Arc CT1 16 C4
Marlowe Av CT1 16 B5
Marlowe Rd,
Ashford TN23 12 B4
Marlowe Rd,
Margate CT9 19 B5
Marlpit Cl TN8 24 C2
Marr Cl ME12 37 A3
Marriott Rd DA1 21 D3
Marsh Cres TN28 38 B3
Marsh La CT14 22 A4
Marsh St, Dartford DA1 21 D1
Marsh St, Dartford DA1 21 D2
Marsh St,
Rochester ME2 52 D4
Marshall Cres,
Broadstairs CT10 15 A4
Marshall Cres,
Queenborough ME11 41 A3
Marshall Gdns TN11 17 B5
Marshalls Land TN30 54 B1
Marsham Cl ME17 30 C2
Marsham St ME14 35 C3
Marsham St ME14 35 C3
Martello Rd CT20 26 E1
Martin Ho DA11 28 A6
Martin Rd ME2 52 C3
Martindown Rd CT5 59 A5
Martins Cl TN30 54 C4
Martyrs Field Rd CT1 16 A6
Marwell TN16 57 B5
Mary Ct ME4 18 C6
Mary Dukes Pl ME15 35 C4
Mary Magdalene Ho
TN9 55 B4
Mary Rd CT14 22 A5

Maryland Ct ME8 42 A6
Mascalls Court Rd TN12 40 C5
Mascalls Pk TN12 40 B5
Masefield Rd DA11 39 C6
Mason Way ME3 52 D1
Masons Rise CT10 15 B3
Matfield Cres ME14 35 D2
Matthews Ct CT14 22 B2
Matthews St ME7 27 B3
Maugham Ct CT5 59 A4
Maxine Gdns CT10 15 A3
Maxwell Pl CT14 22 C4
Maxwell Rd ME7 18 C2
May Rd,
Gillingham ME7 27 A4
May Rd, Rochester ME1 44 B4
May St ME6 49 D2
May Ter*,
Admiralty Ter ME7 18 C1
Mayes Ct BR8 53 E4
Mayfair Cl ME2 52 D2
Mayfair Rd DA1 21 A1
Mayfield Rd CT6 32 C3
Mayfields DA1 21 A5
Mayhew Cl TN23 12 B6
Maynard Av TN9 58 F3
Maynard Pl ME5 27 B6
Maynards TN12 40 A6
Mayors Pl*,
Burgess Row TN30 54 A6
Mayville Rd CT10 15 A2
McCabe Cl TN12 51 B4
McCudden Row ME7 18 C2
McDermott Rd TN15 13 B5
Mead Cl BR8 53 E4
Mead Cres DA1 21 B5
Mead Rd, Dartford DA1 21 B5
Mead Rd,
Gravesend DA11 28 B5
Meades Cl TN12 34 A5
Meadow Bank Rd ME8 18 C4
Meadow Cl TN13 46 A3
Meadow Ct CT9 19 A5
Meadow Hill Rd TN1 56 C5
Meadow La TN8 24 B2
Meadow Rd,
Ashford TN23 12 A2
Meadow Rd,
Gravesend DA11 28 A5
Meadow Rd,
Margate CT9 58 E2
Meadow Rd,
Northfleet DA11 39 B5
Meadow Rd,
Southborough TN4 50 C2
Meadow Rd,
Tonbridge TN9 55 A4
Meadow Rd,
Tunbridge Wells TN1 56 C1
Meadow Walk,
Maidstone ME15 35 C4
Meadow Walk,
Snodland ME6 49 B3
Meadow Way,
Whitstable CT5 59 A6
Meadow Way TN12 34 C5
Meadowside DA1 21 B5
Medina's Way DA12 28 D2
Medway Cl ME10 48 A3
Medway Enterprise
Centre ME2 44 D1
Medway Gdns ME4 18 C5
Medway Rd,
Gillingham ME7 27 A1
Medway Rd,
Rainham ME8 42 B1
Medway Rd,
Sheerness ME12 47 C3
Medway Road Camp
ME4 18 D1
Medway St,
Chatham ME4 18 B3
Medway St,
Maidstone ME14 35 B4
Medway
Trading Est ME16 35 A5
Medway Wharf Rd TN9 55 B3
Meeting House La ME4 18 B3
Meeting St CT11 43 B4
Melbourne Rd ME4 18 C5
Melbury Mews TN28 38 C1
Mellanby Cl CT7 14 D3
Melsetter Cl CT7 14 E2
Melville Cl ME4 18 B2
Melville Rd ME5 35 C4
Mendfield St ME13 25 C2
Mendip Ho DA11 39 C2
Mendip Rise TN24 12 B2
Menzies Ct ME12 37 A4
Mercer Dr ME17 30 D1
Mercers TN18 31 B2
Mercers Cl TN12 40 B4
Mercery La CT1 16 C3

Merchant Pl TN17 34 B5
Mercury Cl ME1 44 A6
Mere Gate CT9 58 E4
Meresborough La ME8 42 C5
Meresborough Rd ME8 42 C5
Mereworth Rd TN4 50 C5
Meridian Pk ME8 42 C5
Meriel Walk*,
Watermans Way DA9 29 B1
Merlewood TN13 46 B3
Merlin Cl ME10 48 C4
Mermaid Cl DA11 39 D3
Merrivale Heights CT10 15 C5
Merryfields ME2 52 B2
Merryweather Cl DA1 21 C3
Meyrick Rd ME12 47 D2
Michael Av CT11 43 C2
Michelle Gdns CT9 58 D3
Mickleburgh Av CT6 32 D3
Mickleburgh Hill CT6 32 D2
Mid Kent
Bsns Centre ME6 49 C4
Middle Deal Rd CT14 22 A3
Middle Garth TN17 20 C5
Middle Row,
Faversham ME13 25 D3
Middle Row,
Maidstone ME14 35 B4
Middle St, Deal CT14 22 D1
Middle St, Deal CT14 22 D1
Middle St,
Gillingham ME7 18 C2
Middle Wall CT5 59 A2
Middleburg St CT20 26 C3
Middlefields ME8 42 C2
Middleton Cl ME8 42 A6
Middleway ME10 48 A4
Middlings Rise TN13 46 A6
Middlings Wood TN13 46 A6
Midsummer Rd ME6 49 A2
Miercourt Cl ME8 42 C2
Miercourt Rd ME8 42 A5
Milburn Rd ME7 27 A1
Mile Town
Ind Est ME12 47 B3
Miles Pl ME1 44 D5
Miles Way CT7 14 C2
Military Rd,
Canterbury CT1 16 D2
Military Rd,
Chatham ME4 18 B4
Military Rd, Dover CT17 23 B2
Military Rd, Hythe CT21 33 A3
Military Rd,
Ramsgate CT11 43 B5
Mill Bank,
Romney Marsh TN29 34 B3
Mill Bank,
Tonbridge TN9 55 C2
Mill Bay CT20 26 D2
Mill Cl, Maidstone ME17 32 C6
Mill Cl, Rochester ME2 52 D2
Mill Cl, Sandwich CT13 45 C1
Mill Cres TN9 55 C2
Mill Ct, Ashford TN24 12 D5
Mill Ct,
Sittingbourne ME10 48 C4
Mill Fld CT10 15 B2
Mill Hill, Deal CT14 22 A6
Mill Hill,
Edenbridge TN8 24 C6
Mill Hill
Sheerness ME12 37 E3
Mill Hill Cotts TN8 24 C6
Mill La, Birchington CT7 14 C3
Mill La, Canterbury CT1 16 C2
Mill La, Dover CT16 23 C2
Mill La, Hythe CT21 33 C3
Mill La,
Maidstone ME14 35 A2
Mill La, Margate CT9 36 C3
Mill La,
Romney Marsh TN29 34 C2
Mill La,
Sevenoaks TN14 46 D1
Mill La, Snodland ME6 49 D2
Mill La, Tenterden TN30 54 C3
Mill La, Tonbridge TN9 55 C2
Mill La,
Westerham TN16 57 C6
Mill Mews CT14 22 B4
Mill Pond Cl,
Rochester ME2 52 D3
Mill Pond Cl,
Sevenoaks TN14 46 D2
Mill Pond Rd DA1 21 C2
Mill Rd, Deal CT14 22 B4
Mill Rd,
Gillingham ME7 18 D2
Mill Rd,
Gravesend DA11 39 D3
Mill Rd, Hythe CT21 33 C3
Mill Rd, Rochester ME2 52 C2
Mill Rd,
Romney Marsh TN29 34 C2
Mill Row CT7 14 C4

Mill St,
Maidstone ME15 35 B4
Mill St, Snodland ME6 49 D2
Mill St,
Westerham TN16 57 D5
Mill Stream Pl TN9 55 D1
Mill Vw, Ashford TN26 60 A1
Mill Vw, Tonbridge TN11 17 A5
Mill Way ME10 48 B2
Millbank TN27 31 A4
Millbrook Cl ME15 35 A6
Milldale Cl CT14 22 B4
Millen Rd ME10 48 A2
Millennium Way ME12 47 C2
Miller Cl TN24 12 D4
Miller Ct ME12 37 A4
Millers Ct CT5 59 A5
Millers Yd CT1 16 A6
Millfield, Dover CT15 41 B4
Millfield,
Folkestone CT20 26 C3
Millfield,
Sittingbourne ME10 48 C4
Millfield Dr DA11 39 D5
Millfield Manor CT5 59 B3
Millmead Av CT9 19 C5
Millmead Gdns CT9 19 C5
Millmead Rd CT9 19 A4
Mills Cl ME12 37 A3
Mills Ter ME4 16 B5
Millside Ind Est DA1 21 A1
Millstead Cl ME14 35 D3
Millstream Cl,
Faversham ME13 25 C2
Millstream Cl,
Whitstable CT5 59 B3
Millstrood Rd CT5 59 B3
Millwall Pl CT13 45 D2
Millwood Ct*,
The Paddock ME4 18 B4
Milner Rd ME7 27 B1
Milroy Av DA11 39 D5
Milsted Cl ME12 47 C5
Milstock Ter ME15 35 A6
Milton Rd,
Gravesend DA12 28 D4
Milton Av, Margate CT9 36 C3
Milton Ct DA12 28 C5
Milton Hall Rd DA12 28 D4
Milton Pl DA12 28 C2
Milton Rd,
Ashford TN23 12 B4
Milton Rd,
Gillingham ME7 27 A5
Milton Rd,
Gravesend DA12 28 C2
Milton Rd,
Sittingbourne ME10 48 B2
Milton Rd,
Swanscombe DA10 29 E2
Milton Rd
Bsns Pk DA12 28 C3
Milton St DA10 29 D3
Minerva Rd ME2 52 B3
Minnis Bay CT7 14 A2
Minnis Rd CT7 14 A2
Minster Cl CT10 15 C6
Minster Dr,
Herne Bay CT6 32 A2
Minster Dr,
Sheerness ME12 37 C2
Minster Rd,
Sheerness ME12 37 A3
Minster Rd,
Westgate-on-Sea CT8 58 C3
Minterne Av ME10 48 A5
Minters
Ind Est CT14 22 B2
Minters Orch TN15 13 D5
Miranda Ct ME12 47 C4
Mirror Ct DA10 29 E2
Miskin Rd DA1 21 A3
Mitchell Av,
Chatham ME4 18 B6
Mitchell Av,
Gravesend DA11 39 C5
Mitchell Cl,
Dartford DA1 21 B6
Mitchell Cl,
Maidstone ME17 32 C6
Mitchell Walk DA10 29 E3
Mitre Ct TN9 55 C2
Mitre Rd ME1 44 C5
Mittell Ct TN29 34 B2
Moat Rd TN1 31 A5
Moat Sole CT13 45 D2
Moat Way ME11 41 B1
Mockett Dr CT10 15 A1
Modesty Cnrs TN4 50 A2
Moles Mead TN8 24 B4
Molyneux Park Gdns
TN4 56 A2
Molyneux Park Rd TN4 56 A2
Monastery St CT1 16 D4
Moncktons Av ME14 35 A1
Moncktons Dr ME14 35 A1

Moncktons La ME14 35 A1
Monks Cl ME13 25 B2
Monks Orch DA1 21 A6
Monks Walk TN27 17 B2
Monks Way TN16 57 D5
Monks Well*,
Watermans Way DA9 29 B1
Monkton Rd TN15 13 B6
Monson Rd TN1 56 C2
Monson Way TN1 56 C3
Mont St Aignan Way
TN8
Montacute Gdns TN4 56 A6
Montague Cl BR8 53 D3
Montague Ct ME12 47 C4
Montague Rd CT11 43 B3
Montague St CT6 32 A1
Montefiore Av CT11 43 C1
Montefiore Cotts CT11 43 C3
Montfort Rd ME2 52 C4
Montgomery Rd,
Gillingham ME7 27 A5
Montgomery Rd,
Tunbridge Wells TN4 50 D4
Montpelier Av CT5 59 A6
Montpelier
Bsns Pk TN23 12 A5
Monypenny CI TN15 17 B5
Moor Park Cl ME8 42 C2
Moor St ME8 46 C1
Moor St ME8 42 D2
Moore Rd DA10 29 E3
Moore St ME2 52 C3
Moray Av CT7 14 D1
Mordaunt Av CT8 58 B3
Morden St ME1 44 C5
Morel Ct TN13 46 C3
Morella Walk ME17 32 B5
Morello Cl BR8 53 B3
Moreton Cl BR8 53 D2
Moreton
Ind Est BR8 53 F4
Morewood Cl TN13 46 A4
Morgan Cl ME8 42 A6
Morgan Rd ME2 52 C3
Morhen Cl ME6 49 A4
Morland Dr ME2 52 C2
Morley Rd TN9 55 D3
Morris Gdns DA1 21 D2
Morrison Rd CT20 26 E1
Mortimer St CT6 32 B1
Mortley CI TN9 55 D2
Mortuary Rd ME12 47 B2
Moss End Mews CT11 15 A6
Mossy Glade ME8 42 A4
Mostyn Rd ME14 35 D3
Mote Av ME15 35 C4
Mote Rd ME15 35 C4
Moultain Hill BR8 53 E3
Mount CI TN13 46 A3
Mount Edgecombe Rd
TN4 56 A4
Mount Ephraim TN1 56 A3
Mount Ephraim CT8 58 A3
Mount Ephraim Rd TN1 56 B2
Mount Fld,
Faversham ME13 25 B3
Mount Fld,
Queenborough ME11 41 B1
Mount Harry Rd TN13 46 B4
Mount Pleasant,
Chatham ME5 18 D5
Mount Pleasant,
Cranbrook TN18 31 A3
Mount Pleasant,
Tenterden TN30 54 C4
Mount Pleasant
Tonbridge TN12 40 B3
Mount Pleasant Av TN1 56 C3
Mount Pleasant Rd,
Folkestone CT20 26 D2
Mount Pleasant Rd,
Tunbridge Wells TN1 56 C5
Mount Rd ME4 18 B5
Mount Sion TN1 56 B5
Mount St CT21 33 B4
Mountfield TN15 13 C6
Mountfield Ct TN1 56 C4
Mountfield Pk TN9 55 C5
Mountfield
Ind Est TN28 38 C4
Mountfield Way CT8 58 A4
Mounts Cl CT14 22 A3
Mounts Rd DA9 29 B2
Moyle Cl ME8 42 B2
Moyle Tower Rd CT21 33 C5
Mozart Ct ME4 18 A6
Mt Pleasant Rd DA1 21 C3
Muir Rd,
Maidstone ME15 35 C5
Muir Rd,
Ramsgate CT11 43 C2
Mulberry Ct CT11 43 C3

Mulberry Ct,
Canterbury CT1 16 B4
Mulberry Ct,
Hythe CT21 33 C3
Mulberry Fld CT13 45 C1
Munday
Works Est TN9 55 C3
Munford Rd DA10 29 F4
Murston Rd ME10 48 B2
Murthwaite Ct ME12 37 A4
Murton Neale Cl TN18 31 C1
Musgrave Rd ME10 48 B1
Musgrove TN23 12 B6
Mutrix Gdns CT9 58 E2
Mutrix Rd CT9 58 E2
Mutton La ME13 25 A4
Myrtle Rd DA1 21 B5

Nacholt Cl CT5 59 D2
Nags Head La ME1 44 D4
Napier Ct ME14 35 B1
Napier Gdns CT21 33 B4
Napier Rd,
Broadstairs CT10 15 D2
Napier Rd,
Gillingham ME7 27 B5
Napleton Rd ME13 25 C2
Napoleon Dr TN12 34 B5
Napoleon Walk ME17 32 B5
Nash Court Gdns CT9 36 C5
Nash Court Rd CT9 36 C5
Nash Gardens CT10 15 D4
Nash La CT9 36 C5
Nash Rd CT9 36 B5
Nasmyth Rd CT7 14 D1
Natal Rd ME4 18 C6
Nativity Cl ME10 48 A3
Nautilus Cl ME12 37 B4
Nautilus Dr ME12 37 B4
Naylands CT9 36 A3
Neale St ME4 18 B6
Neame Rd CT7 14 E2
Nelson Av,
Sheerness ME12 37 D4
Nelson Rd,
Tonbridge TN9 55 A3
Nelson Cl ME12 37 D4
Nelson Cres CT11 43 B5
Nelson Ct CT7 14 B2
Nelson Gdns ME13 25 C4
Nelson Ho DA9 29 D2
Nelson Pl CT10 15 D3
Nelson Rd,
Gillingham ME7 27 A4
Nelson Rd,
Whitstable CT5 59 A3
Nelson St, Deal CT14 22 C1
Nelson Rd,
Faversham ME13 25 C4
Nelson Ter ME13 46 A3
Neptune
Bsns Est ME2 18 A1
Neptune Cl ME2 18 A1
Neptune Gap CT5 59 A2
Neptune Way ME2 18 A1
Ness Rd ME12 34 C2
Nether Av TN28 38 E4
Nevill Pl ME6 49 C4
Nevill Rd ME6 49 C4
Nevill St TN2 56 B5
Neville Rd ME4 18 A6
New Barn Rd BR8 53 D1
New Bri CT16 23 C2
New Covenant Pl ME1 44 D4
New Cross St CT9 36 B2
New Ct TN9 55 C4
New Cut ME4 18 A4
New England Rd TN4 50 D5
New House La,
Ashford TN27 31 A6
New House La,
Gravesend DA11 28 A6
New Hythe La ME20 40 B2
New La TN29 34 B2
New Prospect Rd CT21 33 B4
New Rd, Ashford TN27 31 C5
New Rd, Chatham ME4 18 A4
New Rd,
Cranbrook TN17 20 A5
New Rd,
Gravesend DA11 28 A5
New Rd, Hythe CT21 33 A1
New Rd, Hythe CT21 33 B4
New Rd, Minster ME12 37 C4
New Rd,
Rochester ME1 44 D4
New Rd,
Sheerness ME12 47 B5
New Rd, Swanley BR8 53 D2
New Rd,
Tonbridge TN12 40 C4
New Rents
Ind Est ME12 47 B3
New Rents TN24 12 C4
New Road Av ME1 18 A4
New Romney TN28 38 D3

New Romney Pl CT13 45 D2
New Ruttington La CT1 16 D1
New St, Ashford TN24 12 B3
New St,
Canterbury CT1 16 A6
New St, Chatham ME4 18 A5
New St, Deal CT14 22 C1
New St, Dover CT16 23 C2
New St,
Folkestone CT20 26 D2
New St,
Gravesend DA12 28 C2
New St, Herne Bay CT6 32 C1
New St, Margate CT9 36 B2
New St,
Romney Marsh TN29 34 C2
New St,
Sandwich CT13 45 D2
New St,
Sheerness ME12 47 C3
New St,
Westerham TN16 57 C5
New Stairs ME4 18 B2
New Swan Yd DA12 28 B2
New Wharf Rd TN9 55 B3
Newark Yd ME2 52 C4
Newbury Cl CT7 14 E3
Newcastle Hill CT11 43 B4
Newcomen Rd,
Sheerness ME12 47 D2
Newcomen Rd,
Tunbridge Wells TN4 50 C6
Newgate Lower Prom
CT9 36 D1
Newgate Prom CT9 36 D1
Newhouse Ter TN8 24 B3
Newington Mdw CT21 33 C3
Newland Rd ME12 47 B5
Newlands Ho CT11 15 A3
Newlands Rd,
Ramsgate CT12 43 A1
Newlands Rd,
Tunbridge Wells TN4 50 D5
Newlands Rise TN4 50 D4
Newlyns Way TN4 50 D4
Newmans Cl CT11 15 C1
Newnham St ME4 18 C5
Newton Abbot Rd DA11 28 A5
Newton Cl ME12 40 B3
Newton Rd,
Tonbridge TN11 56 C2
Newtown Grn TN24 12 D6
Newtown Rd TN24 12 D5
Nicholls Av CT10 15 B6
Nicolson Way TN11 46 D3
Nightingale Cl,
Gillingham ME8 42 A4
Nightingale Cl,
Gravesend DA12 39 D6
Nightingale Gro DA1 21 D1
Nightingale Pl CT9 36 D2
Nightingale Rd ME13 25 C3
Nightingale Way BR8 53 D3
Nile Rd ME7 27 A4
Nine Acres TN24 12 D1
Nine Elms Gro DA11 28 A3
Noakes Mdw TN23 12 A6
Nobel St ME13 25 B3
Noble Cl CT9 58 E3
Noble Gdns CT9 58 E3
Nore Cl ME12 47 D3
Noreen Av ME14 37 A3
Norfolk Cl DA1 21 D2
Norfolk Dr TN23 12 A4
Norfolk Heights TN1 56 B3
Norfolk Rd,
Gravesend DA12 28 D2
Norfolk Rd,
Margate CT9 19 A2
Norfolk Rd,
Tonbridge TN9 55 A3
Norfolk Rd,
Tunbridge Wells TN1 56 C5
Norfolk St CT5 59 A4
Norman Cl ME14 35 D1
Norman Rd,
Broadstairs CT10 15 A2
Norman Rd,
Canterbury CT1 16 C6
Norman Rd,
Dartford DA1 21 B5
Norman Rd,
Dover CT15 41 D4
Norman Rd,
Faversham ME13 25 C3
Norman Rd,
Snodland ME6 49 C4
Norman Rd,
Tunbridge Wells TN1 56 D1
Norman Rd,
Westgate-on-Sea CT8 58 D2
Norman Rd,
Whitstable CT5 59 B4

Norman Rise TN17 20 C6
Norman St CT17 23 B1
Normanhurst Rd TN15 13 C6
Normans CI DA11 28 A3
Norreys Rd ME8 42 A3
Norrie ME27 14 D3
Norris CI TN18 31 C1
Norstead Gdns TN4 50 D4
North Av CT11 43 A4
North Barn CI ME2 52 B6
North Barrack Rd CT14 22 C1
North Ct, Deal CT14 22 C1
North Ct,
Maidstone ME15 35 C6
North Down TN12 51 B2
North Foreland Av CT10 15 D1
North Foreland Rd CT10 15 D1
North Gate ME1 44 C3
North Kent Av DA11 39 B2
North La,
Canterbury CT2 16 A2
North La,
Faversham ME13 25 C2
North Lea CT14 22 C1
North Military Rd CT17 23 B3
North Rd,
Chatham ME4 18 C1
North Rd, Dover CT17 23 A1
North Rd, Hythe CT21 33 A3
North Rd,
Queenborough ME11 41 A1
North Rd West CT21 33 A3
North Rd, Ashford TN24 12 C4
North St,
Biddenden TN27 31 C2
North St, Dartford DA1 21 B4
North St, Deal CT14 22 D1
North St,
Folkestone CT19 26 E2
North St,
Gravesend DA12 28 B3
North St,
Headcorn TN27 31 B5
North St,
Herne Bay CT6 32 C1
North St,
New Romney TN28 38 B3
North St, Strood ME2 52 C4
Northbourne TN24 12 C3
Northbrooke TN24 12 C3
Northbrooke La TN24 12 C3
Northcliffe Gdns CT10 15 B1
Northcote Rd,
Deal CT14 22 C3
Northcote Rd,
Strood ME2 52 B4
Northcote Rd,
Tonbridge TN9 55 B4
Northdown TN24 12 C2
Northdown Av CT9 19 A3
Northdown Cl,
Maidstone ME14 35 C1
Northdown Cl,
Tonbridge TN11 40 B3
Northdown Hill CT10 19 D5
Northdown Park Rd CT9 19 A4
Northdown Rd,
Clifftonville CT9 19 A3
Northdown Rd,
Margate CT9 36 C2
Northdown Way CT9 19 C5
Northdowns Vw ME17 30 D1
Northern By-Pass TN27 17 B2
Northfleet
Ind Est DA11 29 F1
Northgate TN18 16 D2
Northgrove Rd TN18 31 B1
Northridge Rd DA12 28 C4
Northumberland Av,
Gillingham ME8 42 B1
Northumberland Av,
Margate CT9 19 B4
Northview ME8 53 C1
Northview Rd TN14 46 D2
Northwall Ct CT14 22 B1
Northwall Mews CT14 22 C1
Northwall Rd CT14 22 B1
Northwood Dr,
Greenhithe DA9 29 A3
Northwood Dr,
Sittingbourne ME10 48 B6
Northwood Rd CT5 59 B1
Norton Rd TN4 50 C2
Norway Ter ME14 35 B1
Norwood Ct DA1 21 D1
Norwood Gdns TN23 12 B4
Norwood Rise ME12 37 C2
Norwood St TN23 12 C4
Nottingham Rd CT7 14 D4
Nunnery Flds CT1 16 C6
Nunnery Rd CT1 16 C6
Nursery Cl,
Sevenoaks TN13 46 C3
Nursery Cl,
Swanley BR8 53 A1

Nursery Cl, Whitstable CT5 59 D3
Nursery Rd TN12 40 B2
Nurserylands CT6 32 B3
Nutfields ME10 48 D4
Nutley Cl TN24 12 D3

Oak Av, Gillingham ME7 27 C2
Oak Av, Sheerness ME12 37 F3
Oak End Cl TN4 50 C1
Oak Farm Gdns TN27 31 B4
Oak Hall Pass CT21 33 B3
Oak La, Ashford TN27 31 C5
Oak La, Romney Marsh TN29 34 B2
Oak La, Sheerness ME12 37 F3
Oak Lodge La TN16 57 D4
Oak Lodge Rd TN28 38 C2
Oak Rd, Gravesend DA12 28 C6
Oak Rd, Rochester ME2 52 A5
Oak Rd, Westerham TN16 57 D4
Oak St CT14 22 D2
Oak Tree Cl TN12 34 C5
Oak Tree Gro CT9 58 E3
Oak Tree Rd TN23 12 A6
Oak Vw TN8 24 B4
Oak Walk CT21 33 B3
Oakdale Rd CT6 32 D3
Oakdene Rd TN13 46 B3
Oakfield TN18 31 B1
Oakfield La DA1 21 A6
Oakfield Park Rd DA1 21 B6
Oakfield Pl DA1 21 A6
Oakfield Rd TN8 31 B1
Oakfields TN27 31 B4
Oakham Dr TN29 34 C1
Oakhill Rd TN13 46 B5
Oaklands Rd TN18 31 B2
Oaklea Rd TN12 40 C4
Oakleigh Cl BR8 53 C2
Oaks Rd TN30 54 B5
Oakum Ct ME4 18 D6
Oakwood CT9 19 C5
Oakwood Dr, Sevenoaks TN13 46 B4
Oakwood Dr, Whitstable CT5 59 D2
Oakwood Mews CT5 59 A5
Oare Rd ME13 25 C1
Oast Ct, Margate CT9 36 C4
Oast Ct, Sittingbourne ME10 48 B5
Oastview ME8 42 A3
Oaten Hill CT1 16 D6
Oaten Hill Pl CT1 16 D5
Oatfield Cl TN17 20 B4
Oatfield Dr TN17 20 B4
Occupation Rd TN25 60 D5
Ocean Cl CT7 14 E2
Ocean Ter ME12 37 E3
Ocean Vw CT10 43 D1
Ocelot Ct ME8 18 D6
Ockley La TN18 31 B1
Ockley Rd TN18 31 B1
Octo Rd CT17 23 A1
Offens Dr TN12 51 B3
Offley Cl CT9 19 C4
Olantigh Rd TN25 60 C5
Olave Rd CT9 19 A4
Old Ash Cl TN24 12 C1
Old Ashford Rd, Ashford TN27 17 B3
Old Ashford Rd, Maidstone ME17 32 D6
Old Boundary Rd CT8 58 D1
Old Bridge Rd CT5 59 B3
Old Cannon Wharf TN9 55 C3
Old Castle Walk ME8 42 A6
Old Crossing Rd CT9 58 E2
Old Dairy Cl CT11 14 D3
Old Dover Rd CT1 16 C5
Old Farm Cl CT5 59 D2
Old Farm Gdns BR8 53 D2
Old Farm Rd CT7 14 B2
Old Gate Rd ME13 25 B2
Old Green Rd, Broadstairs CT10 15 B1
Old Green Rd, Margate CT9 19 B4
Old Ham La ME17 32 A6
Old Kent Rd TN12 40 C4
Old Kingsdown Cl CT10 15 A5
Old Lain ME17 30 C2
Old London Rd TN10 55 C2
Old Manor Dr DA12 28 C4
Old Otford Rd TN14 46 C1
Old Pattens La ME1 18 C4
Old Perry St DA11 39 D5
Old Pond Rd TN3 12 A5
Old Railway Works Ind Est TN24 12 D6
Old Rd ME4 18 B4

Old Rd East DA12 28 B4
Old Rd West DA11 28 A4
Old Ruttington La CT1 16 D3
Old Saltwool La CT21 33 A2
Old School Cl ME17 32 C6
Old School Ct BR8 53 C2
Old School Gdns CT9 36 D4
Old School Pl ME14 35 C3
Old Tannery Cl TN30 54 A6
Old Tovil Rd ME15 35 B6
Old Vicarage Gdns TN25 60 C5
Old Vinters Rd ME14 35 C3
Olive Rd DA1 21 A5
Oliver Cl ME4 18 D6
Oliver Rd, Swanley BR8 53 B2
Oliver Rd, Tonbridge TN12 51 B3
Oliver Twist Cl ME1 44 B5
Olivier Dr ME3 52 D1
Omer Av CT9 19 B3
One Tree Hill ME15 35 D5
Onslow Rd ME1 44 D6
Orange St CT1 16 C3
Orange Ter ME1 44 D4
Orch CT N8 24 A4
Orchard Av, Deal CT14 22 A3
Orchard Av, Rochester ME2 52 B2
Orchard Bsns Centre TN9 55 D3
Orchard Cl, Maidstone ME16 35 C5
Orchard Cl, Sevenoaks TN14 46 D1
Orchard Cl, Sheerness ME12 37 A3
Orchard Cl, Whitstable CT5 59 C1
Orchard Dr, Ashford TN23 12 A2
Orchard Dr, Edenbridge TN8 24 A4
Orchard Dr, Hythe CT21 33 B4
Orchard Dr, New Romney TN28 38 E3
Orchard Dr, Wye TN25 60 C6
Orchard Gdns CT9 58 E2
Orchard Glade TN27 31 C5
Orchard Gro ME12 37 C3
Orchard Heights TN25 12 A1
Orchard Pl, Faversham ME13 25 D3
Orchard Pl, Maidstone ME16 35 A4
Orchard Pl, Sittingbourne ME10 48 C4
Orchard Rd, Gravesend DA11 39 B5
Orchard Rd, Herne Bay CT6 32 C3
Orchard Rd, Margate CT9 58 E2
Orchard Rd, Swanscombe DA10 29 F2
Orchard Rd, Tenterden TN30 54 B1
Orchard St, Dartford DA1 21 B3
Orchard St, Gillingham ME8 42 A3
Orchard St, Maidstone ME15 35 C5
Orchard Villas ME4 18 B5
Orchard Way, Cranbrook TN17 20 A6
Orchard Way, Snodland ME6 49 B3
Ordnance Rd DA12 28 C2
Ordnance St ME4 18 A5
Ordnance Ter ME4 18 A4
Oriel Rd TN23 12 A2
Orient Pl CT2 16 B1
Ormonde Rd, Folkestone CT20 26 E1
Ormonde Rd, Hythe CT21 33 B5
Osborne Cl ME13 25 A2
Osborne Rd, Broadstairs CT10 15 B4
Osborne Rd, Gillingham ME7 27 A3
Osborne Ter CT9 36 C3
Osbourn Av CT8 58 B3
Oscar Rd CT10 15 C4
Osprey Av ME5 27 B6
Osprey Cl ME10 48 C4
Ospringe Pl ME13 25 B4
Ospringe Rd ME13 25 B3
Ospringe St ME13 25 A3
Osterberg Rd DA1 21 C1
Ostlers Cl ME4 49 C2
Otford Rd TN14 46 C1
Otterham Quay La ME8 42 D2
Otway St, Chatham ME4 18 C5

Otway St, Gillingham ME7 27 A2
Otway Ter ME4 18 C5
Outnalls ME12 47 D3
Overcliffe DA11 28 A2
Overmead BR8 53 C4
Overy St DA1 21 C3
Owen Sq CT14 22 B6
Owens Way ME7 27 D1
Ox La TN30 54 C3
Oxenden Rd Dr CT6 32 A2
Oxenden Sq CT6 32 A1
Oxenden St CT6 32 A1
Oxenturn Rd TN25 60 C6
Oxfield TN8 24 C3
Oxford Cl CT1 16 B6
Oxford Rd ME7 27 B5
Oxford St, Margate CT9 36 C3
Oxford St, Snodland ME6 49 C3
Oxford St, Whitstable CT5 59 A3
Oxford Ter CT20 26 C3
Oxney Cl CT7 14 D3
Oyster Cl ME10 48 B1
Oyster Mews*, Skinners Alley CT5 59 A2

Pacific Cl DA10 29 E2
Packers La CT11 43 B3
Paddlesworth Rd ME6 49 A2
Paddock Cl TN29 34 B2
Paddock Rd, Birchington CT7 14 D3
Paddock Rd, Sheerness ME12 47 B2
Paddock Vw CT5 59 B5
Padsole La ME15 35 C4
Paget St ME7 27 A3
Pagitt St ME4 18 A6
Painters Ash La DA11 39 C6
Palace Av ME15 35 B4
Palace Ct ME5 27 B6
Palace St CT1 16 C3
Palladian Circus DA9 29 C1
Palm Bay Av CT9 19 B2
Palm Bay Gdns CT9 19 B2
Palmer Cres CT9 19 B5
Palmers Brook TN11 11 C4
Palmers Yd TN27 31 C5
Palmerston Av, Broadstairs CT10 15 C5
Palmerston Av, Deal CT14 22 B5
Palmerston Ct CT14 22 D6
Palmerston Rd ME4 18 B6
Palmerston St CT11 26 C1
Palting Way CT20 26 A3
Papyrus Way ME20 49 D6
Paradise CT11 43 A4
Paradise Row CT13 45 C1
Paragon CT11 43 A5
Paragon St CT11 43 A5
Parham Rd ME4 18 B6
Parish Rd ME12 37 B4
Park Av, Birchington CT7 14 D3
Park Av, Broadstairs CT10 15 A6
Park Av, Deal CT14 22 B3
Park Av, Dover CT16 23 B1
Park Av, Edenbridge TN8 24 B4
Park Av, Gillingham ME7 27 B6
Park Av, Gravesend DA12 28 C4
Park Av, Maidstone ME14 35 C2
Park Av, Northfleet DA11 39 D4
Park Av, Queenborough ME11 41 B2
Park Av, Sittingbourne ME10 48 A5
Park Av, Whitstable CT5 59 C1
Park Chase CT10 15 A6
Park Cliff Rd DA9 29 C1
Park Cotts TN18 31 C1
Park Crescent Rd CT3 36 D3
Park Dr ME10 48 B3
Park Gate CT10 15 A6
Park House Gdns TN4 50 C2
Park La, Birchington CT7 14 D3
Park La, Margate CT9 36 D3
Park La, Sevenoaks TN13 46 C4
Park La CT14 22 D2
Park Pl, Dover CT16 23 B1
Park Pl, Gravesend DA12 28 C2
Park Pl, Margate CT9 36 D3
Park Rd, Birchington CT7 14 E3
Park Rd, Broadstairs CT10 15 D2

Park Rd, Dartford DA1 21 D4
Park Rd, Faversham ME13 25 D3
Park Rd, Gravesend DA11 28 B5
Park Rd, Herne Bay CT6 32 B2
Park Rd, Hythe CT21 33 B5
Park Rd, Margate CT9 36 D3
Park Rd, New Romney TN28 38 E4
Park Rd, Queenborough ME11 41 A1
Park Rd, Ramsgate CT11 43 A3
Park Rd, Sittingbourne ME10 48 A4
Park Rd, Southborough TN4 50 C2
Park Rd, St Johns TN4 50 D6
Park Rd, Swanley BR8 53 D3
Park Rd, Swanscombe DA10 29 E3
Park Rd North TN24 53 D3
Park St, Ashford TN24 12 C4
Park St, Deal CT14 22 C2
Park St, Dover CT16 23 B1
Park St, Romney Marsh TN29 34 B2
Park Ter DA9 29 C2
Park View Cl TN8 24 B4
Park View Ter TN30 54 B3
Park Villas TN11 17 C5
Park Vw CT9 36 D2
Park Way ME15 35 C6
Park Wood Cl CT10 15 A6
Parker Cl, Ashford TN26 30 B6
Parker Cl, Gillingham ME8 42 A5
Parkfield Rd CT19 26 B1
Parkfield Ct CT10 15 B2
Parklands TN4 50 D3
Parkside CT14 22 C3
Parkside St TN30 54 A6
Parkwood Cl CT10 43 B1
Parr Av ME7 27 B2
Parrock Av DA12 28 C4
Parrock Rd DA12 28 C4
Parrock St DA12 28 B3
Parsonage Chase ME12 37 A4
Parsonage Rd CT6 32 C3
Partridge La ME13 25 D2
Pasley Rd ME7 18 C2
Pasley Rd East ME4 18 C1
Pasley Rd North ME4 18 D1
Pasley Rd West ME4 18 C1
Pattenden La TN12 34 A4
Patterson Ct DA1 21 D2
Pavilion Ct CT20 26 E1
Pavilion Rd CT19 26 C1
Payers Pk CT20 26 D2
Payton Ct CT9 36 D6
Peach Cft DA11 39 D6
Peacock St DA12 28 C3
Pear Tree Cl, Cranbrook TN17 20 C6
Pear Tree Cl, Swanley BR8 53 C1
Pearman Ct ME4 42 C1
Pearson Way DA1 21 C6
Pearsons Way CT10 19 D6
Peckham Cl ME2 52 D3
Pedham Pl Ind Est BR8 53 E4
Peel St ME14 35 B2
Peelers Ct CT21 16 B1
Pegasus Ct DA12 28 C6
Pelham Rd DA1 21 A4
Pelham Ter DA11 28 A3
Pemberton Gdns BR8 53 C2
Pemberton Rd TN24 12 D4
Pembroke Av CT9 58 E2
Pembroke Ct CT20 26 E1
Pembroke Gdns ME8 42 A6
Pembroke Rd, New Romney TN28 38 C2
Pembroke Mews, Sevenoaks TN13 46 C5
Pembroke Rd, Sevenoaks TN13 46 C5
Pembury Gro TN9 55 C4
Pembury Rd TN9 55 B4
Pembury St ME10 48 B3
Pencester Rd CT16 23 C1
Pencroft Dr DA1 21 A3
Pendennis Rd TN13 46 C4
Pender Mews TN30 54 B4
Penderel Rd ME14 35 B2
Penfold Rd CT19 26 F1
Penlee CT N8 24 C4
Penn Cl ME10 48 D5
Penney Cl DA1 21 A4
Pennine Way, Ashford TN24 12 C2

Pennine Way, Gravesend DA11 39 D6
Pennington Pl TN4 50 D1
Pennington Rd TN4 50 C1
Pennyfields TN17 20 C6
Penshurst Rd CT11 43 C3
Penshurst Rise ME13 25 B2
Pentstemon Dr DA10 29 E2
Pepper Hill DA11 39 B6
Pepper Hill La DA11 39 B6
Pepys Av ME12 47 C2
Pepys Cl, Dartford DA1 21 D1
Pepys Cl, Gravesend DA11 39 C6
Pepys Way ME2 52 B3
Perch CT ME20 49 C6
Percy Rd, Broadstairs CT10 15 B3
Percy Rd, Margate CT9 36 D1
Percy Rd, Ramsgate CT11 43 A3
Percy Ter TN4 50 C5
Peregrine Dr ME10 48 C4
Perie Row*, Middle St ME7 18 C2
Periwinkle Cl ME10 48 A2
Perkins Av CT9 36 C4
Perry Gro DA1 21 D1
Perry St, Chatham ME4 18 A5
Perry St, Maidstone ME14 35 B2
Perryfield St ME14 35 B2
Peter St, Deal CT14 22 C1
Peter St, Dover CT16 23 B1
Peter St, Folkestone CT20 26 D1
Peter St, Gravesend DA12 28 C3
Petfield Cl ME12 37 D3
Pett La TN27 17 C2
Pettits Row TN25 25 B3
Pettman Cl CT16 32 C3
Pevensey Ct ME16 35 A3
Pewter Ct CT1 16 C6
Philip Av BR8 53 B3
Philip Corby Cl CT9 19 B3
Phillips Rd CT7 14 D3
Phoenix Ind Est ME2 44 D1
Phoenix Cl DA1 21 B4
Phoenix Pl DA1 21 B4
Pickwick Cres ME1 44 C6
Pickwick Gdns DA11 39 C6
Pier App CT10 15 D4
Pier Approach Rd ME7 27 B1
Pier Av, Herne Bay CT6 32 B1
Pier Av, Whitstable CT5 59 D1
Pier Chine CT6 32 B2
Pier Rd, Gillingham ME7 27 B1
Pier Rd, Greenhithe DA9 29 B1
Pier Rd, Queenborough ME11 47 A6
Pier Rd Ind Est ME7 27 B1
Pierpoint Rd CT5 59 A5
Pierremont Av CT10 15 C4
Pike Cl ME20 49 C6
Pile La TN12 51 D2
Pilgrims Ct, Ashford TN27 17 B3
Pilgrims Ct, Dartford DA1 21 D1
Pilgrims Lakes ME17 30 C1
Pilgrims Rd DA10 29 E1
Pilgrims Vw DA9 29 C3
Pilgrims Way, Ashford TN27 17 C2
Pilgrims Way, Maidstone ME17 32 B5
Pilgrims Way, Rochester ME2 52 A6
Pilgrims Way, Westerham TN16 57 B2
Pilots Way CT14 22 A4
Pin Hill CT1 16 A5
Pine Av DA12 28 D4
Pine Cl BR8 53 D3
Pine Gro, Edenbridge TN8 24 B4
Pine Gro, Maidstone ME14 35 C1
Pine Needle La TN13 46 C3
Pine Rd ME2 52 B5
Pinetree Cl, Birchington CT7 14 E3
Pinetree Cl, Whitstable CT5 59 C1
Pinewood Cl TN12 40 C4
Pinewood Cl CT5 50 C2
Pinewood Gdns TN4 50 C2
Pink Alley TN2 50 C2
Pinks Hill BR8 53 C4
Pinnock La TN12 51 A5
Pinnocks Av DA11 28 B4
Pioneer Way BR8 53 C2

Pit La TN8 24 B2
Pittlesden TN30 54 A5
Pittlesden Pl TN30 54 A5
Pittock Ho CT14 22 B5
Place La TN26 60 B1
Plain Rd TN12 34 B6
Plains of Waterloo CT11 43 B4
Plane Av DA11 39 C3
Plantation La TN12 34 A5
Plantation Rd ME13 25 C3
Platt Ind Est TN15 **13 D4**
Platt Mill Cl TN15 13 D5
Pleasant Row ME4 18 B2
Plenty Brook Dr CT6 32 B3
Pleydell Gdns CT20 26 C4
Plough Walk TN8 24 C3
Ploughmans Way ME8 42 A4
Plover Cl TN8 24 C3
Plover Rd ME12 37 B4
Pluckley Gdns CT9 19 D3
Pluckley Rd TN27 17 B3
Plum Tree Gdns TN26 60 B3
Plymouth Dr TN13 46 C5
Plymouth Pk TN13 46 D5
Poets Corner CT9 36 D3
Pond Dr ME10 48 C4
Pondmore Way TN25 12 A2
Pontoise Cl TN13 46 A3
Poona Rd TN1 56 D5
Pope Dr TN12 51 B3
Poplar Cl ME2 52 B6
Poplar La TN29 34 C1
Poplar Rd, Broadstairs CT10 15 A2
Poplar Rd, Ramsgate CT11 43 A4
Poplar Rd, Rochester ME2 52 A6
Poppy Cl ME7 27 C3
Poppy Mdw TN12 40 D4
Porchfield Cl DA12 28 C5
Port Av DA9 29 B3
Port Rise ME4 18 B5
Porter Cl ME12 37 B3
Portland Av DA12 28 B5
Portland Cl CT21 33 A4
Portland Mews ME10 48 A1
Portland Pl, Greenhithe DA9 29 C1
Portland Pl, Snodland ME6 49 C2
Portland Rd, Gillingham ME7 27 C2
Portland Rd, Gravesend DA12 28 B4
Portland Rd, Hythe CT21 33 B4
Portland Rd, Northfleet DA11 39 C2
Portland St ME4 18 C6
Portman Pk TN9 55 C1
Portree Mews ME7 27 C5
Portway CT5 59 A3
Post Barn Rd ME4 18 B6
Post Office Rd TN18 31 B1
Post Ter CT5 59 B2
Postern La TN11 55 D3
Postley Rd ME15 35 C6
Postmill Dr ME15 35 A6
Potter St CT13 45 D1
Poulders Gdns CT13 45 B3
Poulders Rd CT13 45 A2
Poulsen Ct ME10 48 D3
Pound La, Canterbury CT1 16 B2
Pound La, Sevenoaks TN13 46 C5
Pound Way CT20 26 D3
Pout Rd ME6 49 B4
Povey Av ME2 52 D1
Powder Mill La, Dartford DA1 21 B6
Powder Mill La, Tunbridge Wells TN4 50 D4
Powell Cotton Dr CT7 14 E3
Powlett Rd ME2 52 D2
Poyntell Rd TN12 51 C3
Prestedge Av CT11 43 B1
Preston Gro ME13 25 D4
Preston La ME13 25 D4
Preston Pk ME13 25 D4
Preston Rd, Gravesend DA11 39 D4
Preston Rd, Tonbridge TN9 55 A3
Preston St ME13 25 D3
Pretoria Rd, Chatham ME4 18 B6
Pretoria Rd, Gillingham ME7 27 A5
Prices Av CT9 19 A2
Pridmore Rd ME6 49 B2
Priestfield Rd ME7 27 B1
Priestfields ME1 44 B6
Primrose Walk TN12 40 C5
Prince Andrew Rd CT10 15 A1

Prince Arthur Rd ME7 18 D2
Prince Charles Av ME12 37 D4
Prince Charles Rd CT10 15 A1
Prince of Wales Ter CT14 22 D2
Prince William Ct CT14 22 D1
Princes Av ME12 37 D3
Princes Cl CT7 14 B2
Princes Cres CT9 36 C3
Princes Cres CT9 19 B3
Princes Par CT21 33 D4
Princes Rd, Dartford DA1 21 A5
Princes Rd, Ramsgate CT11 43 A4
Princes St, Deal CT14 22 C1
Princes St, Dover CT17 23 C2
Princes St, Gravesend DA11 28 B2
Princes St, Maidstone ME14 35 C2
Princes St, Margate CT9 36 C2
Princess Rd ME1 44 C5
Princess Vw DA1 21 D5
Princess Walk CT9 19 C2
Princess Anne Rd CT10 15 A1
Princess Margaret Av CT9 19 D3
Princess Mary Av ME4 18 D1
Prioress Cres DA9 29 C1
Priory Cl, Broadstairs CT10 15 B5
Priory Cl, Dartford DA1 21 A2
Priory Cl, New Romney TN28 38 A3
Priory Cl ME8 27 D6
Priory Gate ME14 35 B3
Priory Gate Rd CT17 23 B2
Priory Gdns, Dartford DA1 21 A2
Priory Gdns, Folkestone CT20 26 D3
Priory Gro, Dover CT17 23 B1
Priory Gro, Tonbridge TN9 55 B4
Priory Hill, Dartford DA1 21 A2
Priory Hill, Dover CT17 23 A1
Priory Pl, Dartford DA1 21 B3
Priory Pl, Faversham ME13 25 C1
Priory Rd, Dartford DA1 21 B1
Priory Rd, Dover CT17 23 B1
Priory Rd, Faversham ME13 25 C2
Priory Rd, Gillingham ME8 27 D6
Priory Rd, Maidstone ME15 35 B3
Priory Rd, Ramsgate CT11 43 A5
Priory Rd, Strood ME2 52 B5
Priory Retail Pk DA1 **21 B2**
Priory Row ME13 25 C1
Priory St, Dover CT16 23 B2
Priory St, Tonbridge TN9 55 B4
Priory Station Approach ME17 23 A2
Priory Walk TN9 55 B4
Priory Wy TN30 54 C5
Promenade, Broadstairs CT10 15 C4
Promenade, Deal CT14 22 D4
Promenade, Dover CT16 23 D3
Prospect Av ME2 52 D1
Prospect Cl CT8 58 B3
Prospect Gdns DA12 28 C1
Prospect Hill CT6 32 C1
Prospect Pl TN4 50 B2
Prospect Pl, Broadstairs CT10 15 C4
Prospect Pl, Dartford DA1 21 B2
Prospect Pl, Gravesend DA12 28 D3
Prospect Pl, Maidstone ME16 35 A5
Prospect Rd, Birchington CT7 14 D2
Prospect Rd, Broadstairs CT10 15 C4
Prospect Rd, Hythe CT21 33 B4
Prospect Rd, Sevenoaks TN13 46 C3
Prospect Rd, Southborough TN4 50 B2
Prospect Rd, Tunbridge Wells TN1 50 B2
Prospect Row, Chatham ME4 18 C5

Prospect Row, Gillingham ME7 18 C2
Prospect Ter CT11 43 B5
Providence La ME1 44 C3
Providence St, Ashford TN23 12 C6
Providence St, Greenhithe DA9 29 A2
Puckle La CT1 16 D6
Pudding La ME14 35 B3
Pudding Rd ME8 42 C2
Purbeck Rd ME4 18 B6
Purser Way ME7 27 A1

Quaker Cl TN13 46 D4
Quaker Dr TN17 20 C3
Quaker La TN17 20 C3
Quakers Hall La TN13 46 C3
Quantock Dr TN24 12 B3
Quarry Bank TN9 55 A5
Quarry Cl CT21 33 B3
Quarry Cotts TN13 46 A4
Quarry Gdns TN9 55 A5
Quarry Hill Rd, Sevenoaks TN15 13 A6
Quarry Hill Rd, Tonbridge TN9 55 A5
Quarry La CT21 33 A3
Quarry Rd ME15 35 B6
Quarry Rise TN9 55 A5
Quarry Sq ME14 35 C2
Quay Ct CT5 59 B2
Quay La, Faversham ME13 25 D2
Quay La, Greenhithe DA9 29 B1
Quay La, Sandwich CT13 45 D2
Quebec Av TN16 57 C5
Quebec Sq TN16 57 D5
Queen Anne Rd ME14 35 C3
Queen Berthas Av CT7 14 F2
Queen Elizabeth Av CT9 19 C4
Queen Elizabeth Rd CT16 23 E1
Queen St, Ashford TN23 12 C4
Queen St, Chatham ME4 18 C4
Queen St, Deal CT14 22 C2
Queen St, Dover CT16 23 C2
Queen St, Folkestone CT20 26 D2
Queen St, Gravesend DA12 28 B2
Queen St, Herne Bay CT6 32 B1
Queen St, Ramsgate CT11 43 B4
Queen St, Rochester ME1 44 C4
Queen St, Rochester ME1 44 D4
Queen Victoria Row CT16 23 B1
Queenborough Bsns Centre ME11 **41 A3**
Queenborough Dr ME12 37 B3
Queenborough Rd ME12 41 C1
Queens Av, Birchington CT7 14 A2
Queens Av, Broadstairs CT10 15 C2
Queens Av, Margate CT9 36 C3
Queens Av, Snodland ME6 49 C2
Queens Ct, Ashford TN24 12 C3
Queens Ct, Cranbrook TN18 31 C1
Queens Ct, Edenbridge TN8 24 C5
Queens Ct, Hythe CT21 33 B4
Queens Dr TN14 46 C1
Queens Gdns, Broadstairs CT10 15 D5
Queens Gdns, Dover CT16 23 C2
Queens Gdns, Herne Bay CT6 32 C2
Queens Gdns, Margate CT9 36 D1
Queens Gdns, Tunbridge Wells TN4 50 D5
Queens Mews, Cranbrook TN18 31 C1
Queens Mews, Deal CT14 22 C2
Queens Prom CT9 19 A2
Queens Rd, Ashford TN24 12 C3
Queens Rd, Broadstairs CT10 15 C4

Queens Rd, Cranbrook TN18 31 C1
Queens Rd, Faversham ME13 25 B3
Queens Rd, Gillingham ME7 27 A4
Queens Rd, Gravesend DA12 28 C6
Queens Rd, New Romney TN28 38 D4
Queens Rd, Ramsgate CT11 43 C3
Queens Rd, Romney Marsh TN29 34 B2
Queens Rd, Sheerness ME12 37 D3
Queens Rd, Snodland ME6 49 C2
Queens Rd, Tunbridge Wells TN4 50 C6
Queens Rd, Westgate-on-Sea CT8 58 D2
Queens Rd, Whitstable CT5 59 C2
Queens Way ME12 47 B5
Queensway TN29 34 B2
Quern Rd CT14 22 A6
Quested Way ME17 30 A2
Questor Trading Est DA1 **21 C6**
Quex Rd CT10 58 C3
Quex View Rd CT7 14 D4
Quince Orch TN26 30 B5
Quinnell St ME8 42 B1
Quixote Cres ME2 52 C2

Radley Cl CT10 15 C2
Radnor Bridge Rd CT20 26 E1
Radnor Cl ME14 35 D6
Radnor Park Av CT19 26 B2
Radnor Park Cres CT19 26 B2
Radnor Park Gdns CT19 26 B2
Radnor Park Rd CT19 26 B2
Radnor Pk West CT19 26 A2
Radnor St CT19 26 E2
Raggatt Pl ME15 35 D6
Raglan PT CT10 15 C4
Railway Av CT5 59 B3
Railway Pl DA11 28 B2
Railway Rd ME12 47 C3
Railway St, Chatham ME4 18 B4
Railway St, Gillingham ME7 27 A3
Railway St, Gravesend DA11 39 A1
Railway Ter, Margate CT9 36 B3
Railway Ter, Queenborough ME11 41 A1
Railway Ter, Westerham TN16 57 D4
Rainham Rd ME5 27 A6
Rammell Mews TN17 20 C5
Rampart Rd CT21 33 B4
Ramsgate Rd, Broadstairs CT10 15 B5
Ramsgate Rd, Margate CT9 36 C4
Ramsgate Rd, Ramsgate CT10 43 C1
Ramsgate Rd, Sandwich CT13 45 D1
Rancorn Rd CT9 58 F2
Randall St ME14 35 B2
Randolph Cotts ME2 52 D2
Randolph Rd ME7 27 A3
Ranelagh Gro CT10 15 A3
Ranelagh Rd, Deal CT14 22 C3
Ranelagh Rd, Sheerness ME12 47 D2
Range Rd CT21 33 A5
Range Rd Ind Est CT21 **33 A5**
Ransome Way CT7 14 D4
Raphael Rd DA12 28 B3
Rathmore Rd DA11 28 D2
Raven Ct DA12 22 C3
Ravenscourt Rd CT19 52 D2
Ravenswood Av ME2 52 D2
Rawdon Rd ME15 35 C5
Rayfield Cl ME6 49 C2
Rayford Cl DA1 21 A2
Rayham Rd CT5 59 D4
Rayners Ct ME4 18 B2
Reach Cl CT15 41 B5
Reach Mdw CT15 41 B5
Reach Rd CT15 41 B5
Readers Bridge Rd TN30 54 A1
Reading Street Rd CT10 19 D5
Rec Av ME6 49 B3
Recreation Cl ME14 35 C2
Recreation Ground Rd TN30 54 B5
Rectory Cl, Ashford TN26 60 A1

Rectory Cl, Snodland ME6 49 C3
Rectory Flds TN17 20 C4
Rectory La, Cranbrook TN17 20 C4
Rectory La, Hythe CT21 33 A1
Rectory La, Maidstone ME17 30 C2
Rectory La, Broadstairs CT10 15 D3
Rectory Rd, Deal CT14 22 A4
Rectory Rd, Sittingbourne ME10 48 D4
Rectory Rd, Swanscombe DA10 29 E3
Rectory Walk TN24 30 B6
Rectory Way TN24 12 C1
Reculver Av CT7 14 B2
Reculvers Rd CT8 58 C3
Redcliffe La ME14 35 C1
Rede Court Rd ME2 52 A3
Redfern Av ME7 27 C3
Redhill Rd CT8 58 B3
Redlands Rd TN13 46 A5
Redpoll Walk TN12 40 C5
Redsull Av CT14 22 A5
Redvers Rd ME4 18 C6
Reed Cl ME20 49 C6
Reed Ct DA9 29 D1
Reedland Cres ME13 25 C1
Reeves Cl TN12 51 B2
Reeves Cres BR8 53 B2
Reform Rd ME4 18 D6
Regency Cl CT5 59 C4
Regency Pl ME10 48 A2
Regency Hall TN2 56 A6
Regent Rd ME7 27 A4
Regent St CT5 59 A2
Regents Pl TN23 12 B4
Reginald Rd ME16 35 A5
Rembrandt Dr DA11 39 D6
Rendezvous St CT20 26 D2
Repton Cl CT10 15 A2
Repton Manor Rd TN23 12 A3
Reservoir Cl DA9 29 C2
Reservoir Rd CT5 59 B1
Reynolds Cl CT6 32 D2
Reynolds La TN4 50 B5
Rheims Way CT1 16 A4
Rhodaus Cl CT1 16 B5
Rhodaus Town CT1 16 B5
Rhode St ME4 18 B4
Rhodes Gdns CT10 15 B4
Ribston Gdns TN12 40 B3
Richard St, Chatham ME4 18 B4
Richard St, Rochester ME1 44 B5
Richardson Rd TN4 50 D6
Richborough Dr ME2 52 C2
Richborough Rd, Sandwich CT13 45 C1
Richborough Rd, Westgate-on-Sea CT8 59 A4
Richmond Av TN9 19 A4
Richmond Dr TN28 38 C2
Richmond Rd, Gillingham ME7 27 A2
Richmond Rd, Ramsgate CT11 43 A4
Richmond St CT6 32 B1
Riddlesdale Av TN4 50 D5
Ridge Way, Edenbridge TN8 24 C2
Ridge Way, Gillingham ME7 27 A1
Ridgeway Av DA12 28 B6
Ridley Rd ME1 44 C4
Ringden Av TN12 40 B4
Ringway TN24 12 C4
Ringwood Cl ME8 42 A3
Ripleys Mkt DA1 21 B4
Rising Rd TN23 12 B5
Ritch Rd ME6 49 A3
River Bank Cl ME15 35 C4
River Dr ME2 52 A4
River Lawn Rd TN9 55 B3
River St ME7 18 C2
River Vw, Maidstone ME15 35 B5
River Vw, Queenborough ME11 41 A3
River Walk TN9 55 B3
Riverdale Ind Est TN9 **55 D4**
Riverhead Cl CT9 19 A4
Rivers Walk ME17 32 B5
Riversdale DA11 39 D6
Riverside CT5 24 C5
Riverside Centre TN9 **55 C3**
Riverside Ct, Canterbury CT2 16 B2
Riverside Ct, Edenbridge TN8 24 C5

74

Riverside Ct,
Tonbridge TN9 55 C3
Riverside Est ME2 **18 A2**
Riverside Ind Est,
Ashford TN24 **12 D4**
Riverside Ind Est,
Dartford DA1 **21 B1**
Riverside One ME2 **18 A2**
Riverside Three ME2 **18 A2**
Riverside Two ME2 **18 A2**
Riverside Way DA1 21 B2
Riverview Rd DA9 29 A2
Roach St ME2 52 C4
Road of Remembrance
CT20 26 D3
Roan Ct ME2 52 A3
Robert St CT14 22 C1
Roberts Rd,
Gillingham ME8 42 A2
Roberts Rd,
Snodland ME6 49 B2
Robin Ct CT5 59 D1
Robin Hood La TN29 34 C3
Robin La TN29 34 C3
Robina Ct BR8 53 E4
Robinia Av DA1 39 C3
Robins Av ME17 32 B6
Robins Cl ME17 32 B6
Robyns Way,
Edenbridge TN8 24 C6
Robyns Way,
Sevenoaks TN13 46 A2
Rocfort Rd ME6 49 C3
Rochester Av ME1 44 C5
Rochester Bri ME2 44 C4
Rochester Rd DA1 21 D4
Rochester St ME4 18 A6
Rock Av ME7 27 A4
Rock Rd,
Maidstone ME14 35 C1
Rock Rd,
Sevenoaks TN15 13 B5
Rock Rd,
Sittingbourne ME10 48 A3
Rock Villa Rd TN1 56 B2
Rockdale Rd TN13 46 C6
Rocky Hill ME16 35 A4
Rodmer Cl ME12 37 C2
Rodney St CT11 43 A5
Roebuck Rd,
Faversham ME13 25 A3
Roebuck Rd,
Rochester ME1 44 C4
Roethorne Gdns TN30 54 C4
Roffen Rd ME1 44 C6
Rogers Ct BR8 53 E3
Rogersmead TN30 54 A5
Rolfe La TN28 38 B3
Rolvenden Rd,
Rochester ME2 52 D1
Rolvenden Rd,
Tenterden TN30 54 A6
Roman Cl CT14 22 A2
Roman Ct TN15 13 B5
Roman Heights ME14 35 D1
Roman Rd,
Faversham ME13 25 C3
Roman Rd,
Gravesend DA11 39 B6
Roman Rd,
Snodland ME6 49 B2
Roman Sq ME10 48 B3
Roman Way CT15 41 B5
Roman Way
Ind Est ME2 **44 A4**
Rome Rd TN28 38 B3
Romney Cl CT7 14 D3
Romney Ct ME10 48 A1
Romney Marsh Rd,
Ashford TN23 12 C5
Romney Marsh Rd,
Hamstreet TN26 30 B6
Romney Pl ME15 35 C4
Romney Rd,
Ashford TN26 30 B6
Romney Rd,
Gravesend DA12 39 D6
Rookery Hill ME6 49 B3
Roonagh Ct ME10 48 A5
Rope Walk,
Chatham ME4 18 B3
Rope Walk,
Cranbrook TN17 20 B4
Roper Cl CT2 16 A1
Roper Rd CT2 16 A2
Rose Gdns CT7 14 D4
Rose Hill CT11 43 B4
Rose La CT1 16 C4
Rose St,
Gravesend DA11 39 A2
Rose St, Rochester ME1 44 D5
Rose St,
Sheerness ME12 47 C3
Rose St, Tonbridge TN9 55 C4
Rose Yd ME14 35 B3
Roseacre Ct CT9 19 D3

Rosebank Gdns DA11 39 D4
Rosebery Av CT11 43 C2
Rosebery Ct CT11 28 A4
Rosebery Rd,
Chatham ME4 18 A6
Rosebery Rd,
Gillingham ME7 27 B1
Rosedale Rd CT9 36 D3
Rosehill Walk TN1 56 B3
Roselawn Gdns CT9 58 E3
Roselea Av CT6 32 C3
Rosemary Av CT10 15 B6
Rosemary Gdns,
Broadstairs CT10 15 B6
Rosemary Gdns,
Whitstable CT5 59 D4
Rosemary La CT1 16 A4
Rosemead Gdns TN27 31 A4
Rosemount Ct ME2 52 B2
Rosewood Way CT7 14 E2
Rosherville Way DA11 39 D2
Ross St ME1 44 D4
Rossdale Gdns CT20 26 E1
Rossetti Rd CT20 26 E1
Rossetti Rd CT7 14 D2
Rosslare Cl TN16 57 C4
Rotary Gdns ME7 27 C6
Rothley Cl TN30 54 C4
Rothsay Ct*,
Argyll Dr CT10 43 B1
Rouge La DA12 28 B4
Roundel Way TN12 34 B5
Rowan Cl TN12 40 B4
Rowan Cres DA1 21 A5
Rowan Ct CT20 26 D1
Rowan Rd BR8 53 B3
Rowan Walk ME4 18 A5
Rowe Cl CT9 36 C5
Rowena Rd CT8 58 B2
Rowfield TN8 24 C3
Rowland Cl ME16 35 A4
Roxburgh Rd CT8 58 C2
Royal Av TN9 55 C4
Royal Chase TN4 56 A1
Royal Cl CT10 15 A4
Royal Cres,
Margate CT9 36 A3
Royal Cres,
Ramsgate CT11 43 A5
Royal Eagle Cl ME2 18 A1
Royal Engineers Rd
ME14 35 B1
Royal Par CT11 43 B2
Royal Pier Rd DA12 28 C2
Royal Rd,
Ramsgate CT11 43 A5
Royal Rd,
Sheerness ME12 47 D2
Royal Rise TN9 55 C4
Royal Sovereign Av
ME4 18 D1
Royal Victoria Pl Shopping
Centre TN1 **56 C2**
Royston Gdns CT15 41 B5
Royton Av ME17 32 C5
Ruckinge Rd TN26 30 B5
Rugby Cl CT10 15 A3
Rugby Gdns TN23 12 D6
Rule Ct ME12 47 C4
Runnymede Mews
ME13 25 C3
Rural Vale DA11 39 D3
Ruscombe Cl TN4 50 C1
Rushdean Rd ME2 52 A6
Rushenden Cl ME11 41 A3
Rushenden Rd ME11 41 A3
Rushford CT17 31 B5
Russell Av ME8 42 C2
Russell Ct ME4 18 D5
Russell Mews TN12 40 C3
Russell Rd DA12 28 D2
Russell St, Dover CT16 23 C2
Russell St,
Sheerness ME12 47 C3
Russells Yd TN17 20 C5
Russett Cl ME2 52 A3
Russett Way BR8 53 B1
Ruth St ME4 18 C6
Rutherford Rd TN24 12 C1
Rutland Av CT9 19 B3
Rutland Cl DA1 21 B3
Rutland Gdns,
Birchington CT7 14 C3
Rutland Gdns,
Margate CT9 19 B3
Ruxton Cl BR8 53 C2
Ruxton Ct BR8 53 C2
Rycault Cl ME16 35 A4
Rydal Cl TN4 50 A6
Rydal Dr TN4 50 A6
Ryders Av CT8 58 A2
Rye Rd TN18 31 B2
Ryland Cl CT20 26 E1

Ryland Pl CT20 26 E1
Rylands Rd TN24 12 D2
Rype Cl TN29 34 B3
Rysted La TN16 57 C5
Ryswick Mews TN28 38 C2

Sacketts Gap CT9 19 C2
Sackville Cl TN13 46 B2
Sackville Cres TN23 12 A4
Sackville Rd DA2 21 B6
Saddington St CT9 28 B3
Saddleton Gro CT5 59 A4
Saddleton Rd CT5 59 A4
Saffrons Pl CT20 26 E2
Sage Rd ME1 44 B5
Sail Makers Ct ME4 18 D6
St Agnes Gdns ME12 47 D4
St Albans Cl,
Gillingham ME7 27 C1
St Albans Cl,
Gravesend DA12 28 D6
St Albans Gdns DA12 28 D6
St Albans Rd DA1 21 D3
St Albans Walk ME1 18 A5
St Alphege La CT1 16 C2
St Ambrose Grn TN25 60 C5
St Andrews Cl,
Canterbury CT1 16 A5
St Andrews Cl,
Herne Bay CT6 32 C2
St Andrews Cl,
Margate CT9 36 C5
St Andrews Cl,
Tonbridge TN12 40 C3
St Andrews Cl,
Whitstable CT5 59 B5
St Andrews Ct,
Swanley BR8 53 C2
St Andrews Lees CT13 50 C2
St Andrews Lees CT13 45 D2
St Andrews Park Rd
TN4 50 C2
St Andrews Rd,
Deal CT14 22 C2
St Andrews Rd,
Gillingham ME7 27 B1
St Andrews Rd,
Gravesend DA12 28 C3
St Andrews Rd,
New Romney TN28 38 E4
St Andrews Rd,
Ramsgate CT11 43 C2
St Andrews Rd,
Tonbridge TN12 40 C4
St Annes Cl ME16 35 A3
St Annes Dr CT6 32 A2
St Annes Gdns CT9 36 C5
St Annes Rd CT5 59 C1
St Anns Rd ME13 25 B3
St Anthonys Way CT9 19 B4
St Augustines Av CT9 36 C5
St Augustines Rd CT11 43 A5
St Barnabas Cl ME7 27 B5
St Bartholomews CT17 23 A1
St Barts Rd CT13 45 C3
St Benedict Rd ME6 49 A3
St Benedicts Lawn CT1 43 A5
St Benets CT30 54 B4
St Benets Rd CT8 58 C4
St Benets Wy TN30 54 B4
St Botolphs Av TN13 46 B4
St Botolphs Rd,
Gravesend DA12 39 C6
St Botolphs Rd,
Sevenoaks TN13 46 B5
St Brelades Ct TN8 24 A3
St Catherines Ct*,
Argyll Dr CT10 43 B1
St Catherines Dr ME13 25 D4
St Christopher Cl CT9 19 C5
St Christophers Grn
CT10 15 B3
St Clement Way DA9 45 D2
St Clements CT13 45 D2
St Clements Rd,
Greenhithe DA9 29 C1
St Clements Rd,
Westgate-on-Sea CT8 58 B2
St Crispins Rd CT8 58 B3
St Davids Cl,
Birchington CT7 14 F2
St Davids Cl,
Whitstable CT5 59 C4
St Davids Rd,
Deal CT14 22 C2
St Davids Rd,
Ramsgate CT11 43 C2
St Davids Rd,
Tunbridge Wells TN4 50 D5
St Dunstans Rd CT9 36 C3
St Dunstans St CT2 16 A2
St Dunstans Walk TN17 20 C5
St Eanswythes Way
CT20 26 D2

St Edmunds Rd,
Canterbury CT1 16 B4
St Edmunds Rd,
Dartford DA1 21 D1
St Edmunds Way ME8 42 D1
St Faiths St ME14 35 B3
St Francis Cl,
Maidstone ME14 35 D1
St Francis Cl,
Margate CT9 19 C5
St Francis Cl,
Rochester ME2 52 A5
St Georges Av CT5 59 B5
St Georges Cl CT5 59 B5
St Georges La CT1 16 C5
St Georges Lees CT13 45 D2
St Georges Pl,
Canterbury CT1 16 D4
St Georges Pl,
Dover CT15 41 B5
St Georges Rd,
Sandwich CT13 45 E2
St Georges Rd,
Broadstairs CT10 15 C4
St Georges Rd,
Deal CT14 22 C2
St Georges Rd,
Gillingham ME7 27 A2
St Georges Rd,
Ramsgate CT11 43 C2
St Georges Rd,
Sandwich CT13 45 D2
St Georges Rd,
Sevenoaks TN13 46 C3
St Georges Rd,
Swanley BR8 53 D3
St Georges Sq TN24 12 C4
St Georges St CT1 16 C4
St Georges Ter CT6 32 A1
St Georges Ter*,
St Georges La CT1 16 C5
St Hildas Rd CT21 33 B5
St James Av CT10 15 A3
St James Cl TN11 56 D1
St James Park Rd CT9 58 D2
St James Pl DA1 21 B5
St James Rd TN11 40 C3
St James St, Dover CT16 23 C2
St James St, Dover CT16 23 D2
St James's Av DA11 28 A2
St James's Rd DA11 28 A2
St James's St DA11 28 A2
St Jeans Rd CT8 58 B4
St Johns Church Rd
CT19 26 B1
St Johns Hill TN13 46 C2
St Johns La,
Ashford TN23 12 C4
St Johns La,
Canterbury CT1 16 B4
St Johns Pk TN4 50 C3
St Johns Pl CT1 16 D1
St Johns Rd,
Dover CT17 23 A2
St Johns Rd,
Faversham ME13 25 D3
St Johns Rd,
Gillingham ME7 27 A5
St Johns Rd,
Gravesend DA12 28 D3
St Johns Rd,
Hythe CT21 33 A2
St Johns Rd,
Margate CT9 36 C3
St Johns Rd,
New Romney TN28 38 A4
St Johns Rd,
Sevenoaks TN13 46 C2
St Johns Rd,
Tunbridge Wells TN4 50 C6
St Johns St CT20 26 D2
St Johns Way TN8 24 B3
St Katherines La ME8 49 B3
St Leonards Av ME4 18 B6
St Leonards Cl CT14 22 A4
St Leonards Cl CT21 33 B4
St Leonards Mews CT21 33 B4
St Leonards Rd,
Deal CT14 22 A4
St Leonards Rd,
Hythe CT21 33 B5
St Lukes Av,
Maidstone ME14 35 A3
St Lukes Av,
Ramsgate CT11 43 A2
St Lukes Cl,
Swanley BR8 53 B2
St Lukes Cl,
Westgate-on-Sea CT8 58 C3
St Lukes Cl,
Whitstable CT5 59 B5
St Lukes Rd,
Maidstone ME14 35 C2

St Lukes Rd,
Ramsgate CT11 43 B3
St Lukes Rd,
Tunbridge Wells TN4 50 D5
St Magnus Cl CT7 14 D1
St Margarets Bank ME1 44 D4
St Margarets Mews
ME1 44 C3
St Margarets Rd,
Dover CT15 41 C6
St Margarets Rd,
Westgate-on-Sea CT8 58 C3
St Margarets St,
Canterbury CT1 16 B4
St Margarets St,
Rochester ME1 44 C4
St Marks Cl CT5 59 B4
St Martins Gdns CT17 23 B2
St Martins Path CT17 23 B4
St Martins Rd,
Dartford DA1 21 C3
St Martins Rd,
New Romney TN28 38 C2
St Martins Steps CT17 23 B3
St Marys Av CT9 19 C4
St Marys Cl,
Ashford TN26 30 B5
St Marys Cl,
Gravesend DA12 28 C5
St Marys Ct,
Canterbury CT1 16 A4
St Marys Ct,
Herne Bay CT6 32 B3
St Marys Ct,
Westerham TN16 57 C5
St Marys Gdns ME4 18 D1
St Marys Pass CT16 23 C2
St Marys Rd,
Faversham ME13 25 D3
St Marys Rd,
Gillingham ME7 27 A2
St Marys Rd,
New Romney TN28 38 C2
St Marys Rd,
Strood ME2 52 C4
St Marys Rd,
Swanley BR8 53 B3
St Marys Rd,
Tonbridge TN9 55 B5
St Marys Row ME12 37 A3
St Marys St CT1 16 B4
St Michaels Av CT9 19 C5
St Michaels Cl,
Chatham ME4 18 B5
St Michaels Cl,
Sittingbourne ME10 48 C3
St Michaels Ct ME2 52 D3
St Michaels Rd,
Sittingbourne ME10 48 A3
St Michaels Rd,
Tunbridge Wells TN4 50 D5
St Michaels St TN30 54 B1
St Mildreds Av,
Birchington CT7 14 B2
St Mildreds Av,
Broadstairs CT10 15 B4
St Mildreds Gdns CT8 58 C1
St Mildreds Rd,
Margate CT9 19 A4
St Mildreds Rd,
Westgate-on-Sea CT8 58 B2
St Nicholas Dr TN13 46 C6
St Nicholas Gdns ME2 52 B3
St Nicholas Rd,
Faversham ME13 25 A3
St Nicholas Rd,
Hythe CT21 33 A4
St Nicholas Rd,
New Romney TN28 38 D3
St Patricks Cl CT5 59 B5
St Patricks Rd,
Deal CT14 22 C2
St Patricks Rd,
Ramsgate CT11 43 C2
St Pauls Av ME13 25 A3
St Pauls Cl DA10 29 F3
St Pauls Rd CT9 36 D2
St Pauls St ME10 48 A2
St Pauls Ter CT1 16 D4
St Peter St,
Maidstone ME16 35 A3
St Peter St,
Rochester ME1 44 D4
St Peters Cl DA10 29 F3
St Peters Ct,
Broadstairs CT10 15 B3
St Peters Ct,
Faversham ME13 25 A3
St Peters Footpath CT1 36 C3
St Peters Gro CT1 16 A3
St Peters La CT1 16 B3
St Peters Park Rd CT10 15 B3

St Peters Path*,
King St ME1 44 D4
St Peters Pl CT1 16 A3
St Peters Rd,
Broadstairs CT10 15 A3
St Peters Rd,
Margate CT9 36 C4
St Peters St,
Canterbury CT1 16 B2
St Peters St,
Sandwich CT13 45 D1
St Peters St,
Whitstable CT5 59 A2
St Philips Av ME15 35 C5
St Radigunds Pl CT1 16 C1
St Radigunds St CT1 16 C2
St Richards Rd CT14 22 A5
St Stephens Rd CT2 16 B1
St Stephens St ME16 35 A6
St Stephens St TN9 55 B4
St Theresas Cl TN24 12 B3
St Thomas Rd DA11 39 D5
St Thomas's Av DA11 28 B5
St Vincents Av DA1 21 D2
St Vincents Cl CT5 59 B5
St Vincents Rd DA1 21 D4
St Welcumes Way ME17 30 C2
St Williams Way ME1 44 D6
Salem Pl DA11 39 C3
Salem St ME15 35 C5
Salisbury Av,
Broadstairs CT10 15 B5
Salisbury Av,
Ramsgate CT11 43 B3
Salisbury Av,
Swanley BR8 53 E3
Salisbury Rd,
Chatham ME4 18 C5
Salisbury Rd, Deal CT14 22 B6
Salisbury Rd,
Dover CT15 41 C5
Salisbury Rd,
Maidstone ME14 35 C1
Salisbury Rd,
Whitstable CT5 59 A4
Sally Port ME7 18 C2
Sally Port Gdns ME7 18 C2
Salmestone Rd CT9 36 C5
Salmon Cres ME12 37 A3
Salt Marsh La CT5 59 A2
Salters La ME13 25 D6
Saltings Rd ME6 49 C4
Salts Cl CT5 59 A3
Salts Dr CT10 15 A3
Saltway Ct CT5 59 A4
Saltwood Gdns CT9 19 D3
Saltwood Rd ME15 35 B6
Samphire Ct CT16 23 C1
Samuel Mews TN29 34 C1
Sanctuary Cl,
Broadstairs CT10 15 B6
Sanctuary Cl,
Dartford DA1 21 A3
Sanctuary Rd ME8 27 D5
Sanderling Way DA9 29 A2
Sanders Ct ME12 37 A4
Sanderson Way TN9 55 D3
Sandgate Ct ME8 42 B6
Sandgate Rd CT20 26 A4
Sandles Rd CT7 14 C2
Sandling Rd,
Hythe CT21 33 A1
Sandling Rd,
Maidstone ME14 35 B2
Sandown Dr CT6 32 A2
Sandown Rd,
Deal CT14 22 C1
Sandown Rd,
Sandwich CT13 45 E2
Sandpiper Cl DA9 29 A2
Sandpit Rd DA1 21 A1
Sandringham Mews
TN4 50 D6
Sandway Rd ME17 30 C3
Sandwich By-Pass CT13 45 A2
Sandwich
Ind Est CT13 **45 E1**
Sandwich Rd CT13 45 A3
Sandwood Rd,
Ramsgate CT11 43 C1
Sandwood Rd,
Sandwich CT13 45 C2
Sandy Bank Rd DA12 28 C4
Sandy La,
Sevenoaks TN13 46 D3
Sandy La,
Snodland ME6 49 A4
Sandy La,
Tenterden TN30 54 B5
Sandy La,
Westerham TN16 57 D4
Sandy Ridge TN15 13 C5
Sandycroft Rd ME2 52 B2
Sanger Cl CT9 36 B4
Sanspareil Av ME12 37 A4
Sappers Walk ME7 27 A3

Sara Cres DA9 29 B1
Sarah Gdns CT9 19 C5
Sarre Pl CT13 45 D2
Saunders Cl DA11 39 D5
Saunders St,
Chatham ME4 18 B5
Saunders St,
Gillingham ME7 27 A2
Saunders Way DA1 21 C6
Savoy Rd DA1 21 A2
Sawyers Ct ME4 18 C6
Saxon Av ME12 37 B3
Saxon Cl,
Gravesend DA11 39 C6
Saxon Cl,
Rochester ME2 52 B2
Saxon Pl ME2 52 B6
Saxon Rd,
Faversham ME13 25 C3
Saxon Rd,
Westgate-on-Sea CT8 58 C2
Saxon St CT17 23 B2
Saxons Dr ME14 35 D1
Saxton St ME7 18 D3
Sayer Cl DA9 29 A2
Sayer Rd TN27 17 B2
Sayers La TN30 54 B5
Scanlons Bridge Rd
CT21 33 A3
Scarborough Dr ME12 37 B1
School App TN15 13 B1
School Av ME7 27 B4
School Fld TN8 24 B4
School La,
Ramsgate CT11 43 B4
School La,
Staplehurst TN12 51 C3
School La, Swanley BR8 53 F1
School La,
Tonbridge TN11 55 B2
School Rd,
Ashford TN27 17 B2
School Rd,
Faversham ME13 25 B3
School Rd,
Gravesend DA12 28 C6
School Rd, Hythe CT21 33 A2
School Rd,
Sandwich CT13 45 C1
School Rd,
Sittingbourne ME10 48 D4
School Ter TN18 31 B1
Schrieber Mews ME7 27 B3
Scocles Rd ME12 37 C4
Scotney Gdns ME16 42 C2
Scott Av ME8 27 B5
Scott St ME14 35 C5
Scotteswood Av ME4 18 B6
Scotton St TN25 60 C5
Scotts Terr ME14 18 B6
Scrapsgate ME12 37 A3
Sea App CT10 15 D4
Sea St, Dover CT14 58 D2
Sea St, Herne Bay CT6 32 A2
Sea St, Whitstable CT5 59 A2
Sea View Av CT7 14 B1
Sea View Rd,
Birchington CT7 14 B1
Sea View Rd,
Broadstairs CT10 15 C2
Sea View Rd,
Dover CT15 41 C6
Sea View Sq CT6 32 B1
Sea View Ter CT9 36 A3
Sea Wall CT5 59 A2
Seabrook Rd,
Hythe CT21 33 D3
Seabrook Rd,
Hythe CT21 55 A1
Seacroft Rd CT10 15 C6
Seacroft Rd CT10 15 C6
Seagrave Cres CT19 26 F1
Seal Hollow Rd TN13 46 C5
Seal Rd TN14 46 C2
Seapoint Rd CT10 15 D5
Seaside Av ME12 37 C2
Seathorpe Av ME12 37 D2
Seaton Av CT21 33 A3
Seaton Rd ME7 27 B5
Seaview Rd ME7 27 A4
Second Av,
Gillingham ME7 27 C5
Second Av,
Margate CT9 19 A2
Second Av,
Queenborough ME11 41 A3
Second Av,
Sheerness ME12 47 C4
Seeshill Cl CT5 59 B4
Selah Dr BR8 53 A1
Selbourne Rd CT9 19 A5
Selbourne Rd ME13 25 C2
Selway Ct CT14 22 B5
Selwyn Dr CT10 15 A3

Semaphore Rd CT7 14 C2
Semple Gdns ME4 18 A6
Sene Pk CT21 33 D2
Sermon Dr BR8 53 A2
Serpentine Ct TN13 46 D3
Serpentine Rd TN13 46 D4
Sessions House Sq
ME14 35 B2
Setterfield Rd CT9 36 C4
Seven Stones Dr CT10 43 D2
Sevenacre Rd ME13 25 C1
Sevenoaks TN13 46 A5
Sevenoaks
Bsns Centre TN14 **46 C1**
Sevenoaks Rd TN15 13 A5
Sewell Cl CT7 14 D3
Sexburga Dr ME12 37 B1
Sextant Pk ME2 **18 A2**
Seymour Av,
Margate CT9 58 D2
Seymour Av,
Whitstable CT5 59 A3
Seymour Rd ME5 18 D5
Seymour Walk ME14 29 E4
Shaftesbury Ct CT14 22 C6
Shaftesbury Rd,
Tunbridge Wells TN4 50 C6
Shaftesbury Rd,
Whitstable CT5 59 A3
Shaftsbury St CT11 43 C4
Shakespeare Rd,
Birchington CT7 14 D2
Shakespeare Rd,
Gillingham ME7 27 A5
Shakespeare Rd,
Margate CT9 36 C3
Shakespeare Rd,
Sittingbourne ME10 48 D3
Shakespeare Ter CT20 26 B3
Sheerness
Harbour Est ME12 **47 A3**
Sheerways ME13 25 A3
Sheet Glass Rd ME11 41 B3
Sheffield Gdns CT14 22 C4
Sheffield Rd TN4 50 C1
Shelden Dr ME8 42 B2
Shelley Rise ME1 44 B5
Shellons St CT20 26 C2
Shenley Rd DA1 21 D3
Shepherd St DA11 39 C3
Shepherds Gate CT2 16 A1
Shepherds La DA1 21 A3
Sheppey Cl CT7 14 D3
Sheppey St ME12 47 B2
Sheppy Pl DA12 28 B3
Shepway Cl CT19 26 C1
Sherbourne Dr ME2 52 C2
Sheridan Cl BR8 53 D3
Sheridan Rd DA1 21 D1
Sheron Cl CT14 22 A3
Sherway Cl TN27 31 D5
Sherwood Cl,
Faversham ME13 25 B1
Sherwood Cl,
Whitstable CT5 59 A6
Sherwood Gdns CT11 43 B1
Sherwood Rd CT7 14 C4
Ship La ME1 18 A4
Ship St ST19 26 C1
Shipbourne Rd TN10 55 C1
Shipwrights Lee CT5 59 D4
Shirley Av CT11 43 B1
Shirley Cl DA1 21 A1
Shirlings ME8 42 D1
Shoreham La TN30 54 A1
Shorncliffe Rd CT20 26 A2
Short St, Chatham ME4 18 D5
Short St,
Sandwich CT13 45 D2
Short St,
Sheerness ME12 47 C2
Shortlands Rd ME10 48 D3
Shorts Reach ME1 44 B4
Shorts Way ME1 44 A6
Shottendane Rd CT9 36 A6
Shottenden Rd ME7 27 B1
Shrubbery Rd DA12 28 C4
Shrubcote TN30 54 C5
Shrublands Ct TN9 55 C2
Shrubsole Av ME12 47 D3
Shurland Av,
Sheerness ME12 37 B3
Shurland Av,
Sittingbourne ME10 48 B6

Shurlock Av BR8 53 B2
Shutler Rd CT10 15 D3
Shuttle Cl TN27 13 C2
Sidney Rd ME7 27 A1
Signal Ct ME8 42 C1
Silk Mills Cl TN11 46 D2
Silver Av CT7 14 E4
Silver Cl TN9 55 A6
Silver Hill,
Chatham ME4 18 B5
Silver Hill,
Tenterden TN30 54 C3
Silver St CT14 22 D1
Silverdale Av DA1 37 A3
Silverdale Dr ME8 42 B3
Silverspot Cl ME8 42 B3
Simon Av CT9 19 C3
Simone Weil Av TN24 12 B2
Simpson Rd ME6 49 B4
Sinclair Cl ME8 42 A6
Singapore Dr ME7 18 C3
Singlewell Rd DA11 28 B6
Sion Hill CT11 43 B5
Sir Davids Pk TN4 50 B3
Sir John Hawkins Wy
ME4 18 B4
Sir John Moore Av CT21 33 A3
Sir Thomas Longley Rd
ME2 18 A1
Siskin Gdns TN12 40 C5
Sissinghurst Rd TN27 13 A2
Sittingbourne
Ind Pk ME10 **48 B2**
Sittingbourne Rd ME14 35 C3
Six Bells La TN13 46 C6
Six Flds Path TN30 54 B6
Six Penny Cl TN8 24 C5
Skene Cl ME8 42 D1
Skeynes Rd TN8 24 B5
Skinner Rd TN29 34 C2
Skinner St,
Chatham ME4 18 B5
Skinner St,
Gillingham ME7 27 A3
Skinners Alley CT5 59 A2
Skinners La TN8 24 C3
Skinners Ter TN9 55 B4
Skippers Cl DA9 29 B1
Slaney Rd ME12 51 C3
Slatin Rd ME2 52 C3
Slicketts Hill ME4 18 C4
Sling Ct ME8 42 D1
Slip Mill Rd TN18 31 A1
Slip Pass CT17 23 C2
Slipway Rd ME4 47 B1
Smack Alley ME13 25 D2
Smallhythe Rd TN30 54 A6
Smarden Rd TN27 31 D5
Smarden Walk ME8 42 D1
Smarts Rd DA12 28 C6
Smeed Cl ME10 48 D3
Smetham Gdns ME2 52 C2
Smith St ME2 52 C5
Smithers Cl TN15 17 C5
Smithfield TN8 24 D3
Smugglers TN18 31 C2
Smugglers Way CT7 14 E1
Smugglers Wharf DA9 29 B1
Snargate St CT17 23 B3
Snodland By-Pass ME6 49 C1
Snodland Rd ME6 49 A4
Snowdon Av ME14 35 D3
Snowdon Par ME14 35 D3
Solomans La ME13 25 D3
Solomon Cl CT14 22 B5
Solomon Ho CT14 22 B5
Solomon Rd ME8 42 C1
Solomons Rd ME4 18 B4
Somerhill Rd TN9 55 D4
Somerset Rd,
Ashford TN24 12 C4
Somerset Rd, Deal CT14 22 B5
Somerset Rd,
Tunbridge Wells TN4 50 C5
Somerville Gdns TN4 56 A2
Somerville Rd DA1 21 C3
Sondes Rd CT14 22 D3
Sopers La TN18 31 A1
Sorrell Cl TN8 24 C3
Sort Mill Rd ME6 49 D3
South Av ME10 48 C4
South Bank,
Tonbridge TN12 51 B4
South Bank,
Westerham TN16 57 C5
South Bush La ME8 42 D5
South Cl CT1 16 C3
South Cliff Par CT10 15 C6
South Ct CT14 22 D2
South Eastern Rd,
Ramsgate CT11 43 A4
South Eastern Rd,
Rochester ME2 52 B5
South Gro TN1 56 B5
South Hill Rd DA12 28 C4
South Kent Av CT11 39 B2
South Lodge Cl TN5 60 D6

South Military Rd CT17 23 A4
South Par CT14 22 D2
South Pard Rd ME15 35 D6
South Pk TN13 46 B6
South Rd,
Chatham ME4 18 C1
South Rd, Dover CT14 23 A1
South Rd,
Faversham ME13 25 C3
South Rd,
Herne Bay CT6 32 C2
South Rd, Hythe CT21 33 B5
South Rd,
Tonbridge TN12 34 C5
South St, Deal CT14 22 D2
South St,
Folkestone CT20 26 E3
South St,
Gravesend DA12 28 B3
South St,
Queenborough ME11 41 A1
South St,
Romney Marsh TN29 34 C2
South St,
Whitstable CT5 59 D3
South Stour Av TN23 12 C6
South View CT5 59 A6
South Wall CT1 22 A1
Southbourne Rd CT19 26 F1
Southern Pl BR8 53 B3
Southern Way CT20 26 E1
Southfield Rd TN4 50 C5
Southfields ME1 44 C6
Southfields Way TN4 50 D4
Southgate Rd TN30 54 C5
Southill Rd ME4 18 B5
Southsea Av ME12 37 B1
Southsea Dr CT6 32 A3
Southview Cl BR8 53 C3
Southview Gdns ME12 47 D4
Southwall Rd CT14 22 B1
Southwall Rd
Ind Est CT14 **22 B1**
Southwold Pl CT14 58 B4
Southwood Av TN4 50 D5
Sovereign Blvd ME8 27 C6
Sovereigns Way TN9 55 C3
Sowell St CT10 15 B3
Spa Cl TN11 17 C5
Spanton Cres CT21 33 A3
Speedwell Cl,
Edenbridge TN8 24 C3
Speedwell Cl,
Gillingham ME7 27 C3
Speke Rd CT10 15 A2
Speldhurst Rd TN3 50 A3
Spencer Mews,
Madeira Park TN1 56 B5
Spencer Mews,
Tunbridge Wells TN1 56 D2
Spencer Rd CT7 14 D1
Spencer Sq CT11 43 A5
Spencer St DA11 28 B3
Spenser Rd CT6 32 B2
Spielman Rd DA1 21 C1
Spillett Cl ME13 25 C3
Spinners Cl TN27 13 C1
Spire Av CT5 59 D4
Spire Cl DA12 28 B4
Spital St DA1 21 B3
Spitalfield La TN28 38 A3
Sports Field ME14 35 D2
Spring Gdns CT11 16 A6
Spring Gro DA12 28 C4
Spring Pl TN4 50 B2
Spring Vale North DA1 21 B3
Spring Vale South DA1 21 B4
Spring Walk CT5 59 A5
Springfield Av,
Maidstone ME14 35 A1
Springfield Av,
Swanley BR8 53 E4
Springfield Av,
Tenterden TN30 54 C2
Springfield Cl CT11 43 B5
Springfield
Ind Est TN18 **31 B1**
Springfield Pass CT21 33 A3
Springfield Quays ME14 35 A1
Springfield Rd,
Edenbridge TN8 24 B5
Springfield Rd,
Gillingham ME7 27 B2
Springfield Rd,
Margate CT9 19 D2
Springfield Rd,
Sittingbourne ME10 48 A2
Springfield Rd,
Tunbridge Wells TN4 50 C2
Springfield Ter ME4 18 B4
Springhead
Enterprise Pk DA11 **39 B4**
Springhead Rd,
Faversham ME13 25 C1

Springhead Rd,
  Gravesend DA11 — 39 B4
Springvale ME16 — 35 A4
Springvale Cl DA11 — 39 B5
Springwell Rd TN9 — 55 B5
Springwood Ct TN28 — 38 B3
Sprucedale Cl BR8 — 53 C1
Square Hill ME15 — 35 D4
Square Hill Rd ME15 — 35 C4
Squerryes Mede TN16 — 57 B6
Stable Ct ME13 — 25 D3
Stace Cl TN30 — 54 C2
Staces Cotts TN12 — 40 B5
Stacey Rd TN10 — 55 A1
Staceys St ME14 — 35 B2
Stackfield TN8 — 24 C3
Stade St CT21 — 33 B4
Stafford Cl,
  Ashford TN23 — 12 A4
Stafford Cl,
  Greenhithe DA9 — 29 A2
Stafford Rd TN9 — 55 B2
Stafford St ME7 — 27 A3
Staffordshire St CT11 — 43 B4
Stagshaw Cl ME15 — 35 C6
Staines Pl,
  Broadstairs CT10 — 15 D3
Staines Pl,
  Canterbury CT1 — 16 C4
Staleys Acre TN15 — 13 A5
Staleys Rd TN15 — 13 A6
Stanbridge Rd TN8 — 24 B4
Standen St TN4 — 50 C6
Stangate Quarry Rd TN15 — 13 A5
Stangrove Ct TN8 — 24 B4
Stangrove Rd TN8 — 24 B5
Stanhope Av ME10 — 48 C4
Stanhope Rd, Deal CT14 — 22 C2
Stanhope Rd,
  Strood ME2 — 52 C3
Stanhope Rd,
  Swanscombe DA10 — 29 F2
Stanley Av,
  Queenborough ME11 — 41 B2
Stanley Av,
  Sheerness ME12 — 37 E3
Stanley Cl TN12 — 51 B3
Stanley Gdns CT6 — 32 C3
Stanley Pl CT11 — 43 A3
Stanley Rd,
  Broadstairs CT10 — 15 B2
Stanley Rd, Deal CT14 — 22 D3
Stanley Rd,
  Gillingham ME7 — 27 A2
Stanley Rd,
  Herne Bay CT6 — 32 C2
Stanley Rd,
  Marden TN12 — 34 C5
Stanley Rd,
  Margate CT9 — 36 D2
Stanley Rd,
  Ramsgate CT11 — 43 A3
Stanley Rd,
  Swanscombe DA10 — 29 F2
Stanley Rd,
  Tonbridge TN11 — 50 D6
Stanley Rd,
  Whitstable CT5 — 59 A5
Stanley Sykes Cl CT9 — 19 A5
Staple Cl ME10 — 48 A1
Staple Ford Ct TN13 — 46 A4
Staplehurst Av CT10 — 15 C6
Staplehurst Rd ME10 — 48 A1
Star Hill ME1 — 44 D4
Star Mill Ct ME5 — 27 B6
Star Mill La ME5 — 27 B6
Starboard Av DA9 — 29 C3
Starnes Ct ME14 — 35 B3
Station App,
  Ashford TN27 — 31 C5
Station App,
  Birchington CT7 — 14 D2
Station App,
  Edenbridge TN8 — 24 C4
Station App,
  Maidstone ME16 — 35 A4
Station App,
  New Romney TN28 — 38 D4
Station App,
  Sevenoaks TN15 — 13 B5
Station App,
  Staplehurst TN12 — 51 B1
Station App,
  Swanley BR8 — 53 C3
Station App,
  Tonbridge TN12 — 40 C3
Station Approach Rd CT11 — 43 A3
Station Chine CT6 — 32 B2
Station Ct TN15 — 13 B5
Station Ind Est TN30 — 54 A5
Station Par,
  Birchington CT7 — 14 D2

Station Par,
  Sevenoaks TN13 — 46 B4
Station Pl ME10 — 48 B3
Station Rd,
  Ashford TN23 — 12 C5
Station Rd,
  Birchington CT7 — 14 D2
Station Rd,
  Charing TN27 — 17 B3
Station Rd, Dover CT15 — 41 B4
Station Rd,
  Edenbridge TN8 — 24 B2
Station Rd,
  Faversham ME13 — 25 D3
Station Rd,
  Gillingham ME8 — 42 B2
Station Rd,
  Gravesend DA11 — 39 A1
Station Rd,
  Gravesend DA13 — 39 A6
Station Rd,
  Greenhithe DA9 — 29 A1
Station Rd,
  Harrietsham ME17 — 30 B1
Station Rd,
  Headcorn TN27 — 31 B5
Station Rd,
  Herne Bay CT6 — 32 B1
Station Rd, Hythe CT21 — 33 C3
Station Rd,
  Lenham ME17 — 32 B6
Station Rd,
  Maidstone ME14 — 35 B3
Station Rd,
  Margate CT9 — 36 A3
Station Rd,
  New Romney TN28 — 38 C3
Station Rd,
  Romney Marsh TN29 — 34 C2
Station Rd,
  Sevenoaks TN15 — 13 B5
Station Rd,
  Staplehurst TN12 — 51 B1
Station Rd, Strood ME2 — 52 D3
Station Rd,
  Swanley BR8 — 53 D3
Station Rd,
  Tenterden TN30 — 54 A5
Station Rd,
  Tonbridge TN12 — 40 C3
Station Rd,
  Westgate-on-Sea CT8 — 58 C2
Station Rd,
  Whitstable CT5 — 59 B1
Station Rd East CT1 — 16 A5
Station Rd West CT2 — 16 A2
Station Road Mews TN30 — 54 A5
Stede St ME10 — 48 B3
Stede Hill ME17 — 30 C1
Steele Av DA9 — 29 A2
Steele St ME2 — 52 C3
Steerforth Cl ME1 — 44 C6
Steers Pl TN11 — 17 B4
Stella Cl TN12 — 34 B5
Stembrook CT16 — 23 C2
Step Style ME10 — 48 D5
Stephen Cl CT10 — 15 C4
Stephens Cl,
  Faversham ME13 — 25 B2
Stephens Cl,
  Margate CT9 — 58 E3
Stephens Rd TN4 — 50 D6
Sterling Cl CT10 — 15 A3
Sterling Rd ME11 — 41 B1
Sterndale Rd DA1 — 21 C4
Steven Cl ME4 — 18 C6
Stevens Cl ME6 — 49 C2
Stevenson Cl ME15 — 35 B5
Stiles Cl ME12 — 37 A3
Still La TN4 — 50 C1
Stirling Cl,
  Gillingham ME8 — 42 A6
Stirling Cl,
  Rochester ME1 — 44 A6
Stockbury Gdns CT9 — 19 D3
Stockdale Gdns CT14 — 22 B4
Stockland Green Rd TN3 — 50 A2
Stoke Pl ME16 — 35 C5
Stonar Cl,
  Ramsgate CT11 — 43 B1
Stonar Cl,
  Sandwich CT13 — 45 D1
Stonar Gdns CT13 — 45 E1
Stonar Rd CT13 — 45 E1
Stone Barn Av CT7 — 14 E3
Stone Cross Lees CT13 — 45 D3
Stone Ct CT21 — 33 A3
Stone St CT10 — 15 D3
Stone St,
  Cranbrook TN17 — 20 C4
Stone St,
  Faversham ME13 — 25 C3
Stone St,
  Gravesend DA11 — 28 B2

Stone St,
  Tunbridge Wells TN1 — 56 D1
Stonebridge Rd DA11 — 39 A1
Stonebridge Way ME13 — 25 B3
Stonedane Ct ME13 — 25 C2
Stonegate TN25 — 60 C5
Stonehorse La ME2 — 52 C1
Stonely Cres DA9 — 29 D1
Stones Cross Rd BR8 — 53 A4
Stonewood Cl TN4 — 50 C3
Stoney Alley ME5 — 18 D5
Stoney Path CT14 — 22 C4
Stoneyfield TN8 — 24 C3
Stopford Rd ME7 — 27 A5
Stour Cl ME2 — 52 A4
Stour Ct CT13 — 45 C1
Stour St CT1 — 16 A4
Stour Villas CT1 — 16 B4
Stourfields TN24 — 12 D2
Strand Approach Rd ME7 — 27 C1
Strand St CT13 — 45 C1
Strangford Rd CT5 — 59 C2
Stratford La ME8 — 42 C2
Stratton Ter TN16 — 57 C5
Straw Mill Hill ME15 — 35 A6
Strawberry Flds BR8 — 53 C1
Strawberry Vale TN9 — 55 C4
Stream Walk CT5 — 59 B2
Streetfield TN8 — 24 C5
Streete Court Rd CT8 — 58 C3
Streete Ct CT8 — 58 C3
Streetfield Rd ME8 — 42 B1
Stringer Dr CT7 — 14 E4
Strode Cres ME12 — 47 D2
Strond St CT17 — 23 B3
Strood Retail Pk ME2 — 52 C4
Strover St ME7 — 27 A1
Stuart Cl ME14 — 35 D1
Stuart Rd,
  Gillingham ME7 — 27 B5
Stuart Rd,
  Gravesend DA11 — 28 B2
Sturdee Av ME7 — 27 B4
Sturdy Cl CT21 — 33 C4
Sturges Rd TN24 — 12 C3
Sturla Rd ME4 — 18 C6
Style Cl ME8 — 42 A6
Styles Ct TN12 — 40 C3
Sudbury Pl CT8 — 58 B3
Suffolk Av,
  Gillingham ME8 — 42 B1
Suffolk Av,
  Westgate-on-Sea CT8 — 58 B3
Suffolk Ct ME8 — 42 B1
Suffolk Dr TN23 — 12 B5
Suffolk Mews TN1 — 56 B3
Suffolk Rd, Dartford DA1 — 21 B3
Suffolk Rd,
  Gravesend DA12 — 28 D2
Suffolk St CT5 — 59 A4
Suffolk Way TN13 — 46 C5
Sugar Loaf Hill ME5 — 27 A6
Summer Cl TN30 — 54 D4
Summerhill Av TN4 — 50 B2
Summerhill Rd DA1 — 21 B4
Summerville Av ME12 — 37 A4
Supper Way ME13 — 25 A2
Sun La,
  Gravesend DA12 — 28 C5
Sun La, Hythe CT21 — 33 C3
Sun St CT11 — 16 C3
Sunburst Cl TN12 — 34 B5
Sunderland Cl ME1 — 44 A6
Sunderland Dr ME8 — 42 C2
Sunderland Quay ME2 — 44 D2
Sundew Gro CT11 — 43 B3
Sunningdale Cl ME8 — 42 A4
Sunningdale Cl ME15 — 35 D4
Sunningdale Dr ME8 — 42 A4
Sunninghill DA11 — 39 D5
Sunny Bank ME10 — 48 D2
Sunnyfields Cl ME8 — 42 B3
Sunnymead Av ME7 — 27 C3
Sunnyside TN8 — 24 B2
Sunnyside Av ME12 — 37 A3
Sunnyside Gdns CT13 — 45 B3
Surrenden Rd TN12 — 51 B3
Surrey Gdns CT7 — 14 D2
Surrey Rd CT9 — 19 B2
Susans Hill TN26 — 60 A1
Sussex Av,
  Ashford TN24 — 12 C3
Sussex Av,
  Margate CT9 — 36 C4
Sussex Gdns,
  Birchington CT7 — 14 C3
Sussex Gdns,
  Westgate-on-Sea CT8 — 58 B2
Sussex Mews TN2 — 56 A6
Sussex Rd,
  Dartford DA1 — 21 D4

Sussex Rd,
  Folkestone CT19 — 26 C1
Sussex Rd,
  New Romney TN28 — 38 A3
Sussex Rd,
  Tonbridge TN9 — 55 A4
Sussex St CT11 — 43 B3
Sutherland Cl CT21 — 33 A4
Sutherland Dr CT7 — 14 E3
Sutherland Gdns ME8 — 48 C1
Sutherland Rd,
  Deal CT14 — 22 B2
Sutherland Rd,
  Tunbridge Wells TN1 — 56 C5
Sutton Cl ME8 — 48 C1
Sutton Ct TN12 — 34 B5
Sutton Forge TN12 — 34 B5
Swadelands Cl ME17 — 32 C5
Swaffield Rd TN13 — 46 D3
Swain Cl ME2 — 52 A3
Swain Rd TN30 — 54 C1
Swale Av,
  Queenborough ME11 — 41 A3
Swale Av,
  Sheerness ME12 — 47 C3
Swallow Cl CT9 — 36 A4
Swallowfields DA11 — 39 D6
Swan Bsns Pk DA1 — 21 A1
Swan Cl ME10 — 48 D3
Swan La TN8 — 24 B2
Swan Ridge TN8 — 24 C2
Swanfield Rd CT5 — 59 A3
Swanley By-Pass BR8 — 53 A1
Swanley Centre BR8 — 53 C2
Swanley La BR8 — 53 D2
Swanley Village Rd BR8 — 53 F1
Swanmead Way TN9 — 55 D2
Swanscombe Bsns Centre DA10 — 29 E1
Swanscombe St DA10 — 29 F3
Swanstree Av ME10 — 48 D5
Swanzy Rd TN14 — 46 C1
Sweetlands La TN12 — 51 D2
Sweyn Rd CT9 — 36 D2
Sweyne Rd DA10 — 29 F3
Swifts Vw TN17 — 20 C3
Swinburne Av CT10 — 15 B5
Swinford Gdns CT10 — 19 C5
Sycamore Cl,
  Gravesend DA12 — 28 D3
Sycamore Cl,
  Margate CT9 — 36 B5
Sycamore Cl,
  Romney Marsh TN29 — 34 C1
Sycamore Dr, Deal CT14 — 22 B4
Sycamore Dr,
  Swanley BR8 — 53 C2
Sycamore Gdns TN12 — 40 C5
Sycamore Grange CT11 — 43 C1
Sycamore Rd,
  Dartford DA1 — 21 A4
Sycamore Rd,
  Rochester ME2 — 52 A6
Sydenham Rd CT14 — 22 C1
Sydenham St CT5 — 59 A2
Sydney Rd,
  Chatham ME4 — 18 C5
Sydney Rd, Deal CT14 — 22 A6
Sydney Rd,
  Ramsgate CT11 — 43 A3
Sydney St,
  Whitstable CT5 — 59 B4
Sydney St TN23 — 12 C6
Sylvan Mews DA9 — 29 C1
Symmonds Dr ME10 — 48 D1
Symons Av ME4 — 18 B6
Syndale Pl CT11 — 43 C3

Taddy Gdns CT9 — 19 C5
Tadworth Rd TN24 — 12 D1
Tainter Rd TN11 — 17 B5
Talbot Pl DA11 — 28 B2
Talbot Rd,
  Cranbrook TN18 — 31 A3
Talbot Rd, Margate CT9 — 19 A4
Tamar Dr ME2 — 52 A5
Tams Gdns ME12 — 37 E3
Tangmere Cl ME7 — 27 D3
Tankerton Heights CT5 — 59 B1
Tankerton Mews CT5 — 59 B1
Tankerton Rd CT5 — 59 B1
Tanners Hill CT21 — 33 B2
Tanners Hill Gdns CT21 — 33 B2
Tanners Mead TN8 — 24 B5
Tanners St ME13 — 25 C3
Tannery La,
  Ashford TN23 — 12 C4
Tannery La,
  Sandwich CT13 — 45 C1
Tannery Rd TN9 — 55 C3
Tar Path CT14 — 22 B2
Tarbutts TN17 — 20 C5
Taswell Cl CT16 — 23 C1
Taswell Rd ME8 — 42 C1
Taswell St CT16 — 23 C1
Tates TN18 — 31 B2

Tatsfield Cl ME8 — 27 D6
Taunton Vale DA12 — 28 D6
Tavern Cl TN15 — 13 A5
Taverners Rd ME8 — 42 A3
Tavistock Cl ME8 — 42 B3
Tavistock Rd CT11 — 43 A1
Taylor Cl ME17 — 30 B2
Taylor Rd ME6 — 49 B3
Taylor St TN4 — 50 C3
Taylors La ME2 — 52 D4
Taylors Yd TN25 — 60 C5
Teardrop Ind Est BR8 — 53 F4
Teasels TN27 — 13 C2
Tedder Rd TN4 — 50 D4
Telegraph Rd CT14 — 22 B6
Telford St CT6 — 32 B1
Templar St CT17 — 23 A1
Templar Way TN23 — 12 A3
Templars Ct,
  Canterbury CT2 — 16 A2
Templars Ct,
  Edenbridge TN8 — 24 C3
Temple Gdns,
  Sittingbourne ME10 — 48 D4
Temple Gdns,
  Strood ME2 — 52 B5
Temple Hill DA1 — 21 C2
Temple Hill Sq DA1 — 21 D2
Temple Ind Est ME2 — 52 C5
Tennyson Rd ME7 — 27 A5
Tennyson Walk DA11 — 39 C6
Tensing Av DA11 — 39 D6
Tenterden Rd TN27 — 13 C2
Tenterden Way CT9 — 19 B5
Terrace Rd,
  Maidstone ME16 — 35 A4
Terrace Rd,
  Sittingbourne ME10 — 48 D3
Terrace St DA12 — 28 B2
Terrys La CT5 — 59 A2
Teynham Dr CT5 — 59 C2
Teynham Rd CT5 — 59 C2
Thames Av,
  Gillingham ME8 — 42 A2
Thames Av,
  Sheerness ME12 — 47 C3
Thames Gate DA1 — 21 D1
Thames Way,
  Gravesend DA11 — 28 A2
Thames Way,
  Northfleet DA11 — 39 A2
Thanet Place Gdns CT10 — 15 D2
Thanet Pl,
  Broadstairs CT10 — 15 C4
Thanet Rd, Margate CT9 — 36 C3
Thanet Rd,
  Ramsgate CT11 — 43 C3
Thanet Rd,
  Westgate-on-Sea CT8 — 58 B2
Thanet Way,
  Herne Bay CT6 — 32 A3
Thanet Way,
  Whitstable CT5 — 59 A6
Thatch Barn Rd TN27 — 31 C4
Thatcher Rd TN12 — 51 B2
The Abbots CT17 — 23 A1
The Acorns TN13 — 46 B4
The Avenue, Deal CT14 — 22 C1
The Avenue,
  Dover CT15 — 41 B4
The Avenue,
  Gravesend DA11 — 28 A4
The Avenue,
  Greenhithe DA9 — 29 B1
The Avenue, Hythe CT21 — 33 C4
The Avenue,
  Margate CT9 — 36 D3
The Avenue,
  Sevenoaks TN15 — 13 B4
The Avenue,
  Tonbridge TN9 — 55 B2
The Avenue,
  Westerham TN16 — 57 A1
The Banks CT10 — 15 B2
The Barges CT5 — 59 B1
The Bayle CT20 — 26 D3
The Beach CT14 — 22 D5
The Beeches TN29 — 34 D1
The Bines TN12 — 40 C5
The Birches,
  Swanley BR8 — 53 C1
The Birches,
  Tonbridge TN9 — 55 B5
The Borough CT1 — 16 C2
The Boulevard DA9 — 29 C1
The Bridge App CT5 — 59 C2
The Broadway,
  Broadstairs CT10 — 15 B3
The Broadway,
  Herne Bay CT6 — 32 A1
The Broadway,
  Sheerness ME12 — 37 B1
The Brook ME4 — 18 B3
The Burrs ME10 — 48 C4

The Butts, Sandwich CT13 45 C1
The Butts, Sittingbourne ME10 48 B3
The Causeway, Canterbury CT1 16 B1
The Causeway, Sandwich CT13 45 A1
The Cedars, Canterbury CT1 16 A5
The Cedars, Tonbridge TN12 40 C3
The Chain CT13 45 D2
The Chase, Ramsgate CT11 43 C2
The Chase, Tunbridge Wells TN2 56 D5
The Cherry Orch TN11 17 B5
The Chestnuts TN18 31 A3
The Churchlands TN28 38 B3
The Circus CT6 32 A3
The City Gdn CT1 16 C4
The Cloisters, Maidstone ME17 32 B5
The Cloisters, Ramsgate CT11 43 A5
The Cloisters, Sittingbourne ME10 48 A3
The Close, Ashford TN25 60 C6
The Close, Faversham ME13 25 C4
The Close, Hythe CT21 33 B2
The Close, Rochester ME1 44 C5
The Close, Sevenoaks TN15 13 B4
The Cobs TN30 54 A6
The Cockpit TN12 40 D4
The Colonnade TN18 31 B1
The Common ME1 44 C2
The Conifers CT14 22 A6
The Coppice CT21 33 A1
The Courts CT9 58 D2
The Courtyard CT14 22 B5
The Creek DA11 39 B1
The Crescent, Dover CT15 41 C6
The Crescent, Greenhithe DA9 29 C2
The Crescent, Sandwich CT13 45 C4
The Crescent, Sevenoaks TN15 13 B4
The Crescent, Tonbridge TN9 55 B2
The Crest TN17 20 C5
The Croft, Swanley BR8 53 A2
The Croft, Tenterden TN30 54 B5
The Crofters ME8 42 B3
The Curlews DA12 28 D5
The Dell DA9 29 B1
The Derings TN29 34 A2
The Downage DA11 28 A5
The Drive, Deal CT14 22 C3
The Drive, Sevenoaks TN13 46 B5
The Drive, Tonbridge TN9 55 B5
The Droveway CT15 14 D5
The Durlocks CT19 26 E2
The Exchange CT5 59 C1
The Fairings TN30 54 B5
The Fairway, Gravesend DA11 28 B6
The Fairway, Hythe CT21 33 C4
The Fairway, New Romney TN28 38 E3
The Fairway, Sittingbourne ME10 48 B6
The Fairways TN4 50 D4
The Ferns TN15 13 D5
The Fieldings ME8 48 B5
The Finches ME10 48 C4
The Flats DA9 29 C2
The Flyers Way TN16 57 D4
The Forstal, Ashford TN25 60 C5
The Forstal, Tonbridge TN11 17 C6
The Forum ME10 48 B3
The Freedown CT15 11 C4
The Freehold TN15 17 B5
The Friars CT1 16 B3
The Front CT15 41 D6
The Gateway CT16 23 D2
The Glade TN13 46 B3
The Glebe TN27 17 C2
The Glen, Sheerness ME12 37 B2
The Glen, Tunbridge Wells TN4 50 D1
The Graylings ME1 44 B6
The Green, Hythe CT21 33 A1

The Green, Romney Marsh TN29 34 B3
The Green, Sevenoaks TN13 46 D2
The Green, Westerham TN16 57 C5
The Green, Woodchurch TN26 60 B1
The Green, Wye TN25 60 C5
The Greenways TN13 40 B5
The Grove, Deal CT14 22 B2
The Grove, Gravesend DA12 28 C3
The Grove, Swanley BR8 53 D3
The Grove, Swanscombe DA10 29 F2
The Grove, Tonbridge TN9 55 C2
The Grove, Westgate-on-Sea CT8 58 C2
The Groves ME6 49 B3
The Halt CT5 59 D5
The Hampshires ME17 30 C4
The Haydens TN9 55 A1
The Hedgerows DA11 39 D5
The High St TN27 17 B3
The Hill, Ashford TN27 17 C2
The Hill, Cranbrook TN17 20 C5
The Hill, Gravesend DA11 39 C2
The Homestead DA1 31 A3
The Hoystings Cl CT1 16 D6
The Knole ME13 25 B2
The Lakes ME20 49 C6
The Landway TN15 13 B5
The Lapwings DA12 28 D5
The Larches, Faversham ME13 25 A2
The Larches, Whitstable CT5 59 A4
The Laxey ME15 35 A6
The Leas, Faversham ME13 25 B2
The Leas, Folkestone CT20 26 B4
The Lees ME12 37 C1
The Limes TN8 24 C5
The Lindens TN30 54 B4
The Lowry TN9 55 B4
The Mall ME13 25 C4
The Mallows ME14 35 A1
The Malthouses CT7 14 C2
The Maltings, Canterbury CT2 16 A1
The Maltings, Faversham ME13 25 D1
The Maltings, Gillingham ME8 42 C3
The Maltings, Tonbridge TN11 17 B6
The Maltings*, Station Ter TN16 57 C5
The Maples ME12 37 B3
The Meadows, Ashford TN27 13 C2
The Meadows, Maidstone ME15 35 A6
The Meadows, New Romney TN28 38 C3
The Meadows, Sittingbourne ME10 48 B5
The Meadway TN13 46 A3
The Mews, Ashford TN27 31 B5
The Mews, Calverley Park TN1 56 D4
The Mews, Maidstone ME16 35 A3
The Mews, Sevenoaks TN13 46 B4
The Mews, Sittingbourne ME10 48 B4
The Mews, Strood ME2 52 B4
The Mews, Tunbridge Wells TN1 56 D1
The Middlings TN13 46 A6
The Moat TN27 17 C3
The Moorings ME15 35 B5
The Mortocks ME14 35 B2
The Mount ME4 18 B4
The Musings TN27 17 C6
The Oaks, Broadstairs CT10 15 B1
The Oaks, Swanley BR8 53 C1
The Old Bailey ME17 30 C2
The Old High St CT20 26 E2
The Old Orchard ME8 42 C2
The Orchard BR8 53 B2
The Orchards DA1 21 C3
The Paddock, Chatham ME4 18 B4
The Paddock, Dover CT16 23 C1

The Paddock, Tonbridge TN11 17 B4
The Paddock, Westerham TN16 57 C5
The Paddocks, Ashford TN26 60 B2
The Paddocks, Broadstairs CT10 15 B1
The Paddocks, Margate CT9 19 C4
The Paddocks, Sevenoaks TN15 46 A4
The Pantiles TN4 56 A6
The Parade, Birchington CT7 14 A1
The Parade, Broadstairs CT10 15 D4
The Parade, Canterbury CT1 16 C3
The Parade, Folkestone CT20 26 D3
The Parade, Gravesend DA12 28 D5
The Parade, Margate CT9 36 B2
The Parade, Tonbridge TN12 51 C4
The Parkway CT7 14 E3
The Parrock DA12 28 C4
The Pathway CT10 15 C4
The Pavement TN30 54 B2
The Pavilion TN9 55 B3
The Plat TN8 24 C5
The Priory TN29 34 B2
The Promenade CT10 15 D5
The Quay CT13 45 D1
The Queen Mother Ct ME1 44 B5
The Quern ME15 35 A6
The Rendezvous CT9 36 C1
The Retreat TN7 14 E1
The Ridgeway, Broadstairs CT10 15 A5
The Ridgeway, Margate CT9 19 B4
The Ridgeway, Tonbridge TN10 55 D1
The Ridgewaye TN4 50 D2
The Ridings, Margate CT9 19 D2
The Ridings, Tonbridge TN12 40 C3
The Rise, Dover CT15 41 D4
The Rise, Greenhithe DA9 29 A3
The Rise, Rochester ME1 44 D6
The Rise, Sheerness ME12 41 D1
The Roundel ME10 48 B5
The Rowans ME12 37 B3
The Saltings, Greenhithe DA9 29 C1
The Saltings, New Romney TN28 38 F4
The Saltings, Whitstable CT5 59 A4
The Sandpipers DA12 28 D5
The School CT8 58 B2
The Shires TN12 40 C3
The Shore DA11 39 B1
The Sidings CT5 59 B1
The Slade TN9 55 B2
The Slip TN16 57 C5
The Spinney, Maidstone ME15 35 D5
The Spinney, Margate CT9 19 D4
The Spinney, Swanley BR8 53 C1
The Spinney, Tonbridge TN9 55 A5
The Spires DA1 21 A6
The Square, Birchington CT7 14 D3
The Square, Edenbridge TN8 24 C5
The Square, Maidstone ME17 32 D5
The Square, Swanley BR8 53 B2
The Square, Tonbridge TN11 17 C6
The Stade TN9 26 E3
The Staples BR8 53 F1
The Strand CT14 22 D3
The Street TN26 30 B6
The Tanyard TN17 20 C5
The Terrace, Chatham ME4 18 C1
The Terrace, Gravesend DA12 28 C2
The Terrace, Rochester ME1 44 D4
The Terrace, Tonbridge TN11 17 C6

The Tram Rd CT20 26 E2
The Turnstones DA12 28 D5
The Vale CT10 15 B4
The Vespers CT2 16 B1
The Viaduct CT17 23 B4
The Vine TN13 46 C5
The Vineries ME7 27 C3
The Vines CT5 59 A2
The Violets TN12 40 C5
The Wall ME10 48 B2
The Warren CT5 59 A6
The Warren Dr CT8 58 A4
The Weald TN24 12 C3
The Weavers TN27 13 C2
The Wheelwrights ME17 30 B2
The Willows ME12 37 B1
The Wynd TN27 17 D1
The Yews DA12 28 D5
Theatre Sq*, Bells La TN30 54 B5
Theatre St CT21 33 C3
Theobalds TN18 31 B2
Theodore Pl ME7 27 A3
Theresa Rd CT21 33 B5
Thicketts TN13 46 C4
Third Av, Gillingham ME7 27 C5
Third Av, Margate CT9 19 A2
Thirlmere Cl, Gillingham ME7 27 D3
Thirlmere Cl, Rochester ME2 52 D2
Thirlmere Rd TN4 50 A6
Thirza Rd DA1 21 D3
Thistle Hill Way ME12 37 C4
Thomas Dr DA12 28 D5
Thomas Rd, Faversham ME13 25 C2
Thomas Rd, Sittingbourne ME10 48 D3
Thomas St, Rochester ME1 44 D5
Thomas St, Tunbridge Wells TN4 50 C6
Thompson Cl ME8 42 C2
Thomson Cl ME6 49 C2
Thomson Rd TN24 12 B1
Thorn Gdns CT11 43 B1
Thorn Rd TN12 34 C6
Thornbridge Rd CT14 22 A4
Thornhill Pl ME14 35 B2
Thorold Rd ME5 18 D5
Thrale Way ME8 42 A6
Three Fields Path TN30 54 B6
Thunderland Rd CT6 32 D3
Thurlestone Ct ME14 35 B2
Thurston Pk CT5 59 B3
Tilden Gill Rd TN30 54 C6
Tilghman Way ME6 49 D2
Tillmans TN15 13 C6
Tilsden La TN17 20 D5
Tilton Rd TN15 13 A5
Timperley Cl CT14 22 A3
Tina Gdns CT10 15 C2
Tintagel Cl ME2 52 B4
Tintagel Gdns ME2 52 B4
Tippens CT17 20 C5
Tippledore La CT10 15 A3
Tithe Yd ME17 32 C6
Tivoli Brook CT9 36 B4
Tivoli Gdns DA12 28 B4
Tivoli Park Av CT9 36 B5
Tivoli Rd CT9 36 B5
Toby Gdns TN11 17 B6
Toledo Pad ME7 27 B3
Tolgate La ME2 52 C4
Toll Gate CT14 22 A4
Toll La TN27 17 D3
Tollgate Cl CT5 59 A4
Tollgate Mews TN15 13 C5
Tollgate Pl TN2 31 C5
Tolsey Mead TN15 13 C4
Tom Joyce Cl ME6 49 B4
Tomlin Cl, Snodland ME6 49 B2
Tomlin Cl, Tonbridge TN12 51 B2
Tomlin Dr CT9 19 C6
Tomsons Pas CT11 43 C4
Tonbridge By-Pass TN11 55 A6
Tonbridge Rd, Maidstone ME16 35 A4
Tonbridge Rd, Tonbridge TN11 17 A6
Tonge Rd ME10 48 D3
Tontine St CT20 26 D2
Tookey Rd TN30 38 B4
Tooley St DA11 39 C3
Tormore Mews CT14 22 A4
Toronto Rd ME7 27 C4
Torrington Rd TN23 12 C6
Tournay Cl TN23 12 A6
Tournay Rd TN29 34 A3
Tovil Green Bsns Centre ME15 35 A6

Tovil Hill ME15 35 A6
Tovil Rd ME15 35 A6
Tower Bungalows CT7 14 D1
Tower Gdns, Herne Bay CT6 32 B1
Tower Gdns, Hythe CT21 33 B4
Tower Hamlets Rd CT17 23 A1
Tower Hamlets St CT17 23 A1
Tower Hill, Dover CT17 23 A1
Tower Hill, Whitstable CT5 59 B1
Tower Par CT5 59 B1
Tower Rd, Dartford DA1 21 B1
Tower Rd, Whitstable CT5 59 B1
Tower St CT17 23 A1
Tower Way CT1 16 B3
Town Mdw TN17 20 C5
Town Walk CT20 26 C3
Townfield Cnr DA12 28 D4
Townland Cl TN27 13 C2
Townley St TN11 43 A5
Townsend Farm Rd CT15 41 B4
Townsend Rd ME6 49 A2
Townwall St CT16 23 C2
Trafalgar Rd, Dartford DA1 21 B6
Trafalgar Rd, Gravesend DA11 28 A3
Trafalgar St ME7 27 A3
Tramways ME5 27 A6
Transfesa Rd TN12 40 C1
Travers Rd CT14 22 A3
Trebble Rd DA10 29 E3
Tree Tops TN9 55 B6
Trevelyan Cl DA1 21 D1
Trevithick Dr DA1 21 C1
Tribune Ct ME12 47 C4
Trident Cl ME2 18 A1
Trinity TN9 36 C2
Trinity Cres CT20 26 A4
Trinity Ct, Deal CT14 22 A4
Trinity Ct, Dartford DA1 21 A4
Trinity Gdns, Dartford DA1 21 B3
Trinity Gdns, Folkestone CT20 26 A3
Trinity Hill CT9 36 C2
Trinity Pl, Deal CT14 22 A4
Trinity Pl, Ramsgate CT11 43 C3
Trinity Rd, Sheerness ME12 47 D2
Trinity Rd, Ashford TN24 12 C1
Trinity Rd, Folkestone CT20 26 A3
Trinity Rd, Gillingham ME7 27 A1
Trinity Rd, Gravesend DA12 28 C3
Trinity Rd, Sheerness ME12 47 D2
Trinity Sq CT9 36 C2
Tritton La TN8 38 B3
Trivett Cl DA9 29 A2
Trosley Av DA11 28 A3
Trotts Hall Gdns ME10 48 B4
Trotts La TN16 57 B5
Truro Rd, Gravesend DA12 28 D6
Truro Rd, Ramsgate CT11 43 C4
Tubs Hill TN13 46 B5
Tubs Hill Par TN13 46 B5
Tudeley La TN9 55 C5
Tudor Av ME14 35 D1
Tudor Cl, Birchington CT7 14 F2
Tudor Cl, Gravesend DA11 39 D4
Tudor Ct CT5 59 D1
Tudor Gro ME8 42 B2
Tudor Mews CT14 22 B4
Tufail Rd DA1 21 C3
Tufton Rd, Ashford TN24 12 D4
Tufton Rd, Gillingham ME8 42 B1
Tufton St, Ashford TN23 12 C4
Tufton St, Maidstone ME14 35 C3
Tulip Tree Cl TN9 55 A4
Tunnel Rd TN1 56 C1
Tunstall Rd ME10 48 A6
Tupman Cl ME1 44 B5
Turkey Ct ME15 35 D4
Turmine Ct ME12 37 A4
Turnagain La CT1 16 C3
Turnden Gdns CT9 19 D3
Turner Av TN17 20 C6
Turner Ct DA1 21 A2
Turner Ho DA12 28 C6

Turner St CT11 43 B4
Turners Av TN30 54 B4
Turners Cl ME12 47 D3
Turnpike Cl CT21 33 A3
Tutsham Way TN12 40 B3
Twiss Av CT11 33 C4
Twiss Gro CT21 33 C3
Twiss Rd CT21 33 C3
Twistleton Ct DA1 21 A3
Twyford Rd TN11 17 B5
Tyler Dr ME8 42 A6
Tyler Gro DA1 21 C1
Tyndale Pk CT6 32 D2
Tysoe Ct ME12 37 A4
Tyson Av CT9 58 D2

Ufton La ME10 48 A4
Ulcombe Rd TN27 31 B4
Ulster Rd CT9 54 B4
Underdown Rd CT6 32 C2
Underwood Cl ME15 35 B5
Union Cres CT9 36 C2
Union Ct, Deal CT14 22 C2
Union Rd, Ramsgate CT11 43 C2
Union Rd, Sheerness ME12 37 D3
Union Row CT9 36 C2
Union Sq TN4 56 A6
Union St, Canterbury CT1 16 D2
Union St, Chatham ME4 18 C4
Union St, Dover CT17 23 B3
Union St, Faversham ME13 25 D3
Union St, Maidstone ME14 35 B3
Union St, Ramsgate CT11 43 B4
Union St, Rochester ME1 44 C4
Union St, Sheerness ME12 47 B2
Unity Pl CT11 43 C3
Unity St ME10 48 A4
Upbury Way ME4 18 C4
Uplands Cl TN13 46 A4
Uplands Way, Sevenoaks TN13 46 A3
Uplands Way, Sheerness ME12 41 C1
Upper Approach Rd CT10 15 C5
Upper Brents ME13 25 D2
Upper Bridge St, Ashford TN25 60 C5
Upper Bridge St, Canterbury CT1 16 C5
Upper Britton Pl ME7 18 D3
Upper Chantry La CT1 16 D5
Upper Dane Rd CT9 19 A4
Upper Denmark Rd TN23 12 C6
Upper Dumpton Rd CT11 19 A4
Upper Dunstan Rd TN4 50 D5
Upper Field Rd ME10 48 D2
Upper Gro CT9 36 C2
Upper Grosvenor Rd, Tonbridge TN11 50 D6
Upper Grosvenor Rd, Tunbridge Wells TN1 56 C1
Upper Luton Rd ME5 18 D5
Upper Malthouse Hill CT21 33 B3
Upper Maltings Pl CT7 14 C2
Upper Rd ME15 35 C5
Upper St Anns Rd ME13 25 B4
Upper Stone St ME15 35 C4
Upper Strand St CT13 45 D2
Upton Rd CT10 15 B3
Uptons TN27 31 B4
Uridge Rd TN10 55 C1
Ursuline Dr CT8 58 A4
Usborne Cl TN12 51 B4

Vale Av, Southborough TN4 50 C2
Vale Av, Tunbridge Wells TN1 56 B4
Vale Ct TN4 50 C1
Vale Pl CT11 43 A4
Vale Rd, Broadstairs CT10 15 A4
Vale Rd, Cranbrook TN18 31 B1
Vale Rd, Gravesend DA11 39 C3
Vale Rd, Ramsgate CT11 43 A4
Vale Rd, Southborough TN4 50 C1
Vale Rd, Tonbridge TN9 55 B3
Vale Rd, Tunbridge Wells TN1 56 B4
Vale Rd, Whitstable CT5 59 B4

Vale Rise TN9 55 D4
Vale Sq CT11 43 A5
Valenciennes Rd ME10 48 A4
Valetta Way ME1 44 B4
Valley Dr, Gravesend DA12 28 D6
Valley Dr, Sevenoaks TN13 46 C6
Valley Dr, Tonbridge TN11 17 C4
Valley Gdns DA9 29 B3
Valley Heights*, Trevelyan Cl DA1 21 D1
Valley Rd, Broadstairs CT10 19 C6
Valley Rd, Gillingham ME7 27 A3
Valley Vw, Greenhithe DA9 29 B3
Valley Vw, Tunbridge Wells TN4 50 D1
Vange Mews ME1 44 B4
Vauxhall Cres ME6 49 B5
Vauxhall Gdns TN11 55 C5
Vauxhall La TN11 55 C6
Vauxhall Pl DA1 21 B4
Veles Rd ME6 49 B3
Vere Rd CT10 15 C4
Vereth Rd CT11 43 A4
Vernon Pl CT1 16 D5
Vernon Rd DA10 29 F3
Vesty Ct CT8 58 C2
Vicarage Cres CT9 36 C4
Vicarage Dr DA11 39 B2
Vicarage Hill TN16 57 C5
Vicarage La, Ashford TN23 12 C4
Vicarage La, Dover CT15 41 B5
Vicarage La, Faversham ME13 25 A4
Vicarage La, Sandwich CT13 45 D1
Vicarage Rd, Gillingham ME7 27 A3
Vicarage Rd, Sheerness ME12 37 D3
Vicarage Rd, Strood ME2 52 D3
Vicarage Rd, Tunbridge Wells TN4 50 C1
Vicarage St ME13 25 D2
Victor Av CT9 19 D3
Victoria Av, Broadstairs CT10 19 D6
Victoria Av, Dover CT15 41 D4
Victoria Av, Gravesend DA12 28 B3
Victoria Av, Hythe CT21 33 A4
Victoria Av, Margate CT9 19 A4
Victoria Av, Westgate-on-Sea CT8 58 C3
Victoria Cl TN8 24 C6
Victoria Cotts TN17 20 C4
Victoria Cres, Ashford TN23 12 C5
Victoria Cres, Dover CT17 23 B1
Victoria Cl ME16 35 A4
Victoria Gro CT20 26 C2
Victoria Ind Pk DA1 21 B2
Victoria Mews CT14 22 C2
Victoria Par, Broadstairs CT10 15 D5
Victoria Par, Deal CT14 22 D2
Victoria Par, Maidstone ME14 35 B2
Victoria Par, Ramsgate CT11 43 C4
Victoria Park Mews CT16 23 D1
Victoria Pk, Dover CT16 23 D1
Victoria Pk, Herne Bay TN6 32 C1
Victoria Pl ME13 25 C3
Victoria Rd, Ashford TN23 12 C5
Victoria Rd, Broadstairs CT10 15 A2
Victoria Rd, Chatham ME4 18 D6
Victoria Rd, Dartford DA1 21 B2
Victoria Rd, Deal CT14 22 D3
Victoria Rd, Edenbridge TN8 24 C6
Victoria Rd, Folkestone CT19 26 B2
Victoria Rd, Hythe CT21 33 B4
Victoria Rd, Margate CT9 36 C3
Victoria Rd, New Romney TN28 38 E4
Victoria Rd, Ramsgate CT11 43 B3
Victoria Rd, Sevenoaks TN13 46 C6
Victoria Rd, Southborough TN4 50 A2
Victoria Rd, Tonbridge TN11 17 D6
Victoria Rd, Tunbridge Wells TN1 56 C1
Victoria Rd Ind Est TN23 12 C5
Victoria Rd West TN28 38 E4
Victoria Row CT1 16 D1
Victoria St, Gillingham ME7 27 A3
Victoria St, Maidstone ME16 35 A4
Victoria St, New Romney TN28 38 B3
Victoria St, Rochester ME1 44 D4
Victoria St, Sheerness ME12 47 D4
Victoria St, Strood ME2 52 D4
Victoria St, Whitstable CT5 59 A2
Victoria Yd CT1 16 D2
Victory Bsns Pk ME2 44 D2
Victory St ME12 47 C2
Viewlands ME5 18 D5
Viking Cl CT7 14 A2
Viking Ct CT10 15 C5
Viking Rd DA11 39 B6
Villa Cl DA1 21 C5
Village Vw ME5 27 A6
Village Way TN26 38 C6
Villiers Ct CT17 23 A3
Vincent St ME4 47 D4
Vincent Gdns ME12 47 D4
Vincents Rd DA1 21 D3
Vine Av TN3 46 C5
Vine Cl CT11 43 B1
Vine Court Rd TN13 46 C4
Vine Lodge Ct TN13 46 B4
Vine Walk TN12 51 B4
Vinelands TN29 34 B2
Viners Cl ME10 48 B5
Vines La ME1 44 C3
Vineyard Cres ME8 42 D1
Vineys Gdns TN30 54 B5
Vinters Rd ME14 35 D3
Virginia Rd, Gillingham ME7 27 A1
Virginia Rd, Whitstable CT5 59 A4
Vulcan Cl CT5 59 A4

Wades Cl TN12 34 C5
Wadham Pl ME10 48 D5
Waghorn Rd ME6 49 C2
Waghorn St ME4 18 D6
Wagon La TN12 40 D1
Waid Cl DA1 21 D3
Wainhouse Cl TN8 24 C3
Wainwright Pl TN24 12 D6
Wakefield Rd DA9 29 C2
Wakefield Walk CT21 33 C4
Wakefield Way CT21 33 A5
Wakeley Rd ME8 42 C1
Waldeck Rd DA1 21 D3
Waldeck Rd CT10 15 C6
Waleys Cl ME8 42 D1
Walker La CT7 14 A2
Wall Rd TN24 12 C3
Wallace Gdns DA10 29 E3
Wallace Way CT10 15 A4
Wallers Rd ME13 25 A3
Wallis Pk DA11 39 A1
Wallwood Rd CT11 43 C2
Walmer Gdns, Deal CT14 22 A6
Walmer Gdns, Sittingbourne ME10 48 A2
Walmer Rd CT5 59 B4
Walmer Way CT14 22 A6
Walmsley Rd CT10 15 B3
Walner Gdns TN28 38 C2
Walner La TN28 38 C2
Walnut Cl TN12 40 C4
Walnut Tree Av DA1 21 B5
Walnut Tree Cl, Birchington CT7 14 D3
Walnut Tree Cl, Westerham TN16 57 C5
Walnut Way BR8 53 B1
Walpole Rd CT9 19 A4
Walters Farm Rd TN9 55 C3
Wansbury Way BR8 53 B4
Wanstall Ct CT7 14 D2
Wantsume Lees CT13 45 C1
Warblers Cl ME2 52 C4
Warden House Mews CT14 22 A4
Warden Rd ME1 44 C6
Wardona Ct DA10 29 F3
Wardour Cl CT10 15 C4

Wards Hill Rd ME12 37 B1
Warehorne Rd TN26 30 A6
Warlingham Cl ME8 42 D1
Warner St ME4 18 B5
Warnett Ct ME6 49 C2
Warren Cl TN13 46 C5
Warren Dr CT10 15 A3
Warren La TN24 12 B2
Warren Rd, Dartford DA1 21 C6
Warren Rd, Folkestone CT19 26 F1
Warren Rd, New Romney TN28 38 D3
Warren Retail Pk TN24 12 B2
Warren Vw TN25 12 A2
Warrington Rd TN12 40 B4
Warsop Ind Est TN8 24 D6
Warten Rd CT11 43 C1
Warwick Cl TN13 46 B6
Warwick Pk TN2 56 B6
Warwick Pl, Gravesend DA11 39 A1
Warwick Pl, Maidstone ME16 35 A4
Warwick Rd, Deal CT14 22 C6
Warwick Rd, Margate CT9 19 B3
Warwick Rd, Tunbridge Wells TN1 56 B5
Warwick Rd, Whitstable CT5 59 A2
Warwick Way DA1 21 C6
Wat Tyler Way ME15 35 C4
Watchmans Ter ME5 27 A6
Water La, Canterbury CT1 16 B4
Water La, Cranbrook TN18 31 D2
Water La, Faversham ME13 25 A6
Water La, Faversham ME13 25 D2
Water La, Westerham TN16 57 C6
Water Side Dr CT8 58 C2
Water Slippe TN11 17 B5
Water St CT11 22 C1
Watercress Cl TN14 46 D1
Watercress Dr TN14 46 D1
Waterdales DA11 39 C5
Waterlaakes TN8 24 C6
Waterloo Cres CT17 23 C3
Waterloo Hill ME12 37 D3
Waterloo P CT11 43 C4
Waterloo Pl, Cranbrook TN17 20 C4
Waterloo Pl, Tonbridge TN9 55 B4
Waterloo Rd, Cranbrook TN17 20 C3
Waterloo Rd, Gillingham ME7 27 A4
Waterloo Rd, Sittingbourne ME10 48 A2
Waterloo Rd, Tonbridge TN9 55 B4
Waterloo St, Whitstable CT5 59 A2
Waterloo St, Gravesend DA12 28 C3
Waterloo St, Maidstone ME15 35 C5
Waterlow Rd ME14 35 B3
Watermans La TN12 40 C6
Watermill Cl ME2 52 D3
Waters Edge ME15 35 B5
Waterside, Faversham ME13 25 D1
Waterside, Gravesend DA11 39 D2
Waterside, Maidstone ME15 35 B3
Waterside Ct ME2 18 A2
Waterside Gate ME16 35 A3
Waterside La ME7 27 D1
Waterstone Way DA9 29 A3
Watkins Cl TN12 51 B2
Watling Av ME5 27 B6
Watling Pl ME10 48 C4
Watling St, Canterbury CT1 16 B4
Watling St, Gillingham ME7 27 B6
Watling St, Gravesend DA11 39 A5
Watling St, Rochester ME2 52 A4
Watsons Hill ME10 48 A2
Watts Av ME1 44 C4
Watts Cl ME6 49 D2
Watts St ME4 18 A5
Watts Yd CT13 45 D2

Waverley Av ME12 37 B2
Waverley Rd CT9 58 F2
Waylands BR8 53 D3
Wayne Cl CT10 15 A3
Wayside TN30 54 C2
Wayside Av TN30 54 C1
Wayside Dr TN8 24 C3
Weald Ct ME10 48 A5
Weald View Rd TN9 55 B5
Wealden Av TN30 54 C3
Wealden Cl ME5 18 D6
Wear Bay Cres CT19 26 F2
Wear Bay Rd CT19 26 F2
Weatherly Cl ME1 44 C4
Weatherly Dr CT10 15 B6
Weavering Ct ME14 52 D1
Weavers Cl, Gravesend DA11 28 A4
Weavers Cl, Tonbridge TN12 51 C2
Weavers La TN14 46 D1
Webbs Alley TN13 46 D6
Webbs Mdw TN13 46 D6
Webster Rd ME8 42 B1
Week St ME14 35 B3
Weld Cl TN12 51 C3
Weldon Way DA9 29 B2
Well La CT15 41 B5
Well Rd, Maidstone ME14 35 C2
Well Rd, Queenborough ME11 41 A3
Well Rd, Queenborough ME11 41 B1
Wellcome Av DA1 21 C1
Weller Av ME1 44 D6
Wellers Cl TN16 57 C6
Wellesley Av CT14 22 C6
Wellesley Cl, Broadstairs CT10 15 A5
Wellesley Cl, Westgate-on-Sea CT8 58 C4
Wellesley Cl, Ashford TN24 12 C4
Wellesley Rd, Dover CT16 23 C2
Wellesley Rd, Margate CT9 19 A4
Wellesley Rd, Westgate-on-Sea CT8 58 C4
Wellington Cl CT8 58 B2
Wellington Cres CT11 43 C4
Wellington Pav CT14 22 C5
Wellington Pl, Maidstone ME14 35 B2
Wellington Pl, Tenterden TN30 54 B4
Wellington Rd, Dartford DA1 21 A3
Wellington Rd, Deal CT14 22 C3
Wellington Rd, Gillingham ME7 27 A4
Wellington Rd, Westgate-on-Sea CT8 58 C3
Wellington St DA12 28 C3
Wellingtonia Way TN8 24 B4
Wellis Gdns ME4 36 A4
Wells Cl, New Romney TN28 38 D3
Wells Cl, Tenterden TN30 54 A5
Wells Cl, Tonbridge TN10 55 D1
Wells Cl, Westerham TN16 57 C6
Wells Way ME13 25 B1
Wellwinch Rd ME10 48 A2
Welsdene Rd CT9 58 E3
Wentworth Av CT9 58 D2
Wentworth Dr ME8 42 A4
West Cliff CT5 59 A3
West Cliff Av CT10 15 C5
West Cliff Gdns CT20 26 D3
West Cliff Prom, Broadstairs CT10 15 C6
West Cliff Prom, Ramsgate CT11 43 A6
West Cliff Rd, Broadstairs CT10 15 C5
West Cliff Rd, Ramsgate CT11 43 A6
West Crescent Rd DA12 28 C2
West Cross TN30 54 A6
West Cross Gdns TN30 54 A5
West Cross Mews TN30 54 A6
West Dumpton La CT11 43 B1
West End TN3 34 A5
West Fld TN13 46 C2
West Hill DA1 21 A3
West Hill Dr DA1 21 A3
West Hill Rise DA1 21 A3
West Kent Av DA11 39 B2
West La, Sheerness ME12 47 B2
West La, Sittingbourne ME10 48 D3

West La
Trading Est ME10   **48 C2**
West Lea CT14   22 B1
West Lea Ct CT14   22 C1
West Mill DA11   28 A2
West Norman Rd CT16   23 D1
West Par CT21   33 B5
West Park Av,
   Margate CT9   19 C4
West Park Av,
   Tunbridge Wells TN4   50 C2
West Park Rd ME15   35 D5
West Rd ME4   18 C1
West Ridge ME10   48 A4
West Roman Ditch CT16   23 E1
West St, Ashford TN23   12 B4
West St, Deal CT14   22 C1
West St, Dover CT17   23 A1
West St,
   Faversham ME13   25 C2
West St,
   Gillingham ME7   27 B2
West St,
   Gravesend DA11   28 B2
West St,
   Maidstone ME17   30 A2
West St,
   New Romney TN28   38 A3
West St,
   Queenborough ME11   41 A1
West St, Rochester ME2   52 D2
West St,
   Sheerness ME12   47 B2
West St,
   Sittingbourne ME10   48 A3
West Ter CT20   26 C3
West View Rd,
   Dartford DA1   21 C3
West View Rd,
   Swanley BR8   53 E3
West Wood Way TN13   46 A3
Westbourne Rd ME10   48 A2
Westbrook Av CT9   58 D2
Westbrook Cotts CT9   36 A3
Westbrook Gdns CT9   58 F1
Westbrook Prom CT9   58 F1
Westbrook Rd CT9   36 A3
Westbrooke Cl ME4   18 C6
Westbury Rd CT8   58 C2
Westbury Ter TN16   57 B5
Westcliff Cl CT9   58 F1
Westcliff Dr ME12   37 D2
Westcliff Rd CT9   58 F1
Westcott Av DA11   28 A6
Westcourt St ME7   18 B2
Wested La BR8   53 E4
Westergate Rd ME2   52 A2
Westerham Hill TN16   57 B1
Westerham Rd TN16   57 A6
Western Av,
   Ashford TN23   12 B4
Western Av,
   Cranbrook TN18   31 B1
Western Av,
   Herne Bay CT6   32 A2
Western Cl CT17   23 A1
Western Cross Cl DA9   29 C3
Western Esp,
   Broadstairs CT10   15 C6
Western Esp,
   Herne Bay CT6   32 A1
Western Link ME13   25 A2
Western Rd,
   Cranbrook TN18   31 B1
Western Rd, Deal CT14   22 C2
Western Rd,
   Margate CT9   19 B5
Western Rd,
   Sevenoaks TN15   13 B5
Western Rd,
   Tunbridge Wells TN4   50 C2
Westfield Rd,
   Birchington CT7   14 D2
Westfield Rd,
   Margate CT9   58 F3
Westgate Bay CT8   58 A2
Westgate Bay Av CT8   58 B2
Westgate Gro CT2   16 A2
Westgate Hall Rd CT1   16 B2
Westgate Rd DA1   21 B3
Westgate Terr CT9   59 B2
Westharold Br ME8   53 B2
Westhill Cl DA12   28 B4
Westleigh Rd CT8   58 A2
Westmarsh Dr CT9   19 D3
Westmead ME20   49 D6
Westmeads Rd CT5   59 B1
Westmount Av ME4   18 B5
Weston Rd ME2   52 B4
Westonville Av CT9   58 E2
Westover Gdns CT10   15 A1
Westover Rd CT10   15 A1
Westree Ct ME16   35 A4
Westree Rd ME16   35 A4
Westrise TN9   55 A5

Westways,
   Edenbridge TN8   24 B4
Westways,
   Westerham TN16   57 C5
Westwell Ct TN30   54 A6
Westwell La TN27   17 D3
Westwood
Ind Est CT9   **36 D6**
Westwood Pl ME13   25 D4
Wharf Rd,
   Gillingham ME7   27 A1
Wharf Rd,
   Maidstone ME15   35 A5
Wharf Way ME15   48 B2
Wharfedale Rd CT9   36 D3
Wharfedale Sq ME8   35 A6
Whatman Cl ME14   35 D1
Wheatcroft Cl ME10   48 D3
Wheatcroft Gro ME8   42 B3
Wheatfield Cl TN17   20 B4
Wheatfield Dr TN17   20 B4
Wheatfield Lea TN17   20 B4
Wheatfield Way TN17   20 B4
Wheatley Cl DA9   29 C4
Wheatley Rd CT5   59 C2
Wheatsheaf Gdns ME12   47 C4
Wheelbarrow
Pk Est TN12   **34 A4**
Wheeler La,
   Ashford TN27   31 C5
Wheeler St,
   Maidstone ME14   35 C3
Wheeler Street Hedges
   ME14   35 C2
Wheler Rd TN27   17 B2
Whetsted Rd TN12   40 A1
Whiffens Av ME4   18 B3
Whiffens Av West ME4   18 B3
Whitby Cl DA9   29 A2
White Bear Pas TN1   56 B5
White Horse La CT1   16 B3
White Lodge Cl TN13   46 C4
White Marsh Ct CT5   59 B2
White Oak Cl TN9   55 B6
White Rd ME4   18 C6
White Rock Pl ME16   35 A4
Whitecroft BR8   53 C1
Whitedyke Rd ME6   49 B1
Whitefield Rd TN4   50 C6
Whitefriars Mdw CT13   45 D2
Whitefriars St CT1   16 C4
Whitefriars Way CT13   45 D2
Whitefriars Wharf TN9   55 C3
Whitegate CT1   50 C3
Whitegate Ct ME8   42 A5
Whitehall Gdns CT2   16 A3
Whitehall Rd,
   Canterbury CT2   16 A3
Whitehall Rd,
   Sittingbourne ME10   48 A5
Whitehill La DA12   28 D6
Whitehill Par DA12   28 D6
Whitehill Rd DA12   28 C5
Whitehorse Hill ME5   18 D5
Whiteoak Cl BR8   53 C2
Whiteoak Ct BR8   53 C2
Whitepost CT5   59 A2
Whites Cl DA9   29 C3
Whites La TN18   31 C1
Whitewall Rd,
   Chatham ME2   18 A1
Whitewall Rd,
   Rochester ME2   44 D1
Whiteway Rd ME1   47 A6
Whitewell La TN17   20 B1
Whitfield Av CT10   19 D6
Whitfield Cotts TN23   12 C6
Whitfield Rd TN23   12 C6
Whiting Cres ME13   25 A2
Whitstable CT5   59 A1
Whybornes Chase
   ME12   37 C3
Whytecliffs Par CT10   15 C6
Wickenden Rd TN13   46 C2
Wickham Av CT11   43 C2
Wickham Pl ME17   30 C2
Wickham St ME1   44 D6
Widred Rd CT17   23 A1
Wigwam Padds CT7   14 E1
Wilbrough Rd CT7   14 E2
Wilderness Hill CT9   36 D2
Wildish Rd ME13   25 A2
Wiles Av TN28   38 B4
Wilfred St DA12   28 C2
Wilkes Rd CT10   15 A5
Wilkie Rd CT7   14 D2
Wilkinson Cl DA1   21 D1
Wilkinson Dr CT14   22 C5
Wilks Av DA1   21 C6
Willement Rd ME13   25 B2
Willesley Gdns TN17   20 C3
William Av CT9   19 C5
William Judge Cl TN30   54 D5
William Pitt Av CT14   22 B2
William Pitt Cl CT21   33 C3

William Rd TN23   12 B6
William St,
   Faversham ME13   25 D3
William St,
   Gillingham ME8   42 C1
William St,
   Gravesend DA12   28 B3
William St,
   Herne Bay CT6   32 C2
William St,
   Sittingbourne ME10   48 A3
William St,
   Tunbridge Wells TN4   50 C6
Willis Ct ME12   37 A4
Willow Av,
   Faversham ME13   25 A3
Willow Av,
   Swanley BR8   53 D3
Willow Cl CT9   19 C4
Willow Cres TN12   51 C1
Willow Dr TN26   30 B6
Willow Rd,
   Dartford DA1   21 A5
Willow Rd,
   Rochester ME2   52 A5
Willow Way,
   Maidstone ME15   35 D5
Willow Way,
   Margate CT9   36 A4
Willowside ME6   49 C2
Wilman Rd TN4   50 D5
Wiltie Gdns CT19   26 B1
Wilton Cl CT14   22 B3
Wilton Rd CT19   26 A1
Wimborne Ho DA12   28 D6
Wimbourne Dr ME8   42 A4
Winch Cl TN17   20 C6
Wincheap CT1   16 A6
Winchester Cres DA12   28 D6
Winchester Gro TN13   46 B4
Winchester Mews CT14   22 B5
Winchester Rd TN18   31 B1
Winchester Way ME8   42 C2
Winchs Garth TN12   51 C1
Wincliff Rd TN9   55 B4
Windermere CT TN24   12 C2
Windmill Cl ME2   52 D2
Windmill Cotts TN17   20 C3
Windmill Ct CT5   59 A5
Windmill Rd,
   Chatham ME4   18 D5
Windmill Rd,
   Gillingham ME7   27 A5
Windmill Rd,
   Sittingbourne ME10   48 A1
Windmill Rd,
   Whitstable CT5   59 A5
Windmill Rise ME12   37 F3
Windmill St,
   Gravesend DA11   28 B2
Windmill St,
   Gravesend DA12   28 B2
Windmill St, Hythe CT21   33 B4
Windsor Av,
   Rochester ME2   52 C2
Windsor Av,
   Chatham ME4   18 B6
Windsor Av,
   Margate CT9   19 A4
Windsor Cl,
   Broadstairs CT10   15 A3
Windsor Cl,
   Maidstone ME14   35 D2
Windsor Ct ME7   27 B3
Windsor Mews TN28   38 C2
Windsor Rd ME7   27 B3
Wingfield Bank DA11   39 B5
Wingfield Rd DA12   28 B3
Wingrove Dr ME2   44 C1
Wings Cl CT10   15 D2
Winstanley Cl ME7   18 C3
Winstanley Cres CT11   43 A2
Winstanley Rd ME12   47 D3
Winston Ct CT7   14 D1
Wintergarden Cres DA9   29 A4
Winterstoke Cres CT11   43 C3
Winterstoke Undercliff
   CT11   43 C3
Winterstoke Way CT11   43 C3
Winton Ct BR8   53 C3
Wisteria Gdns BR8   53 B1
Witham Way ME2   52 B4
Wodehouse Cl ME20   49 B6
Wollaston Rd CT14   22 C4
Wolseley Pl TN24   12 C3
Wolsey Cres DA9   29 A3
Wombwell Gdns DA11   39 D5
Wood End BR8   53 A3
Wood Lodge Grange
   TN13   46 C3
Wood Rd CT21   33 B4
Wood St, Dover CT16   23 B1
Wood St,
   Gillingham ME7   18 C1
Wood St,
   Sheerness ME12   47 D3

Wood St,
   Tunbridge Wells TN1   56 D1
Woodberry Dr ME10   48 D3
Woodbridge Dr ME15   35 A6
Woodbrook TN27   17 C3
Woodbury Cl TN16   57 B5
Woodbury Gdns TN30   54 A6
Woodbury La TN30   54 A6
Woodbury Park Gdns
   TN4   50 C6
Woodbury Park Rd TN4   50 D6
Woodbury Rd TN18   31 B1
Woodchurch Ct ME17   30 B2
Woodchurch Rd TN30   54 C4
Woodcocks TN27   31 B5
Woodcourt CT ME18   48 A5
Woodfield Av DA11   28 B4
Woodfield Rd TN9   55 B4
Woodford Av CT12   43 A2
Woodford Ct CT7   14 E3
Woodgate Cl ME13   25 C1
Woodgate Way TN11   55 D6
Woodgers Gro BR8   53 C1
Woodland Av CT7   14 E3
Woodland Dr,
   Edenbridge TN8   24 C3
Woodland Dr,
   Sheerness ME12   37 B2
Woodland Way DA9   29 A1
Woodlands,
   Swanley BR8   53 B3
Woodlands,
   Tonbridge TN12   40 B3
Woodlands Av ME6   49 B2
Woodlands Cl BR8   53 D2
Woodlands Cl TN4   50 C2
Woodlands Rd,
   Gillingham ME7   27 D3
Woodlands Rd,
   Sittingbourne ME10   48 D4
Woodlands Rd,
   Tonbridge TN9   55 D6
Woodlands Rise BR8   53 D2
Woodlawn St CT5   59 A2
Woodlea TN24   12 D3
Woodnesborough Rd
   CT13   45 A3
Woodpecker Cl TN8   24 C3
Woodside Rd,
   Sevenoaks TN13   46 B3
Woodside Rd,
   Tonbridge TN9   55 B5
Woodstock Rd,
   Deal CT14   22 C4
Woodstock Rd,
   Sittingbourne ME10   48 A6
Woodstock Rd,
   Strood ME2   52 B4
Woodview Rd BR8   53 B1
Woodview Rise ME2   52 B2
Woodville Pl DA12   28 B3
Woodville Rd ME15   35 C5
Woolaston Cl ME15   35 B6
Woolcomber St CT16   23 D2
Woollett St ME14   35 B3
Woolley Cl TN4   50 B2
Woolley Rd TN4   50 B2
Worcester Cl,
   Greenhithe DA9   29 B1
Worcester Cl,
   Rochester ME2   52 A3
Worcester Cl,
   Sheerness ME12   37 C3
Worcester Dr ME10   48 A1
Worcester Gro CT10   15 B3
Worthington St CT16   23 B2
Wreight Ct ME13   25 B1
Wright Cl DA10   29 E3
Wrights Cl TN30   54 B4
Wrotham Av ME4   15 C4
Wrotham Rd,
   Broadstairs CT10   15 C4
Wrotham Rd,
   Gravesend DA11   28 A6
Wrotham Rd,
   Sevenoaks TN15   13 B5
Wyatt Cl TN15   13 A6
Wyatt Pl ME2   52 B4
Wyatt St ME14   35 C3
Wye Rd,
   Gravesend DA12   28 D5
Wye Rd,
   Sevenoaks TN15   13 B4
Wyke Manor Rd ME14   35 C3
Wykeham Cl ME11   41 A3
Wykeham St ME2   52 D2
Wyles St ME7   27 A1
Wyndham Av CT9   19 B3
Wyndham Rd ME4   18 A6
Wynn Rd CT5   59 D1
Wyvern Cl, Dartford DA1   21 A3
Wyvern Cl,
   Snodland ME6   49 C3
Wyvill Cl ME8   42 A5

Yardley Cl TN9   55 D1
Yardley Park Rd TN9   55 C1
Yarrow Cl CT10   15 C5
Yeoman Gdns TN12   40 B4
Yeoman Gdns TN12   41 B1
Yevele Cl ME11   41 B1
Yew Tree Cl CT14   22 B4
Yew Tree Gdns CT7   14 D2
Yew Tree Mews,
   Deal CT14   22 A5
Yew Tree Mews,
   Westerham TN16   57 C5
Yew Tree Rd TN4   50 C3
Yoakley Sq CT9   36 C4
York Av,
   Broadstairs CT10   15 C4
York Av,
   Gillingham ME7   27 A4
York Cl CT6   32 A2
York Ct ME15   35 D6
York Hill ME4   18 C4
York Rd,
   Canterbury CT1   16 A6
York Rd, Dartford DA1   21 D4
York Rd, Deal CT14   22 C5
York Rd,
   Gravesend DA12   28 C6
York Rd, Herne Bay CT6   32 A1
York Rd,
   Maidstone ME15   35 D6
York Rd,
   Northfleet DA11   39 C3
York Rd, Rochester ME1   44 C5
York Rd,
   Tunbridge Wells TN1   56 B3
York St,
   Broadstairs CT10   15 C4
York St, Dover CT17   23 B2
York St, Ramsgate CT11   43 B4
York Ter CT17   14 E2
Young Cl CT14   22 B2

Zetland Av ME7   27 C6
Zion Pl,
   Gravesend DA12   28 B3
Zion Pl, Margate CT9   36 C2

80